Legends of People
Myths of State

Smithsonian Series in Ethnographic Inquiry
William L. Merrill and Ivan Karp, Series Editors

Ethnography as fieldwork, analysis, and literary form is the distinguishing feature of modern anthropology. Guided by the assumption that anthropological theory and ethnography are inextricably linked, this series is devoted to exploring the ethnographic enterprise.

Legends of People

Myths of State

Violence, Intolerance,
and Political Culture in
Sri Lanka and Australia

Bruce Kapferer

Smithsonian Institution Press
Washington and London

Library of Congress Cataloging-in-Publication Data

Kapferer, Bruce.
  Legends of people, myths of state, violence,
intolerance, and political culture in Sri Lanka and
Australia.

  (Smithsonian series in ethnographic inquiry ; 7)
  Bibliography: p.
  Includes index.
    1. Nationalism—Case studies. 2. State, The—Case
studies. 3. Ethnic relations—Case studies.
4. Political culture—Sri Lanka. 5. Political culture—
Australia. I. Title. II. Series.
JC311.K28 1988 320.5'4'0926   87-42558
ISBN 0-87474-566-7

ISBN 0-87474-565-9 (pbk.)

British Library Cataloging-in-Publication Data available

Manufactured in the United States of America

Cover: The Lion of State: A Sorcery Shrine in Sri Lanka

For
Clyde Mitchell

Contents

Preface

I explore in this book the culture of nationalism in Australia and in Sri
Lanka. The general aim is to achieve a comparative understanding of the
nationalist process, the force of nationalist ideas and traditions in motivating human action—action which is often violent and intolerant—and
to demonstrate the value of a cultural approach to the understanding of
modern societies. The discussion of these nationalist ideologies is also
intended to reveal some of the cultural assumptions that are ingrained
within the interpretations which students in the humanities and social
sciences, most frequently in the West, make of the action of human
beings.

Nationalism, I think, throws into relief some of the ways in which
human beings comprehend their realities. This is so in Sri Lanka and in
Australia where nationalist feeling is at high tide. This is most tragically
apparent in Sri Lanka, where the majority Sinhalese population and the
large Tamil minority are in violent conflict. I focus on Sinhalese Buddhist
nationalism and in particular investigate the logic of what I understand
to be its hierarchical form. I contrast this with the nationalism of white
Australians specifically, what I describe as Anzac nationalism. There
have been many new directions in Australian nationalism over recent
years but despite this I consider that it is still developing within the
egalitarian ideology of those First World War Australian soldiers who
inspired the tradition of Anzac. Nationalist feelings are currently being
generated in Australia as the country approaches the bicentennial of the
arrival of the First Fleet from England with its cargo of convicts in 1788.
The nationalist mood in Australia is happier than that in Sri Lanka. But
its egalitarianism has been integral in the development of racial intolerance
and in the structure of state violence.

The overall perspective essayed here is one developed in comparative
anthropology. I develop a particular comparative approach in an attempt

to examine nationalist ideologies on their own terms and in the contexts of their ideas. But the objective is also to indicate how an understanding of one nationalist or cultural form is extended by placing it into a critical and dialectical relation to another. The organization of this book derives from this comparative position. My view is that vital dimensions of Australian life are thrown into general significance through the lens of Sri Lanka and vice versa. Much of the Australian description, in other words, depends on a reading of the Sri Lankan ethnography and the same applies the other way around.

This book is part of a larger project having to do with the cultural complexities of power and their relation to the anguish and suffering of human beings. It is a project which I am pursuing in Australia, Sri Lanka and elsewhere. This analysis, therefore, is preliminary. I have deliberately chosen a broad brush to paint the argument, for I want to present the parameters of ideological schemes, the principles which guide the logic of action within them. The variations within Australia and Sri Lanka are enormous but if one sometimes stands back a little from the canvas, a distancing which may be further facilitated in comparison, another or further understanding of important cultural and ideological forces may be achieved.

In the first instance, it was the tragedy of the current strife in Sri Lanka, a country that has given so much in knowledge and human understanding, a country I regard as a second home, that provoked me to write about nationalism. I share in the great sadness which people from all communities in Sri Lanka feel at the present situation. My stress on the cultural processes engaged in the conflict highlights their importance in effecting any solution to the present crisis.

Obviously, any book directed to a contemporary situation is likely to be overtaken by the flow of events. But it is the structure of the argument rather than the events in themselves that is critical in a book like this. The argument I have presented for the nationalisms of Sri Lanka and Australia seems to be gathering additional relevance in the unfolding of events that have occurred subsequent to the final preparation of the manuscript.

The first draft of the Sri Lankan part of the book was written while I was in Colombo in 1985. Slight additions were made to keep the discussion up to date, but none was made after April 1987. In July 1987, while I was responding to editorial suggestions preparatory to going to press, news was announced of the signing of an accord between India and Sri Lanka bringing the ethnic war to an official close. Indian troops and police are forcing a peace in the northern and eastern provinces of the island and there is hope for a general return to equanimity. Readers of this book will note that Sinhalese Buddhist cultural metaphors of evil give significance to some of the events surrounding the ethnic struggle; the present intervention of India is no exception.

Thus a ritual, the Suniyama, which overcomes the destructive violence of sorcery, portrays an event called the Vadiga Patuna. Here Indian Brahmin healing magicians—dressed liked Punjabis in the ritual—come from abroad to cure the disease of the original act of evil sorcery. In the logic of the rite, the magicians have intimate connection with the agent of evil but their magical power is such, following their incorporation within a Sinhalese Buddhist order, that they transform a condition of annihilating fragmentation (which is also their own possibility) into one of wholeness and health. If the logic of Sinhalese antisorcery ritual commands the further unfolding of social and political events in Sri Lanka, the accord should succeed. But the accord could fan the flames of ethnic suffering. This is so by the legitimacy it may give to the political polarization of communities founded on ethnic identity and the meaning such polarization could achieve in the hierarchical nationalism I describe. The conditions of the accord may give added potency to destructive forces designed to restore a hierarchical unity within the Sinhalese population and this may turn Sinhalese violently against one another. There are already some indications of this, as for example in the escalation of Sinhalese civilian disturbance and political murder following the accord.

Political events in Australia are giving additional shape to my discussion concerning the logic of egalitarian nationalism. In August 1987, following the successful reelection of the Labour government, an issue concerning the Australia Identity Card is gathering momentum. Legislation is being proposed whereby every Australian must be registered and issued with an identity card. The proposal is backed by egalitarian argument. Thus, it is held that it will facilitate the equalitarian treatment of individual Australians in government bureaucratic matters. Some officials argue that it will prevent tax-dodging and especially big business and corporation "bottom of the harbor schemes" and "rorts" that favor the economically better-off groups furthering social and economic inequality. There is a growing feeling across the Australian political spectrum, however, that the Australia Card represents an undue degree of state surveillance into individual private matters. The issue follows the major ideological contradiction, ingrained in Australian political culture, that opposes state and nation.

August 1987 also saw the outbreak of serious rioting involving Aborigines and whites in the Australian country town of Brewarrina. This followed the "suicide" in jail of a young Aborigine. The rioting embarrassed the Australian government internationally, more especially because of the approaching bicentennial celebrations in which Australia is presented as the egalitarian dream. The rioting drew attention to the plight of Aborigines living in Australian towns and elsewhere. White Australians hold urban Aborigines in lower regard than tribal Aborigines. This is an attitude, I suggest, generated in an egalitarian ideology such as

that manifest in Australia where individual equality is viewed as fundamental in nature. Tribal Aborigines are symbolic of the white Australian
valuation of the essential harmony of the individual with nature. In so
far as urban Aborigines are not manifestations of such unity, they can be
the objects of legitimate disapprobation. Egalitarianism can underlie
white prejudice and was an aspect of the Brewarrina situation as it has
been of numerous other black-white confrontations in Australia.

I might add that Aborigines, and predominantly urban Aborigines,
are protesting the bicentennial as marking the beginning of the destruction
of Aboriginal society. In perfect, if cynical, egalitarian vein, Prime
Minister Hawke is proposing a signing of an accord, a kind of symbolic
treaty, with Aboriginal groups. Theoretically, such a treaty would give
recognition of "equal" political status to Aborigines vis-à-vis whites.
There is a nonalcoholic "whiskey" in Australia called Claytons. It was
advertised as the drink one has when one is not having a drink. Claytons
has entered the vernacular and Hawke's accord, rooted in the principles
of an Australian egalitarian consensus, is being referred to as a Claytons
treaty—the treaty you have when you don't have a treaty.

I have received the help of numerous persons in the development of
the arguments in this book. Many Sri Lankans have discussed the ethnic
situation with me and continue to do so. These include Mahen Vaith-
ianathan, who also welcomes me into his home with the warmest
friendship and hospitality, Newton Gunasinghe, I. V. Edirisinghe, Charles
Abeyesekera, Kumari Jayawardena, and Leslie Gunawardena. As usual,
much of my argument about Sri Lanka would have been impossible
without the indefatigable support of Chandra Vitarana. All these persons
are not, of course, responsible for any of the opinions expressed in this
book and, indeed, disagree sharply with several of them.

Llyn Smith and Rohan Bastin have discussed most of the Sri Lankan
and Australian materials with me. Their own research knowledge of Sri
Lanka has been invaluable as has their understanding as native Australians.
Michael Roberts, whose own work on nationalism in Sri Lanka is of
central importance, has also given me the advantage of his comparative
understanding of Australia.

Michaela Kapferer joined me in Sri Lanka during 1984 when I was
researching into sorcery shrines. Her questioning provoked me into
making enquiries I otherwise would not have bothered about. People
also told her things they already thought I would know. Consequently,
much new information was revealed to me. Her interest and presence
improved my research immeasurably.

In Australia and in England many friends and colleagues have commented on the manuscript at various stages. Barry Morris, Tom Ernst,
Susan Barham, Andrew Lattas, Jadran Mimica, and Michael Muetzelfeldt
have all been exploring or researching Australian society and have freely
shared their knowledge. Roland Kapferer has forced me to sharpen some

of the analytical points and I learn from him. Don Handelman, Andrew Roberts, Kirsten Alnaes, Phil Burnham, Rob Jones, Michael Rowlands, John Gledhill, Danny Miller, Allen Abramson, and Josep Llobera have helped me. Some of the ideas were worked out in a series of seminars given at the Department of Social Anthropology at the University of Stockholm. Stefan Molund, Bawa Yamba, Karen Norman, Eva Rosanders, Yngve Lithman, and Tomas and Eva Gerholm were full of ideas and stimulating company. Dr. Michael McKernan of the Australian War Memorial has given me much food for thought and I am grateful to him and the Memorial for permission to publish some photographs. Leslie Dharmaratne, Executive Director, Upali Newspapers Limited, and Rex de Silva, Editor of the *Sun*, have kindly given me permission to publish the cartoons reproduced in this volume. David Beatty provided me with some of his outstanding photographs of the Suniyama rite. David Howell-Jones and Hong Yoke Lim have gone to considerable trouble to prepare this manuscript for publication and they have my gratitude.

The staff of the Smithsonian Institution Press have been indefatigable in the preparation of this manuscript for publication. Ruth Spiegel and Linda McKnight have persevered through all my anxieties. Daniel Goodwin's enthusiasm for the idea of the book spurred me to complete the project. The research for the book both in Sri Lanka and in Australia was supported by generous grants from the University of Adelaide and from the Australian Research Grants Scheme.

Judith Kapferer must bear the chief responsibility for forcing me in a comparative direction. She has always insisted that a cultural anthropological perspective should be directed toward Australia. We have been doing joint research into aspects of Australian society and many of the directions taken in this analysis have been suggested in discussion with her.

This book is dedicated to Clyde Mitchell, who introduced me to anthropological research in Zambia, to the significance of ethnicity in industrial society, and to the importance for anthropology to address critical social and political issues confronting the worlds that anthropologists study.

Bruce Kapferer
University College, London

I

Cultures of Nationalism

Political Cosmology and the Passions

Nationalism makes the political religious and places the nation above politics. The nation is created as an object of devotion and the political forces which become focused upon it are intensified in their energy and passion. The religion of nationalism, wherein the political is shrouded in the symbolism of a "higher" purpose, is vital to the momentum of nationalism. This momentum, which if anything is on the increase, has been among the most liberating, but also among the most oppressive and destructive, political energies of this century. The religious form of nationalism which is so much part of this process has engulfed social and other religious and political ideas and doctrines—liberal democracy, communism, socialism, fascism, and anarchism—in its path. These have all become subordinate to the nationalist purpose and have received renewed energy and have been transformed or fashioned within the religion of nationalism.

Culture has assumed pride of place in the litany of nationalisms everywhere. Almost universally the culture that nationalists worship is those things defined as the founding myths and legends of the nation and the customs and traditions and language of the nation. These are at once constituted within the nation and constitute the nation. They are integral to national sovereignty and are made sacred in the nation as the nation is made sacred in them. The customs, language, and traditions of the nation are often referred to as primordial, the root essence of nationalism and national identity, those that generate the feeling or sentiment of national unity and legitimate national independence. This primordial value of culture is intrinsic to nationalist religion. It is a value emergent in the historical circumstances of the growth of nationalism. The primordialism of the cultural in nationalism is the construction of nationalism itself and is not to be regarded as independent of nationalism.

Culture in nationalism is seen in a particular way. It becomes an object, a reified thing, something which can be separated or abstracted from its embeddedness in the flow of social life. Made into a religious object, culture becomes the focus of devotion. It can have the character of a religious fetish, an idol, a thing which has self-contained magical properties capable of recreating and transforming the realities of experience in its image. This appearance of culture in the religion of nationalism has a basis in fact. Culture spiritualized has indeed become an instrument in the forging and defining of nation and in the perpetration of some of the most appalling crimes against humanity the world has yet known (Mosse 1970). Such nationalist passion can be seen to be generated in the act of religious contemplation of culture in which a national self and a national other are defined and receive significance in the explanation of evil and suffering. This, as Hegel foresaw in his examination of the French revolutionary Jacobin Terror, can be seen as being at the root of the modern human devastations of nationalism. Hegel likens the Terror to a "Hindu fanaticism of pure contemplation," which is not apart from the world but is rather engaged in the practices of lived political and social realities.

> It takes place in religion and politics alike as the fanaticism of
> destruction—the destruction of the whole subsisting social order—as
> the elimination of individuals who are objects of suspicion to any
> social order, and the annihilation of any organization which tries to
> arise anew from the ruins. Only in destroying does this negative will
> possess the feeling of itself as existent (Hegel 1952, 5:22).

In this book I shall explore two modern nationalisms, Sinhalese Buddhist nationalism and Australian egalitarian nationalism. Both have realized their existence in destruction. Death and extinction are key symbolic aspects of their life, as Benedict Anderson (1983) has noted for nationalism more widely. Sinhalese nationalism is constructed out of its myths of history and the deeds of its heroes, wherein Tamils threaten to destroy or subsume Sinhalese but are themselves conquered and destroyed. These ideas are integral to the modern social and political practice of nationalism in Sri Lanka and are part of a current tragedy, and in the fires of its passions, Sinhalese, and especially Tamils, are being consumed. Australian nationalism gathers its religious focus in the flames of the destruction of war. In the midst of death and extinction are born the legends of Australian national identity. These legends, which contain the spirit of national liberation no less than do the myths of Sinhalese nationalists, also have force in the cause of human suffering. The passion of their ideas in practice bears a relation to certain forms of intolerance and prejudice in Australia. These are destructive and are certainly instrumental in the anguish of those against whom they are directed, as they may also be of those who engage them.

Australians may object that the ideas and practice of their nationalism should be brought into association with that which is being experienced in Sri Lanka at present. The scale of human suffering in the present nationalism of Sri Lanka hardly bears comparison, and most Australians would not consider such internal conflagration thinkable, let alone possible. After all, to cite the title of a well-known book critical of Australian serendipity—a word derived from Serendib, the Arab name of Sri Lanka—Australia is a Lucky Country, free from the suffering of other far-distant realities. But Australians should be conscious of the terrible destruction in the past of the Australian Aborigines, a destruction made possible in the practice of ideas that underline much Australian nationalist thought. I should add that the argument of Australian nationalism is cognate with European nationalisms that have wrought the greatest human destruction of this century.

I am concerned with the religious form of nationalism and with the influence of culture, as defined by nationalists, in this religious form. Their conjunction in the production of nationalist passions which can manifest great human anguish and suffering is a primary focus of this analysis. Australia and Sri Lanka are the settings in which I explore this issue and through which I consider modern nationalism more generally. Their nationalisms highlight what I think has been obscured in scholarly and more popular debate concerning the phenomenon of nationalism. There has been a tendency to assume that because nationalism is a worldwide phenomenon it is necessarily universal in form. This is so in the hard-nosed, down to earth, sociological universalism of Gellner (1983), who considers all nationalism to be basically founded in the same social and material conditions, and in the culturism of Geertz (1973; see also Anderson 1983), who conceives of nationalism broadly as cleaving to a similar religious attitude and form (Kapferer 1987). Kedourie (1985) in an important work on European nationalism almost takes a diffusionist stance. Nationalism born in the emergence of a European individualism is an exported spiritual commodity which varies around the same ideological themes. From the Marxist point of view it is generally argued that nationalism is a product of European colonialism, capitalist expansion, the creation of international and local bourgeoisies, an instrument in class domination, and so on. I do not dispute the significance of these views of the nature and force of modern nationalism.

There is much that is common to nationalism throughout the world in its cultural and social process. Many nationalisms have spawned yet other nationalisms, which have assumed variant form in the cultural dialectics of their political resistance and reaction. Many aspects of Sinhalese and Australian nationalism are similar. Their roots are in the circumstances of British colonialism and their elites are often inclined toward English values despite their overt rejection of these values. The internal political forces of their nationalisms are to be seen in the context of wider capitalist processes in which the conflicts of class in both countries are constituted. Both Australian and Sinhalese nationalism, in their specific historical settings, obscure the grounds of class conflict and unite otherwise opposed classes in the force of their nationalism.

Despite their similarities some nationalisms are radically distinct in their religious form and in what I describe as their political culture. In other words, what is reified as the culture of particular nationalisms sometimes contains an argument that is far from reducible to nationalism, generally. It is an argument that elaborates a specific political universe which points to or highlights certain significant meanings over others in the social and cultural worlds of experience. The meanings accentuated, moreover, carry implications for further action and, I suggest, can motivate action in accordance with the direction of the nationalist argument. I am not presenting an idealist view, one which gives to nationalist ideas a determination of their own. They gain their determination through the political and social structures and processes of the worlds of which they are already a part. Their force is generated, as I shall demonstrate, by their action within and upon a wider spectrum of situated ideas and meanings which are possibly more complex, multivalent, and various than those present and selected within a culture of nationalism—its particular collection of significant myths and traditions.

The "cone of light" that a culture of nationalism casts over a diverse cultural and social reality is one that illuminates the same insistent message. The culture of nationalism or the meanings of a nationalist ideology tend to be coherent and systematic. They are totalitarian in form or tend increasingly in this direction in the historical and political settings in which they gather force. As such, supported dialectically by the political events to which they yield significance and further impetus, they mold diverse realities within their uniform message. Realities once multiple and even distinct begin to refract similar messages and to shine with the same burning light that is shone over them. The political and social settings in which a culture of nationalism finds significance begin to assume its totalitarian form and with all too frequent tragic result. In this sense nationalism is vital in the creation and transformation of cultural and political realities. It conditions what it reflects, and this is critical to my understanding of the power of the cultures of nationalism in giving direction to action and in firing the passions.

The religions of Sinhalese and Australian nationalism are distinct in their argument and these arguments, or what I shall refer to at different points as their logic or structures of reasoning (Hacking 1982, Rabinow 1986), are part of their religious form and integral to their religious passion. Here I expand on the discussion of Benedict Anderson (1983) on the religion of nationalism. Anderson, I think correctly, identifies some of the distinctive religious features of nationalism in general. He concentrates upon the universalization of temporal and spatial schemes in modern nationalism whereby all in the nation are conceived of as progressing in unison through the one space and time. The historical circumstances that yield these conceptions account, in Anderson's analysis, for the spread of the religion of nationalism and for its power in human action and emotion. I agree with this view and with Anderson's important statement that nationalism is very different in form from the universalizing cosmic religions it has apparently supplanted. The specific directions taken by the actions of certain nationalisms, however, boil down eventually to a consideration of historical specificities. While this is valid, Anderson undervalues aspects of the particular arguments which modern nationalisms may transformationally incorporate into their religious schemes. These arguments extend an understanding of the force of the nationalist imagination which Anderson explores.

Before I outline those arguments of Sinhalese and Australian nationalism that are important to the discussion of this book, I wish to stress that the religions of nationalism I shall examine are not religious by virtue of the religions they may incorporate. Much modern nationalism declares its religion to be synonymous with the religion it subsumes—an Islamic nationalism, a Christian Democratic nationalism, Hindu nationalism. I note, however, that the religions so harnessed to nationalism are often regarded as purified and more orthodox than before. Here is the point, they are purified in their nationalist incorporation. Nationalists, in effect, declare their nationalism to be a higher religious form than those erstwhile universalist religions they appear to supplant. The religious fundamentalism, moreover—the purification of religion or religious "revitalization" or revivalism—that is so often linked to modern nationalist movements highlights the fundamentalist and revivalist character of nationalism itself. I suggest that it is the fundamentalism of nationalism—of which the primordialism of nationalism and the search for the essence of national identity are aspects—which conditions the fundamentalism of the religions that are incorporated into nationalism. The fundamentalism of nationalism is, of course, directly connected with the totalitarian form of nationalist religion, by no means intrinsic to the religion subsumed by nationalism, and with the systematic coherence of nationalist political culture to which I have already referred.

It follows from the foregoing that one modern nationalism is not necessarily more or less religious than another. Australians assert a secular nationalism, Sinhalese an expressly Buddhist nationalism. What I stress is that the religion of nationalism is in nationalism per se and not in the religious ideas it may incorporate. Australian nationalism displays its religious form in its rejection of the religious, in the same way that Sinhalese nationalism develops its religious form in the assertion of Buddhism and the active incorporation of it.

I do not state that the religious ideas that may be included in modern nationalism are irrelevant to an understanding of the religious form of nationalism and its political process. Far from it. Such a suggestion would contradict much of the thrust of my discussion in this book.

Australian nationalism, its secularism notwithstanding, derives some of the force behind its argument from its elaboration within the historical and cultural world of Western Christianity quite as much as Sinhalese nationalism gains its power within a Buddhist historical world. What I am saying is that the religion of nationalism, in relation to its historical, social and political context, transforms or interprets the import of the religious ideas and themes it incorporates within its own religious scheme.

Buddhism, for example, gains its significance within the religion and practice of Sinhalese nationalism and not vice versa. While Sinhalese nationalism may be Buddhist, the Buddhism which is brought to consciousness is that conditioned within the nationalist process. The Buddhist ideas practiced by Sinhalese and to which they refer are wide and various. Sinhalese nationalism selects within the many possibilities of Buddhism in practice and realizes a particular logic, a logic made integral to Sinhalese nationalism and forceful to its process.

Tambiah makes a similar point in the setting of Thai Buddhist nationalism. I cite his statement for its relevance especially to my later analysis of Sinhalese Buddhist nationalism, which extends from a discussion of some of the important Sinhalese religious chronicles.

> It must be stated at the outset that the canonical texts of Buddhism
> (just as the Bible of Christianity or the core texts of any other religion)
> are complex and rich in meaning . . . capable of different levels of
> interpretation. . . . Any perspective that naïvely assumes that there are
> certain unambiguous prescriptions and value orientations in Buddhism
> from which can be deduced behavioral correlates that bear an intrinsic
> and inherent relation to the religion is inaccurate, usually misguided,
> and sometimes pernicious. In other words, the question of the nexus
> between Buddhism and this-worldly conduct is more open than has
> been imagined by certain scholars, including the illustrious Max Weber
> (Tambiah 1976, 402.)

To clarify my own argument as well, the import of Buddhism or any religion is inextricably part of its practice, which includes its interpretation. The Buddhism of Sinhalese nationalism is a Buddhism of nationalist practice and interpretation, a Buddhism reconstituted in the religion of nationalism. The violence, destruction, and prejudice of Sinhalese and Australian nationalisms are not to be reduced to an essential Buddhism or Christianity, for example, which exist outside the import and significance they achieve within nationalism. The energy and force of Buddhist and Christian themes are formed and realized in the religious order of nationalism itself.

The reasoning of Sinhalese and Australian nationalism is contained in their respective cosmologies, in the myths, legends, and other traditions to which these nationalisms accord value. The logic of their cosmologies is revealed in the hermeneutics of the rites of the nation, in the interpretations of the cultural world of the nation offered by such rites, and in other ritual events that nationalists may value or to occurrences in daily experience which their myths and traditions may render sensible.

The conceptions of the nation, of the state, of power, and of the person are very different in Sinhalese Buddhist nationalist cosmology from their conception in Australian nationalist cosmology. The thesis of this book is centered on this difference, for I shall argue that the dynamics of the respective nationalisms, their religious ideological force within the wider cultural worlds of which they are a part, the character of the suffering they can engender, and the significance that the human beings caught in their schemes routinely attach to events in their lives influencing their action, are integral to the arguments elaborated within these nationalist cosmologies. I shall outline some of the critical differences.

Broadly, I consider that in Sinhalese Buddhist nationalist cosmology the nation and the state compose a unity. In cosmological conception the state protectively encloses the nation of Sinhalese Buddhists, whose integrity as persons is dependent on this encompassment. The state in such a conception encloses other peoples or nations who are not Sinhalese Buddhists. But critical here is that these peoples are maintained in hierarchical subordination to Sinhalese Buddhists. The encompassing and ordering power of the state is hierarchical, and the integrity of nations, peoples, and persons within the Sinhalese Buddhist state is dependent on the capacity of the state to maintain by the exercise of its power the hierarchical interrelation of all those it encloses. The failure in the power of the Sinhalese Buddhist state to maintain hierarchy in the whole order it circumscribes threatens the integrity of persons. Thus the fragmentation of the state is also the fragmentation of the nation and is also the fragmentation of the person.

Australian nationalist cosmology places the nation and the state in ambivalent relation. In the populist traditions of Australian nationalism, the nation includes the state. The state achieves its integrity in the will of the nation and the people. The integrity of persons as autonomous and discrete individuals is a property of individuals per se. Indeed, the ordering power of the state potentially disorders the integrity of persons. This is so when the state moves into dominant and inclusive relation to the nation. Ideally, I suggest, in Australian nationalism the power of the state mediates between nations, peoples, and persons. Australian identity is not founded in an Australian state, as it is in Sinhalese Buddhist nationalism, but in the Australian nation conceived as separate from the state. In Australian nationalism the subsumption of the Australian nation within the power of the state can be a manifestation of the malign force of the state whereby personal autonomy and integrity are destroyed. The conception is radically different from Sinhalese Buddhist nationalism wherein the state is a benign force in its ordering encompassment. The nation and the person are vital and whole within such ordering power. Unlike the Australian conception, the incapacity of the state to encompass and to establish an hierarchical order in Sinhalese Buddhist nationalism transforms the state, for example, into a malevolent form that destroys the person.

The contrast I have drawn builds upon the comparative work of Louis Dumont (1977, 1980, 1986), which is based on his researches into Indian and European ideological systems. He makes a distinction between the hierarchical world of India and the conceptual realities of European and North American ideologies founded in egalitarianism and the valuation of the individual. I shall not develop upon Dumont uncritically. Neither, I should add, am I concerned to argue within his schema alone. Tambiah (1976) and many others are important to my understanding of the Sinhalese Buddhist material. But it is Dumont more than any other anthropologist of whom I am aware who has directed his ethnographic researches and related knowledge of the texts toward the comparative understanding of ideology. This is so in the sense that he has explored the inner logic of different and variant ideological forms and with reference to such burning modern issues as nationalism. I must freely acknowledge Dumont's influence, but at the same time the reader should note that there are aspects of Dumont's larger intellectual project which I do not share.

I am not concerned to demonstrate that hierarchy, for example, is universal or to show that Western egalitarianism and individualism are later transformations upon hierarchical conceptions. This has been an issue of wide scholastic discussion, and the argument made by Dumont is but one among many. In the ideological context of political debate Dumont's position scares some hares. It opposes political positions right across the modern political spectrum from radical Marxists through anarchists to conservative populists.[1] This is especially so where such positions are that equality and inequality are natural within humankind, integral to the autonomous individual as an empirical, biological, species being. Dumont demonstrates that such a position is an ideological construction, and he is committed to showing that its social forces are prejudice and the imprisonment of humanity, not necessarily its release. Much of his argument is that egalitarianism engages hierarchical conceptions within it and that it is the very ideological suppression of hierarchy and, it should be stressed, the transformation of the meaning of hierarchy in egalitarianism, which is part of the potential dehumanizing power of egalitarianism. More mundanely, Dumont is attacking conceptions commonly taken for granted in the West and ingrained in Western philosophy and social science that egalitarianism in any of its versions is grounds for asserting the superiority of Western knowledge and practices over others. In pursuing this argument to the limit, Dumont has exposed himself to the charge of being reactionary in a Western sense; that is, he has opposed himself to forces that from whatever position they are considered have indeed been active in the material and spiritual improvement of humankind. Dumont has countermanded great liberating ideals. Some would say, following the implications of Dumont's work, that he has valued hierarchy above equality. While not conceiving either to be natural to humankind in its species being, hierarchy, even if always as ideology, is intrinsic to society. This is an egalitarian's nightmare.[2]

In my own argument egalitarianism is not valued above hierarchy or vice versa. One is not necessarily prior to the other. What can be discovered as hierarchical in egalitarianism, for example, may be a logical possibility of egalitarianism in practice and not a transformation of hierarchy, as Dumont conceives it. Most important, I do not wish to deny the great liberating ideals that are a feature of many egalitarian ideologies and also of hierarchical ideologies. What I shall explore is their different capacity in practice and under specific historical circumstances to be integral to the causation of great human suffering. Dumont does suggest that the human destruction of the partition of India in 1947 was a consequence of processes connected with the Westernization of India. He indicates that it was the combination of egalitarian ideas with those of Hindu hierarchy that were instrumental in the racial conflagration. This supports his view that racism is egalitarian and specifically Western. My argument, certain aspects of which are anticipated by Dumont, is that hierarchy and egalitarianism, separately or in combination, are potentially destructive and dehumanizing. This potential is realized in nationalism itself, which takes particular direction through hierarchical ideology or egalitarian ideology.

One of the most important criticisms of Dumont is that he reduces complex, highly variant cultural and historical ideas to rather simple, coherent schemes. I think there is much validity in this criticism, though I do not consider that it negates the overall importance of Dumont's scholarship. It certainly does not validate a return to an open-ended, anything-goes, cultural voluntarism which is becoming fashionable in modern anthropology. My view is that the insight of Dumont's approach to an understanding of modern political ideas as well as the internal coherence of the ideological schemes he investigates may have much to do with modern nationalism and the colonialism that preceded it. Colonialism and nationalism are totalitarian ideological forms. They are forces by virtue of the demands of their own orders, which, I suggest, tend to the construction of internally coherent, simplified ideologies upon more complex cultural ground. That the ideologies described by Dumont may have grown up in colonial or modern nationalist conditions in no way reduces their importance in analysis. Quite the contrary. It is by recognizing their totalitarian form and exploring their inner logic that we may be able to understand some of the destructive force of egalitarianism and hierarchy in nationalism.

It is because the conceptions of nation, state, power and person in Sinhalese Buddhist and Australian nationalist cosmologies gain their momentum in particular ideologies of hierarchy and egalitarianism that

I shall now draw out some of their distinct principles. I do this to alert the reader to certain ideas which are important to a grasp of the argument of the book as a whole.

The distinction between hierarchical and egalitarian ideologies is centered in a set of principles that govern the relations of parts to wholes. In hierarchical systems society is conceived of broadly as a whole. The principles that govern the whole determine both the nature of the parts and their interrelation. In Dumont's example of Hindu India, the whole comprises a cosmic unity founded in accordance with the opposing but complementary principles of purity and pollution. They define, in their dynamic union, the internal hierarchical differentiation of the parts and their composition into a unified whole. Thus the Indian caste system is defined by the purity-pollution opposition. The highest castes are the purest and the lowest are the most polluted. Brahmans and Untouchables, in Dumont's analysis, describe the boundaries of the system and manifest in the action of caste members and the cultural attitudes of others toward them the system-determining and encompassing principles of purity and pollution.[3]

In Hindu India, hierarchy and differentiation unify the whole; they do not divide it. The hierarchy and differentiation of castes in the ideology of Hindu India constitute the logic of coherence of the system, the reintegration of the parts into the whole even as they are distinguished and differentiated.

A cornerstone of Dumont's argument relating to the purity-pollution opposition is that status encompasses power and that power is determined by virtue of its subordinate relation to status. Thus, Brahmans are superior to kings (*kshatriya*). This Brahman precedence and encompassment is a condition, however, of the king's power. It should be stressed that the status of the Brahman is a cosmic-ritual status. It is not a status-honor in a Weberian sense, an individual quality of prestige, for example, which accrues to or is achieved by the individual, independent of forces in the cosmic whole. This is a Western ideological notion of status, Dumont might claim, which is to be distinguished from Hindu conceptions. Fundamental to the Hindu scheme is that the dominance of status is a principle of the cosmic whole and not of those worlds encompassed and determined by this whole.

The ideology of hierarchy I have outlined here is not strictly applicable to Buddhist Sri Lanka. Dumont virtually excludes Sri Lanka from his analysis for this reason, although some would challenge his judgment (Yalman 1967). The pure-impure complementary opposition is less determinate in the Sri Lankan system, wherein power is ideologically recognized as less subordinate to status. The location of Sinhalese castes in hierarchy is determined in their relation to the king; power affects status. This point has been made for India as well by some of Dumont's critics (Heesterman 1985, Dirks 1987). Over all, however, I take Sinhalese

Buddhist cosmological conceptions, while representing an important variation from Dumont's depiction of Hindu India, as nonetheless being broadly consistent with it.

Sinhalese Buddhist cosmology, like the Hindu system interpreted by Dumont, articulates a hierarchical argument.[4] The whole is determinate of the parts and their interrelation. The holistic principles are those of the religio-cosmic encompassment, which places knowledge and reason (*dharma*) in the dominant relation to political power (*artha*). Reason, the teaching and way of the Buddha, can be seen as standing in a relation of virtual complementary opposition to nonreason, the demonic. In everyday Sinhalese Buddhist conception, the Buddha is pure and the demonic is polluting. The Buddha and the demonic both define the boundaries of existence, the point of entry into nonexistence or extinction. The worlds of existence and of social relations that involve human beings and a plethora of supernaturals have their places in hierarchy determined by the degree of their orientation to the Buddha or to the demonic. I stress that the encompassing principles defined by the Buddha and the demonic are engaged in dynamic tension throughout the realities they encompass and are present to varying degrees in all the various elements of existence and their relation. In all this the cosmic principles defined by the Buddha are dominant and determinate. Ultimately they encompass the demonic. Some of the myths I have collected in the south of Sri Lanka make this explicit, for the Buddha is presented as having a demonic manifestation. These myths could have come from North Indian Mahayana Buddhism, which has had a historical influence in this part of the island. What I have indicated as the nature of the encompassment of the Buddha also defines an important aspect of Sinhalese Buddhist hierarchical conception, which is also that of Hindu India.

The logic of Hindu and Sinhalese Buddhist hierarchy is what I call one of progressive encompassment and transformation. This is one of upward movement in hierarchy, motivated by the forces that govern the apical unity of the system, whereby lower forms of existence are incorporated by higher forms and transformed in accordance with those principles that determine the higher form. In Sri Lanka this is the logic of rituals of healing and community protection. An important Sinhalese Buddhist goddess is Pattini (Obeyesekere 1984a). She is recognized as having a number of different manifestations, some of them demonic and destructive. The rituals which address her move her progressively from a low to a high possibility of being, the highest representing her most incorporative and encompassing stage.

The kind of hierarchical scheme I am discussing is consistent with religious systems such as Hinduism and Buddhism, in which the cosmos is conceived of as being in a condition of continual flux, process, and transformation. Given the incorporative logic of hierarchy and the tensions between the defining forces of the whole, what is unified at one

moment can break down into a less unified and more fragmented form
(Kapferer 1983). A deity or a human being can become demonic, reduced
to a lower fragmented possibility of itself, but can be reconstituted once
again into a higher encompassing possibility. In my understanding of the
Sinhalese Buddhist cosmic hierarchy, purity can be conceived of as
equivalent to encompassing unity and pollution to a fragmented, decom-
posed, encompassed reduction.

    As I have suggested, nation and state have a particular significance
in Sinhalese Buddhist hierarchical conception. The nation is encompassed
by the state symbolized in the kingship. These in turn are encompassed
by the Buddhist religion or the Triple Gem (Buddha, dharma, sangha). In
this unity of the whole is the integrity of the parts. Thus the nation or
the people who compose a hierarchically interrelated social order discover
their unity in the power of the state, which is enabled in its unifying
power by its subordination to the Buddha. The most unifying of Buddhist
kings, as Tambiah (1976) shows, are the renouncers, who leave society or
who give up their pursuit of artha and assert the principles of encompassing
Buddha dharma. A failure in the principles that determine the cosmic
whole, for whatever reason, causes fragmentation and a reduction to
dislocating demonic forces and powers, which were overcome and transformed in a hierarchical cosmically determined unity. The world becomes
ahierarchical and the principle of encompassment is attacked. The Buddha
dharma is opposed by the state, and the state and the people are brought
into mutual conflict. The situation is returned to its former order by the
assertion of the ultimate determinate cosmic principles of the whole, the
way of the Buddha. The demonic and destructive conditions of existence
are also the source of the regeneration of the hierarchical order of society.
The reduction is one that intensifies the conflict between the cosmic
determining forces of reason and nonreason, Buddha and the demonic,
and in the violence of their struggle hierarchy is renewed through the
greater encompassing powers of the Buddha. I emphasize that the demonic
gives rise to ordering processes connected with Buddhism. The two are
unified in dynamic tension as determining the cosmic whole. Their
tension, differentiation, and separation and the progressive encompassment by the Buddha of the demonic recreates the ordered worlds of
existence. All this will be examined in some detail in the following
chapters.

    The cosmic hierarchical scheme I have outlined involves a distinct
valuation of the individual or person. I must distinguish, following
Dumont, between the individual as an empirical unit and the individual
as culturally or ideologically valued. The empirical statement that all
societies are composed of individuals, separate biologically integrated
behaving units, is in general unproblematic. It becomes problematic
when it is stated as a cultural value or it is assumed that all societies, for
example, carry dominant conceptions of the primacy of the individual in

society or of the autonomy of the individual in society that are essentially the same despite superficial cultural differences.

In the hierarchical conceptions of Sinhalese Buddhist traditions the constitution of the individual is conditioned in the motion of a hierarchical world determined within an encompassing cosmic process. Individuals outside society or in a society that is becoming asocial through the failure of its hierarchical encompassing order confront extinction. Buddhist monks and Sinhalese demons outside society are oriented toward nonexistence, monks move toward nirvana through the achievement of an ultimate transcendental unity, and demons move toward a fragmented annihilation. It is within society that monks and demons come back from the brink of extinction to realize the force of the principles they embody in society. Thus the demons become potent as independent beings in society and begin to recast it in their ahierarchical image. Monks reentering the social world are activated in its processes and may restore its order according to the ideals of cosmic encompassment which they embody. This notion, of course, receives explicit Buddhist recognition in the concept of bodhisattva, the enlightened who turn beneficently and recreatively back to the social world. The existence of individuals, therefore, the continuity of their selves, is determined by society. Society gives life to the individual.

The empirical, physical individual does not circumscribe within itself the properties of autonomy, coherence, or power independent of cosmic hierarchical principles and processes within which both the society and the individual are formed. Put another way, autonomy, coherence, and power are properties of hierarchy rather than intrinsic aspects of individuals. This reflects a hierarchical process. Thus the failure of hierarchy and its ordering cosmic principles is revealed in the destructive, demonic power of kings. The restoration of hierarchy is manifest in the benevolence of the king. The hierarchical principle of incorporation is vital to individual integrity and coherence. Outside the hierarchical order of society human beings can become weak and impotent or destructive of themselves and others. With reference to medieval Europe, in many ways a hierarchical universe, Bloch (1973) describes the way kings and other royal personages were able to heal the skin disease scrofula by their royal touch. By this act the bodies of the royal subjects were made whole, ordered once again, through their incorporation into the body of the king. Something similar occurred in Sri Lanka. Leprosy (*kushta*) was known as the king's disease. It was cured in rituals that asserted the embodiment of the king in the cosmic order and engaged the sufferer in the same process.

In Australia the word *hierarchy* is used to refer to that order to which Australian egalitarian nationalists consider themselves opposed. In their ideology it is characterized by the political and social order of England, which is variously described as a class society, one ruled by aristocrats of good birth and riddled with the fopperies of status and status convention. Hierarchy for the Australian indicates the extreme of inequality and is almost symbolic of evil and personal destruction. It symbolizes the colonial domination and unfounded superiority of the British. Hierarchy in Australian ideology is at the root of almost all stupidity and irrationality, oppressing individuals, and can deny humanity itself.

The hierarchy that many Australian nationalists find offensive is tied to a conception of inequality ingrained within egalitarian ideology. It bears no relation to the hierarchical ideology of Hindu India or of Sri Lanka as I have described it. This is so even though some Australians, like the influential Professor Blainey, whose views will be examined in chapter 7, assume that their commonsense notions of hierarchy refer to Asian systems. Hierarchy, as Australians use the word, has some connection to more analytical Western sociological conceptualizations of social stratification, of status, power, and prestige, which Dumont has shown to be in general consistent with Western egalitarianism and individualism. Thus Australians who recognize hierarchy to be part of their own social world generally describe it as being related to individual, category, or group differences arranged along an ordinal scale to indicate levels of superiority and inferiority in wealth, social background, education, property, occupational status, power, and so on. Hierarchy in Australia is about stratification, and perhaps the ideological conception of inequality in egalitarianism can be called stratificational to distinguish it from the hierarchical universe of Sinhalese Buddhist ideological conception.

In the discussion of Australian nationalism I must use the word *hierarchy* because it is used by Australian egalitarians in their efforts to understand their realities. I stress that its Australian sense should not be confused with the idea of hierarchy in the hierarchical logic of Sinhalese nationalism. In Australia hierarchy receives its import in a logic of egalitarianism, not in one of hierarchy.

In egalitarianism the individual is the fundamental unit of value. The individual is ideologically conceived of as preceding society and as the building block upon which society is constituted. Egalitarians will often conflate what I have distinguished as the empirical, physical individual with the individual—or more accurately in this context, the person—as valued in culture. In this conflation, one which is ideologically motivated, the various culturally constituted properties of the person are conceived of as given and intrinsic to the individual in nature, to be a matter of empirical fact. At this point, I hasten to add that the hierarchical conceptions of Buddhist Sri Lanka are not without concepts of the individual or the person. What I am stating is that in hierarchical logic the individual is valued differently, and the world order is not conceived of as constructed out of individuals so much as of individuals being constituted, instead, in an encompassing cosmic process. The nature of this cosmic order is often taken as empirical fact by Sinhalese Buddhist nationalists, who cling to it with all the commitment that such a factual attitude can inspire.

Intrinsic to the individual in egalitarianism are the integrity and coherence of the individual, the autonomy of the individual, and the capacity to act as a free, self-determining, and moral unit or agent. In Buddhist hierarchy, by way of contrast, the person achieves moral agency by virtue of a cosmic encompassment. If he or she acts alone in the egalitarian sense, then the person can be conceived of in amoral terms and regarded as acting demonically (Kapferer 1986b). Ideally, in egalitarianism, the part should determine the whole. Should the reverse be true, then all that is valued in the individual may be lost, and what can be understood as morally intrinsic or potential may be destroyed. This is especially so in Australian egalitarianism. Integral to such a point of view are the related concerns common in Western societies of careful social engineering to bring out or create the best in individuals or the interest to restrict interference in individual lives.

The egalitarian conception of the social whole is ordered from within the ideological terms of the autonomous individual. Society in the egalitarian view may be likened to a succession of Chinese boxes, each social category, group or unit of organization more inclusive than the one before. The individual is the basic starting point from which successively larger units of ordering are built up. The greater inclusion of the larger units is not the same as the principle of encompassment in hierarchy. In the logic of encompassment the individual is not the elemental unit nor does it persist virtually unchanged through the successive orders as it does in egalitarianism. Change or transformation through encompassment is critical to hierarchy, for it is part of the definition of the higher in relation to the lower, the capacity to determine by virtue of the cosmic forces that constitute the whole. A fear expressed in egalitarian ideology is that the individual will be consumed, obscured, and will lose its identity in more inclusive orders and that those who command such orders will negate the autonomy of subordinates. This fear is often expressed in egalitarian worlds—in American democratic individualism, for example, and in the extreme individualism of Australian nationalism—by the incessant assertion of the sanctity of individuals, their uniqueness, and so on. Australian egalitarians abhor the boss who effaces the autonomy and identity of subordinates. In hierarchical ideology the fears are somewhat different. The individual in society can be an object of fear and terror. This is clearest in the idea of the demonic, an outsider within, which asserts the determination of its individuality against encompassing and incorporating forces. Australian egalitarianism often values the outsider within society positively as symbolic of the ultimate value of individuality. Buddhist monks can in the Sinhalese conception be seen as outsiders in society when they choose to live in its midst rather than in monasteries or forests. But they are regarded with less respect by some Sinhalese (Gombrich 1971, Carrithers 1983) because the ultimate encompassing principles they represent are inextricably linked to their being external to society. In Sinhalese thought an outsider in society is virtually a contradiction in terms, so the demon must be expelled and the monk should be in the monastery. It is when the social order is itself fragmented and in disarray that beings of the outside, demons and monks, enter and further destroy in the instance of the former or, as in the instance of monks, act restoratively. In effect they are not outside, for society in its fragmentation is rendered outside itself.

The popular Australian film *Crocodile Dundee* perhaps clarifies the distinction of the egalitarian view. The qualities of the unique individual, Dundee, are defined in the context of the outside, the bush. He then enters the society of New York. His uniqueness is maintained and his individuality is even determinate and instrumental in reordering some aspects of the disorder of New York and in asserting the ultimate correctness of natural individual value. The film closes with the egalitarian conquest of the chief egalitarian fear. Dundee on a crowded subway platform clambers over the backs of the crowd, which is packed like so many faceless sheep. Dundee's transcendent Australian individualism, ultimately including that which threatens to subsume it, is consummated in his consequent embrace of his American love.

A possible additional interpretation of Dundee's last act is of essential unity in identity. He and his love, Australia and America, are basically the same in their uniqueness, despite superficial cultural differences. Both worship the autonomous individual, which is fundamental to society. Identity, by which I mean here essential likeness or similarity, is an important principle of egalitarianism in general and of Australian egalitarianism especially. It is linked to the way egalitarians often construct their social realities according to a logic of inclusion. Thus the successive social units of greater inclusion are constituted from like individual elements. The more inclusive forms are congeries of linked like elements, which as wholes are virtually individuals in aspect and action. Groups, and sometimes society, may be referred to by egalitarians as if they had the qualities of individuals. So, too, the nation that egalitarians often conceive of as a super individual which gains its unity in a unique character, which is also the principal quality of each of the component units of the nation.

Identity and difference, the critical principles of individual and social coherence in egalitarianism, are perfectly complementary. Thus identity or likeness constitutes that which is to be regarded as different, while difference marks out that which is to be classed as the same. Difference is a principle of separation, which identifies those who are to be associated, the principle of association being identity or similarity. They operate simultaneously to create the closure which Weber (1978) argued is the particular tendency in status groups and in ethnicity. By closure Weber referred to the pattern according to which status and ethnic groups become exclusive in their membership, distinguish themselves, and separate themselves from others. Weber considered such closure to be a universal, almost primordial tendency. What I note here is that complementarity of identity and difference, which produces closure, is consistent with an egalitarian individualism wherein the parts compose and determine the whole. The society of egalitarian ideology is a collection of coherent independent parts which are eventually integrated into an organic unity.

I emphasize that in Australian egalitarian ideology similarity and difference ideally reduce to a single principle whereby the one is a manifestation of the other. Such a principle, in the Australian egalitarian view, is achieved in nature and in the individual outside society. This, I should add, is integral to the Australian conception of nation. In nature, individuals manifest their uniqueness and unite by virtue of an elective affinity, a fundamental similarity in nature. This ideological conception is consistent with the view that the individual is prior to society and with the Australian egalitarian value that ideally society should be an extension of nature. Suffering in society is conceived of as an instance of society going against the grain of nature. Conflict in society is regarded as a suppression by society of what should be natural within it or a manifestation of the natural in society. The practice of this ideology has many implications for the understanding of Australian political culture, not least among them the Australian nationalist dislike of socially produced inequalities. What I note here, however, is that the essential unity of similarity and difference is fundamental to the Australian conception of nation. The nation is the transcendent manifestation of society as the perfect realization of nature, of what is at the root or base of society, and is the unity of natural difference in essential similarity. The logic of such a conception relates to the Australian nationalist view of the nation as above society and the state. The nation for Australians is the exemplification of nature as the cosmically unifying principle. It is outside "real" society, the social order of daily experience, and the state and theoretically generates and regenerates them both. Ideally the state must transform in the direction of the nation as the embodiment of universal nature. This is in contrast to the Sinhalese Buddhist conception whereby the nation transforms by virtue of its incorporation within the state as the embodiment of universal cosmic principles.

The nationalisms and wider political cultures of Sri Lanka and Australia are very different in the logic of their reasoning. Without a grasp of this reasoning much that appears ordinary or extraordinary in their worlds would elude understanding. Arguments in Australia concerning the legitimacy of state policies, the appropriate use of government power, and the issue of multiculturalism achieve some significance and direction in the egalitarianism of Australian nationalism. In Sri Lanka the Sinhalese Buddhist logic of hierarchy yields some insight into the violent destruction of Tamils in rioting by Sinhalese, of the violence of Buddhist monks, and of the ideological weight behind various public pronouncements of politicians.

Some scholars and political commentators may protest that the nationalist ideas to which I have referred gain their force and achieve their full comprehension only in the complex specifics of their historical, political, and economic settings. They would be perfectly correct. The ideologies I have discussed were formed in history and continually gain new meaning in the historical processes and particular social and political contexts in which they are very much engaged. This is a point that I shall reiterate throughout this volume.

What I am concerned to show, however, is that what anthropologists generally understand by culture is deeply ingrained in practices and is a primary factor giving direction and force to such practices. This is a point that numerous anthropologists have not tired of making. In their view and in mine, culture is not a mere adjunct of other forms of analysis and interpretation, such as economics, politics, and the like. It is not another factor to be added to the battery of methodological considerations which clutter the armory of modern social science. The role of culture is fundamental, for its logic can be integral to the very way analysts interpret their social worlds.

One of the general arguments I shall pursue in this volume is that the cultural reasoning which is involved in nationalism is also ingrained in the serious, objective analyses of modern social science. The dualism of Australian nationalist thinking, which makes distinctions between individual and society, ideal and real, nature and society, and even nation and state, is not necessarily vastly different from the dualism to be found in a Durkheim or a Levi-Strauss. This observation does not invalidate the analyses that flow from such reasoning. On the contrary, it may account for their apparent explanatory success and even their durability in a discipline such as anthropology, which is notorious for its changes in theoretical fashion. Thus the very fact that the conceptualizations of a Levi-Strauss, or a Freud, or a Marx, or a Weber are deeply embedded in the cultural worlds of their historical realities gives such conceptualization force in explanation and in understanding. This is all the more true because the power of their thought especially is connected with their deep concern to explore the logic of their realities. But this kind of awareness is also their limitation. A reasoning bound within history and integral to its flow cannot easily transcend these limitations except through the force of history itself. Marx and Weber, for example, may add to their relevance in a world increasingly subordinated to the outward thrust of those very cultural and historical worlds within which they wrote. And so in my analysis of aspects of Sinhalese Buddhist nationalism I shall indeed draw upon analytical frameworks that have been used to explore nationalism in the West. Sri Lanka is in many ways part of the same expanding and transforming capitalist world.

But I have focused on the distinct dimensions of Sinhalese Buddhist and Australian nationalism to underline the fact that there are aspects of their political realities which must be explored through the logic of their ideologies. These cannot be passed off and left to one side, regarded as mere variations upon the same general pattern. They are not to be dismissed as cultural templates imposed from above and aesthetically suasive (Geertz 1973). Neither are they simply the constructive artifice of the dominant—instances of the "big fix," as one wag has described those Marxist approaches unmodified by Gramsci or Weber (Wright 1985). Nationalist ideologies, like many of the social theories that are engaged to fathom the world, operate at depth. There are critical features of the cultures of nationalism that are ingrained in the historical realities of nationalist potency.

Here is the method behind my elaboration of the arguments of Sinhalese hierarchy and Australian egalitarianism. The reasoning or logic of the respective nationalist ideologies has ontological dimensions;[5] that is, these ideologies contain logical elements relevant to the way human beings within their historical worlds are existentially constituted. The being of the myths and legends bears a connection with an ontology of being as this is constituted and reconstituted in the everyday world. I mean by this only that the nationalist myths and legends have a logical connection with the ontologies of being in routine realities. I do not mean that their meaning is identical. Indeed I shall argue that the logic of the myths as I explore them could hardly be described as having meaning at all. Its meaning is confined to the structure of the myths alone and has no necessary import beyond them. A potentiality of meaning, a range of possibilities of meaning, awaits them in context. When they are engaged in nationalism they become linked with identical logics of being that orient experience in everyday realities. The myths and legends contextualized politically and made to ring with a systematic nationalist message begin to override the multiple meanings in ontology of the ordinary contexts of existence. In this process the meaning of everyday logic can become transformed to the terms of the nationalist ontology of myth and rite. Nationalist myths and legends therefore begin to work at great depth and within the very vitals of the person and, perhaps, reorient persons toward the horizons of their experience. Acting through the logic of myth and rite, the religion of nationalism can even reconstitute the meaning of ontologies in daily life, forcing a consistency upon them, and expanding the contextual relevance of ontology. It is a feature of nationalism and of its totalitarian ideological form that it is highly redundant in meaning; that is, the meaning with which its logic is imbued and in which the very being of its audience becomes reconstituted can threaten to become the totality of meaning for all contexts. In a way the gathering tide of redundancy in the meaning of nationalist ontology drowns out a hitherto great diversity of meaning. And thus action in a variety of contexts becomes driven, often destructively, in the force of a nationalist logic which has become the only truth.

The being of the person potentially constituted in nationalism is available, I suggest, through the analysis of the logic of nationalist legend and rite. In other words the psychology of the nationalist person is present in the logic of those cultural artifacts that make up the traditions of the nation. The nationalist bricolage made up of bits and pieces of a cultural world, as Levi-Strauss (1966) explains in a different context, can never be independent of the logic of those realities in which the bric-a-brac of nationalist imagination were gathered. In a way, therefore, the logic of the myths is also in the world. It is through attention to nationalist traditions and to the practices of everyday life that I search for the potency of nationalism. This potency is not in the individual psychology of persons independent of the world in which they are embedded. The potency of nationalism and the psychology with which it resonates is there in the world that extends around the person, a world in which the person is constituted in the deepest recesses of his or her being.

I am interested in the passions of nationalism, on which my focus upon ontology has direct bearing. The passions are often seen as moments of irrationality or as moments when reason is lost. In such a view either the world is suffering under a monstrous delusion, is somehow deranged, or the person is regarded as maddened and apart from all sense of reality. Various forms of the cultural action of human beings, from witchcraft to millenarian movements and cargo cults and to the furies of the Nazis, have often been explained by some appeal to a concept of irrationality. My argument is that the passions—and the often furious passions of nationalism—manifest reason and are conditioned in the ontology of being essayed by the logic of the traditions of nationalism. I am not saying that the destruction in Sri Lanka or the ethnic prejudice in Australia is sane because it manifests reason. Either can, indeed, be seen as madness, but a madness filled with a reasoning of its own and produced in the ideas and practices of an otherwise routine and compassionate world. It is the very reasoning in nationalism that creates it as such a powerful, even all-consuming beast.

The discussion of the relation between ontology and the passions of nationalism, therefore, is intended as a general contribution to an understanding of the force of nationalist ideology. Ideology for me gains its power in the historically and politically formed contexts of a cultural world. It does so additionally through the logics that are inscribed in its traditions and by the nature of their connection and transformation of the ontologies of the everyday world in which those captured in nationalism must live.

The book is divided into two parts. In part 1 I shall explore Sinhalese Buddhist nationalism and its relation to the current Sinhalese-Tamil violence in Sri Lanka. Part 2 is a description of Australian cultural nationalism, a nationalism crystallized in the violence and metaphors of war and relevant to current discussions of intolerance toward ethnic identity. The myths and legends that I shall examine in both parts are those taken by nationalists to be vital in the comprehension of their historical worlds. I stress this in the context of my own awareness that anthropologists in their analyses of cultures are engaged in the act of construction. They are bricoleurs who participate in the act of creating the very objects they investigate. No anthropologist or serious student of culture could ever escape such a charge, and I cannot avoid it here. But, I do claim that I have taken the myths that most Sinhalese and Australians would point to as the key myths of nationalist identity. They are the ones through which Sinhalese and Australians interpret the significance of their social and political realities.

The myths and legends stand as significant, independent of my assertion of their importance. Furthermore, the myths and legends are readily available, which is one of the advantages of the anthropological study of something as public as nationalism. The idiosyncrasy that some are bound to detect in my analysis of often sensitive matters is open to independent investigation. The reader is not completely reliant on the ethnography I choose to divulge, as he is in respect to much anthropological description. I cannot avoid the fact, however, that my interpretation of the myths is my interpretation. What I do claim, though, is that my understanding is within the ideological terms of those who use the myths. This is apparent in the hermeneutics of the rites that engage the myths to their purpose and in the hermeneutics or analysis that the events of daily social and political life reveal in the myths. I underline this point. Ritual and everyday practices, in my view, constitute an ongoing analysis by cultural actors of the terms of their own cultural existence. My reference to these practices, practices that are within the ordinary experience of Sinhalese and Australians, is not merely to illustrate the argument of my analysis. It is to indicate that the logic or reasoning of the myths and legends of nationalism I detect is consistent with the interpretations placed by Sinhalese and Australians on their realities, interpretations revealed in the structure of their cultural practices. Insofar as this is so, my understanding of the reasoning of the myths and legends is not to be dismissed as a product of my own imaginative construction, somehow independent of the realities lived by others.

The great myths of the origin of the Sinhalese people, of the foundation of their state, and of the triumphant reconquest by a Sinhalese Buddhist king of Sri Lanka, are the stories that provide the focus of my analysis of Sinhalese Buddhist nationalism. These myths are recounted in the famous religious chronicles of Sinhalese Buddhism. My interpretation centers on the versions in the *Mahavamsa*, the fifth-century chronicle most often referred to by Sinhalese nationalists. I do not begin the analysis with my interpretation of these myths. Rather, I begin with a discussion of some of the main approaches to an understanding of the historical significance that Sinhalese and Tamil nationalists and scholars from these communities accord to the chronicles. The purpose is both to establish the importance of the histories in nationalist debate and to demonstrate the potential value of an alternative approach to the myths of history for understanding their force in the current conflict.

Tambiah, in his study of the historical and political background to the riots of 1983 (1986, 6), drew attention to the need to "deconstruct" the legends contained in the *Mahavamsa*. The task he suggests is complex, involving archeological research untrameled by nationalist interest and careful historical reconstruction. My deconstruction is a modest beginning indeed. But it is one that is for the most part untried in Sri Lanka and, I think, worthy of much greater elaboration than I am able to give it.

The argument of the myths, I claim, is being worked out anew in the modern situation of ethnic conflict. My demonstration of this does not give the myths causative power. The present disasters are born of historically produced political and social conditions. These have been excellently detailed by Tambiah and many others. Such work is indispensable to a full understanding of the current tragedy of the island. Rather, I shall show how the logic of the myths can be a factor in giving forces which are already powerfully present in the situation particular direction and added impetus.

Evil and the state are an important theme of the Sinhalese Buddhist myths of history. They are inextricably bound, and the one is generated in the other. Evil in the arguments of the Sinhalese myths is to be distinguished from other conceptions of evil—those of Western Christianity, for example. Some scholars have claimed that the idea of evil in Hindu and Buddhist societies is less radical than the Christian kind.[6] I think they are mistaken. Evil in the Sinhalese myths is the fragmentation of the cosmically instituted political order, and this fragmentation is manifest in the destruction of the person. The evil suffering of person, and of the nation as well, sets in train their own process of violent regeneration. In this process the evil of fragmentation is reversed and the hierarchy of the world order encompassed by the benevolent Buddhist state is restored.

This argument of the myths is a factor that lends significance to the collective violence of nationalism in Sri Lanka. It is, I contend, of relevance to the passions of ethnic destruction in rioting, in terrorism, and in the military action of the state. The penetration of the logic of the myths into the depths of personal suffering is evident in the ideas and practices of sorcery. Sinhalese from all social classes visit the sorcery shrines, where they ask the demons of sorcery to address all manner of problem. Chief among these demons is Suniyam, a being who is also a god. His dual character is symbolic of his power, the power of the state, which is at once destructive and fragmenting and regenerative and ordering.

I shall trace a connection between the personal fear, suffering, and violence of sorcery and the collective violence of ethnic strife. The connection is not simply in the logic of the myths, however; it is made in modern social and political processes that actively tie personal suffering to the politics of nation. I shall examine some of these processes and the new meaning and force which they yield to the myths of history.

The religion of Australian nationalism is crystallized in the legends of suffering of Australian people. Australian national history often appears as a tale of despair rooted in the nation's founding in convict abjection, in the harshness of climate and soil, in the thirsty wandering of explorers, in the destruction of defiant bushrangers, and so to the present day. The legend of Anzac, the story of Australian and New Zealand soldiers in the First World War, is a tale of horrendous suffering. But it is also the legend in which the ideals of the Australian nation receive perhaps their greatest expression. Anzac is the foremost legend of Australian identity. Its key events are centered upon the defeat by Turkish forces of the Australian and New Zealand troops at Gallipoli in the Dardanelles. Unlike other defeats suffered by Australians—of the bushranger Ned Kelly, a supreme symbol of individual autonomy, who, suited in armor, is shot by police, or the gold miners of Eureka stockade, who as symbols of collective individualism are routed by the agents of state order—the Anzacs are ultimate victors. This victory, I must add, is not necessarily a glorification of war and its violence but the apotheosis of the Australian people transcendent in the midst of state destruction.

I shall discuss the accounts of Anzac in the official Australian war histories and the events of Anzac as interpreted by modern nationalist writers. The war histories have the status of religious chronicles comparable to the great religious histories of the Sinhalese. My analysis of the Anzac legend will be concentrated on what I regard as a central theme, the nation or people as recreative and regenerate of the state. The nation, consistent with the logic of egalitarianism, stands independent of the state. The Anzac legend declares the nation to be whole and unified, outside the mechanism of the state, and this autonomous integrity is reproduced in its parts, in individual Australian citizens.

The argument of Anzac will then be shown to be part of Australian political culture, perhaps out of proportion to the numbers of people who may actually celebrate the occasion or who have knowledge of the Anzac events. The logic of Anzac is part of the person and vital to the process of interpersonal practices, even for those who purport to analyze and interpret the Australian scene objectively—historians and other social scientists. I shall investigate some of the possibilities of the logic of

Anzac egalitarian nationalism and its presence in ethnic prejudice and in the ideas and practices of those who may abhor such prejudice yet whose arguments may be instrumental in reproducing its energy.

I have chosen to compare Sri Lanka and Australia for numerous reasons: they are clearly relevant to scholarly debate on the nature and excesses of nationalism; they are appropriate to my general theme concerning the different ways in which nationalist ideology may be shaped in accordance with hierarchy or egalitarianism, and of course Australia and Sri Lanka are countries in which I have done field work.

But further, equally important reasons have to do with methodological questions, the nature of anthropological comparison and anthropology as criticism. Some of my colleagues and friends have registered surprise at the very thought of comparing Sri Lanka and Australia. One distinguished colleague commented jokingly at the absurdity of comparing a great world civilization such as Buddhist Sri Lanka, with its centuries of recorded history, with Australia, a new world with a brief history and an "uncultivated" reputation. Other scholars, mainly in Australia, have recorded astonishment that an advanced industrial society should be brought into contrast with a third world nation and on the same analytical terms. Such attitudes, of course, are produced in the very nationalisms I shall discuss and in the ideological commitments that in various ways are part of us all despite our struggles to escape them. I stress that the comparison I shall present is concerned with structures of reasoning or the logics of conceptualization within the cultures of nationalism. I am not comparing societies as they may exist in their full empirical reality in an objectivist sense, although I see no reason that this should not be attempted. This aside, however, I note that implicit in the surprise at the kind of comparison I shall attempt here is a notion that the units of comparison should be of like empirical kind. How this is to be determined before the comparison actually takes place strikes me as problematic, for it is only through the comparison that what is like and what is unlike can be determined. This is the reason behind the idea of comparison in much anthropology. More generally, the logic of comparison in the anthropology I practice here is founded on the exploration of those aspects that may radically distinguish human beings in their action yet simultaneously manifest them as united in a single humanity. The idea of anthropological comparison that I shall pursue is directed to an investigation of the assumptions that are integral to the cultural worlds in which human beings live and by which they interpret their realities. This approach is at the heart of the critical possibility of anthropology: an anthropology that can directly address issues of political and social moment that affect the lives of the very people who give anthropologists their imaginative inspiration.

Anthropological criticism, unfortunately too often self-indulgent and narcissistic, has drawn attention to the fact that anthropologists engage their own realities in their construction of the realities of others (Fabian

1983; Clifford and Marcus 1986). The dangers of this are particularly evident in an analysis in which cultural practices are addressed in relation to their involvement in the production of human anguish and suffering. The anthropologist risks a kind of moral absolutism wherein the values of his or her own world are given an ultimate validity which they do not necessarily have. This is so regardless of the anthropologist's politics or social views or social and cultural origins.

The point was driven home to me excellently by a close Sinhalese friend, a man of considerable personal courage, who has openly criticized the current situation and who is active in other humanitarian causes. Once when I was commenting on aspects of the present ethnic strife he remarked, in disagreement with a few of my points, "The trouble with you, Bruce, is that you are an Australian egalitarian." The truth of the remark shocked me and made me realize more powerfully than the numerous anthropological arguments that I had read on the subject the depths to which my own historical ideological constitution was undoubtedly integral to my interpretation of modern events in Sri Lanka. This is a personal reason for my having chosen to include an analysis of Australian nationalism in the same volume with a discussion of Sri Lanka. By attempting an anthropological analysis of my own native culture I have been able to apprehend, but always only in part, the extent to which the logic of my own cultural world enters into the understanding of another.

But consideration of Australia in juxtaposition with Sri Lanka has a methodological import that transcends my personal reasons. While a common criticism of anthropology is that its practitioners impose their own cultural assumptions upon those whom they study, it is never clear what these assumptions may be. The cultural reasoning of their political worlds is not subjected to the same kind of analysis as those they study or upon which they freely comment. I cannot claim that I have avoided such a charge here. But I have attempted to explore aspects of my own cultural reality anthropologically and in the spirit of criticism which I think can be facilitated by the comparativist perspective in anthropology. A vital aspect of the anthropological point of view that I value is not only an insistence on the cultural constitution of political and social realities but also an understanding, by virtue of such a point of view, that these realities are arbitrary and have no strict determining necessity (Kapferer 1986a).

There is a further methodological point to the manner in which the ethnography in this volume is presented. The comparative method in anthropology is at its weakest if it is merely a system for what Gluckman called "apt illustration" or what Leach called "butterfly collecting." These anthropologists were complaining of a tendency in anthropology and in other disciplines in which cultural materials are used to compare cultures without close attention to the settings in which these cultures achieved their significance or to the principles engaged in the structures of meaning. Cultures analyzed in this way are drained of their particular import and are reduced to each other: they become subordinated to theory, repetitively drumming out theoretical themes which remain oblivious to the arguments that cultures may themselves present. Our understanding of humanity in general is impoverished rather than enriched.

My juxtaposition of Sinhalese Buddhist and Australian egalitarian nationalism in one volume is intended to place the two nationalist religions, as I understand them, into dialogical relation. In other words each is to realize its distinction and similarity in its refraction through the other. I aim, therefore, to realize a potential of anthropological comparison whereby the nature and import of cultural ideas and practices are drawn into clear focus through the lens of other cultural ideas and practices. In this analysis, moreover, Sinhalese Buddhist nationalism comes to play an analytical role in the interpretation of Australian nationalism and vice versa. Sinhalese and Australian cultural and political worlds are not merely placed alongside each other but are brought into active dialectical relation within the structure of the entire volume and participate together in extending an understanding of social and political processes of immediate moment.

Part I

Evil and the State

Sinhalese Nationalism, Myth, Violence, and the Power of Hierarchy

To inquire into the "truth" of the political myths is, therefore, as meaningless and as ridiculous as to ask for the truth of a machine gun or a fighter plane. Both are weapons; and weapons prove their truth by their efficiency. If the political myths could stand this test they needed no other and no better proof. In this respect the theory was beyond attack and invulnerable. All it had to do was to put the political myths into action and to show their constructive and destructive power.

Ernst Cassirer, *"Judaism and the Modern Political Myths"* 1944

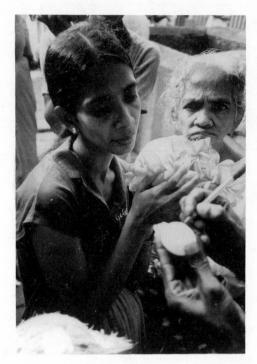

The Passion of Destruction. A woman at a sorcery shrine in Colombo watches as a shrine priest writes the name of her deserting husband on an egg. The egg, powerfully symbolic of cosmic origin, will be smashed and her husband extinguished in fragmentation. The woman holds lotus blooms indicative of the regeneration of her life simultaneous with her act of destruction. Her mother looks on furiously. (Photo by Bruce Kapferer)

2

Ethnic Violence and the Force of History in Legend

In July 1983 riots against the Hindu Tamil minority in Sri Lanka erupted throughout the island. They were of a savagery unparalleled in the recent history of ethnic conflict in Sri Lanka.[1] The highland tea estate areas, where Tamils descended from indentured laborers recruited during the nineteenth century are concentrated, and the capital, Colombo, were the most severely affected. Gangs of Sinhalese thugs roamed the streets with lists of Tamil houses, buildings and businesses, systematically burning them and slaughtering their inhabitants. Added to this horror was the sight of large gatherings of ordinary Sinhalese who looked on while, in some instances, Tamil victims were burned alive. By the end of July most of the 300,000s Tamils of Colombo had fled the city or were in refugee camps. Many of the 800,000 Tamil tea-estate laborers were similarly driven away. The Sri Lankan government admits that something in the region of 350 Tamils were killed. The numbers are certainly far greater.[2] Some Sinhalese did shelter and protect Tamils, but the systematic way Tamils were attacked, the fact that it was Sinhalese murdering Tamils—virtually no Sinhalese were killed—and the fact that for two or three days the government and its agents took no preventive action while the killing continued has led some members of the Tamil population to draw stark parallels with Nazi pogroms.

The fury of the riots was demonic. Indeed it was this demonic fury that led me to wonder whether there could be a connection between this action and Sinhalese Buddhist ideas concerning the demonic, the subject of an earlier study of mine (Kapferer 1983). My recent work on sorcery rites in Sri Lanka (Kapferer 1986b) indicated that I should pursue the possibility further. This was especially in view of the fact that the demonic passions of the rioting were fuelled in a Sinhalese Buddhist nationalism that involved cosmological arguments similar to those in exorcism, particularly in the rites of sorcery.

*Oddi Raja, the Transformer of
Evil.   (Photo by Bruce Kapferer)*

    Sorcery rites in Sri Lanka engage the cosmology of the state and the
symbolism of the destructive and reconstituting power of the embodiments
or prime agents of the state—typically, kings, queens, princes, and
merchant princes.   Anthropologists have long noted the connection
between forms of political authority and power and sorcery.[3] Obeyesekere
(1976, 1981) has remarked on the link for Sri Lanka in his important
work, though he has argued that an apparent increase in the practice of
sorcery in the island is related to the decline in traditional authority
structures, among other factors.[4] What struck me, however, was the nature
of the myths surrounding Suniyam, the most dangerous of the demonic
figures of evil destruction.   The main myths for this principal Sinhalese
Buddhist being of sorcery parallel in their form and content the great
heroic legends.   These myths, like the heroic legends, are about cosmic
origin, the beginning of the state, the institution of kingship at the apex
of hierarchy, the attack by the agent of evil upon the state, and the
consequent decline and subsequent regeneration of the state.   Associations
such as these between the myths of evil and the myths of the state led

Suniyam, the God of Sorcery, wielding the punishing sword of state. He grips a fire viper in his mouth. (Photo by Bruce Kapferer)

me to explore the possibility of a deeper connection, an ontological connection, which may expand an understanding of the current circumstances of state terror and personal suffering, terror and violence that are part of the ethnic conflict and of sorcery as well.

Obeyesekere (1975) has drawn powerful attention to the murderous sentiments that Sinhalese Buddhists engage in their everyday sorcery and antisorcery practice at shrines throughout the island. My own work at these temples, and my observation of the several important sorcery rites, confirms much of what Obeyesekere has to say. The following is an invocation to Suniyam at a shrine in a shanty area at the edge of Colombo city. It was uttered loudly by the shrine priest (*kapurala*) on behalf of a woman recently deserted by her husband. His departure was believed to have been through the evil agency of her in-laws. The woman was destitute.

> O Siddha Suniyam, king of the gods, victorious hero
> You who have the power of fiery destruction.
> I tell you lord that someone has threatened this
> holder of life (*prana karaya*), beaten her and disappeared.

Cast your divine eye upon the maker of this trouble.
Gather your demon army. Raise your sword of Vaḍiga in judgment.
Take hold of this evil husband.
Seize him by the neck, squeeze the breath from his body.
Crush his wind pipe. Give him up as a sacrifice to the the Blood
Demon.
We do this incantation (*kannalavva*) so that you will give the
appropriate punishment (*sudusu danduwama*).
If he [the husband] should climb a tree, a rocky mountain, or any high
place, drag him down.
When he walks in the street, let him meet with an accident.
Smash his skull into pieces, no larger than grains of rice. Tear his
body apart.
If he goes near the sea, a river, or stream, make him drown.
O God! Infect him with disease—smallpox, eczema, leprosy. Cause his
skin to itch.
Give him the thirty-two sufferings.
Make this woman's heart full of happiness by meting out this
punishment.

This kind of violent curse is common at the shrines. It is a passionate
violence not confined to the priest but quite apparent in the demeanor
and expressive action of the supplicants. Certain priests are very popular
because they give powerful expression to personal sentiment. But as
Obeyesekere argues forcefully, the action of the priest is not merely
expressive, it is performative. Supplicants often expect their victims
actually to experience the horrors of their terrible curses.

I consider that there is a relation between the passion of sorcery and
the furious passion of ethnic violence. Both, I suggest, find their force in
ideologically driven concerns, founded in a Sinhalese Buddhist ontology
of the state, of the person, and of evil. Through this ontology personal
suffering places the other in a particular destructive relation to the self,
unleashing almost cosmic powers of regeneration. The passions of the
ethnic strife in Sri Lanka manifest the violence of such cosmic regeneration.

In drawing on this connection for my argument I intend to further
an understanding of the reasons ordinary people should sometimes be
consumed by horrendous and senseless destructive rage. The issue I raise
has particular poignancy in the Sri Lankan setting. I am concerned with
Sinhalese Buddhists who practice perhaps the most peaceful, nonviolent
of the world's great religions. Some commentators on the current political
scene have simply asserted that the Sinhalese rioters "forgot" their
Buddhism. They were just not being Buddhist, presumably in the sense
of those who have explained the action of Christians who have murdered

Jews as being a suspension of their Christian morality! This kind of argument is perhaps most difficult as an explanation for the action of some Buddhist monks, the presumed epitome of Buddhist nonviolence. But Buddhist monks assisted and even urged Sinhalese thugs to attack marked areas of Tamil residence. In the aftermath of the bombing of the Colombo bus station in April 1987 in which around 120 Sinhalese were reported killed, groups of monks have been seen leading the public clamor for bloody vengeance.

Most Sinhalese did not participate in the killing of July 1983. Nontheless, many watched, without acting, while Tamils burned. Compassionate Sinhalese sheltered Tamils in their homes. But I have heard the very same people state that "they [the Tamils] got what they deserved." There is a faintly hollow sound to statements that rioters were acting irrationally or were following political orders. There is evidence that much of the destruction was caused by organized gangs of hoodlums, some of which were actively encouraged by political leaders (Obeyesekere 1984b). But none of this mitigates the fact that Tamils were for a while engulfed by the flames of a passionate Sinhalese Buddhist violence which was directed against them alone.[5]

Four years later after a rash of Tamil separatist attacks on Sinhalese there is widespread Sinhalese pressure for total war against the Tamil minority. It seems that the government of Sri Lanka can prevent another violent outbreak of Sinhalese rioting only by demonstrating its ability to destroy Tamils in bombing raids on Jaffna. The deaths caused in such raids are being used to legitimate government authority among the Sinhalese population as a whole.

The ethnic violence that is consuming Sri Lanka, like the violence of sorcery, gains its force and its meaning in the turbulence of a historical political and social world. Sorcery and the symbolic distortions of its ideas and practices takes form in the contradictions and transformations of class relations, among other things. So does the ethnic violence. To explore some of the class processes that underlie ethnic tension is essential, for the force and intensity of individual and communal fear, hatred, and destruction are fueled in the structure of class relations. In a significant way the fury of ethnicity, and sorcery too, is the fury of class suffering.

But the anger of ethnic tensions is obviously born of ethnic nationalism, which has other passions, not just those of class. The analysis begins with an account of the import of some of the main Sinhalese Buddhist legends in current political rhetoric, though no account could possibly convey a full sense of the ubiquitous presence of the legends in daily political discourse in Sri Lanka. As I shall show, the political myths are treated by ideologues and academicians alike as constituting legitimations of different political claims and perceptions of reality. The view is basically of myth and legend as cultural or historical resources to be manipulated. This is not entirely wrong, but myths are also considerably more than this. The logic of the myths is deeply ingrained in the practices of everyday life and is part of a more embracing cosmology. Factors such as these not only account for the recurrent force of the myths in legitimizing action but also their continual appearance as the focus of public, often heated, debate.

Legends, History, Political Rhetoric, and Scholarship

The Vijaya and Dutugemunu legends recorded in the great Sinhalese chronicle, the *Mahavamsa*, are among the most common themes of political rhetoric of modern Sri Lanka. The Vijaya story is the myth of origin of the Sinhalese people. It tells of an unruly prince, the eldest son of twins, themselves the offspring of a union between a lion and the errant and wandering daughter of the King of Vanga, in India. Vijaya, because of his unruly and destructive behavior, is banished from India by his father, Sihabahu (lion-arm). It is from Sihabahu that the Sinhalese claim their name, the people of the lion. After various misadventures Vijaya and 700 male companions arrive on the shores of Lanka. Here they encounter the Yakkas (demons), whom Vijaya slaughters with the aid of a demoness, Kuveni. Vijaya abandons Kuveni, who is his lover (wife), and establishes a new order and various settlements in Lanka. He then marries his men to women brought from India himself consecrating an Indian princess as his queen, and establishes the royal line of Sinhalese kings. Vijaya is transformed from an unruly prince into a righteous king.

The Dutugemunu legend is about Sinhalese political and religious resurgence. Through Dutugemunu's military leadership, the Sinhalese rid themselves of their vassal status under a foreign overlord. Lands lost to them are reconquered, and King Dutugemunu makes the full light of Buddhism shine over Lanka. Confined to the southeastern part of the island, at Magama, near the now famous religious shrine to the god Kataragama, Dutugemunu, with his ten mighty champions, breaks out and overpowers the Tamil king, Elara. Dutugemunu recaptures the ancient Sinhalese capital, Anuradhapura. This city, so legend has it, was one of the cities establishd by Vijaya. It is of cosmic centrality in the present consciousness of Sinhalese, for it is the place to which the sacred branch of the Bodhi tree was brought, the tree under which Gautama Buddha achieved his Enlightenment.

Professor Suriyakumaran, in a newspaper article, states, "History, the basis of many nation's strengths, has been our bane. Myths, legends, truths and untruths have been freely mixed and that which has flourished least, expectedly, has been the truth" (Colombo *Island*, 21 July 1984). In Sri Lanka myth has become historical reality and history myth, in ways that superficially parallel the wonderful analysis of the historical emergence of modern Hawaii of Marshall Sahlins (1981).

The Vijaya and Dutugemunu myths are frequently treated as historical fact or as having foundation in fact. Overt political propaganda, commentary in the press, popular histories, and the learned argument of Buddhist priests and some lay scholars are full of references to these stories as if they were factual accounts of historical events. The Vijaya and Dutugemunu stories as told in the ancient chronicles are reproduced in school texts and presented as fundamental to Sinhalese identity and to Sinhalese political rights (Siriweera 1984, 67–68).

In the present horrifying setting of ethnic warfare symbolic themes of the myths appear to be repeating themselves as historical reality. Since 1956 the Sri Lankan military units fighting the Tamil separatists have borne such names as the Gemunu Watch, the Sinha Regiment, and the Rajarata Rifles, names filled with mythic and Sinhalese nationalist significance. In 1985, when I wrote the first draft of this book, news broke that Tamil liberationist guerillas had attacked Anuradhapura, shooting large numbers of civilians, some near the sacred Bo tree. What did not receive as much press coverage was that local Sinhalese retaliated. Not only were Tamil civilians killed in response but Tamil *kovils* (Hindu temples) in Anuradhapura were destroyed and their incumbent priests killed.

The centrality of the Vijaya and Dutugemunu legends in political discourse is nowhere more evident than in the fury of propaganda. Thus a widely circulated pamphlet, entitled "Eelam—the Truth" (Eelam is the Tamil name for Sri Lanka), attacking the manifesto of the Tamil independence organization, the Tamil United Liberation Front, has this to say:

> They have disrupted families and severed friends. In fact the Sinhala and the Tamil people even of the Eastern and Northern provinces are one and the same race. They are descended from King Vijaya's Ministers, from whom the Sinhala people take pride of descent. After sending Ambassadors to the King at Madurai in the South of the Madras Presidency, which is now Tamil Nadu, the King of Pandi, who "when he had thus ordained many maidens ... sent his daughter ... to the conqueror Vijaya. Then King Vijaya consecrated a daughter of the Pandu King with solemn ceremony as his queen." After that the youngest son of the King of Madras was sent to Ceylon as the Prince Panduvasdeva who became ruler of Lanka and from them and their ministers are the Sinhala and Tamil people descended. This is the descent of the two nations according to the *Mahavamsa* (Dhammaruchi 1979).

In a few strokes of the pen the Vijaya story is used to demonstrate that the Sinhalese and the Tamils are of the same origin. This would probably be hotly denied by many Tamil nationalists, some of whom claim that their ancestors were the yakkas whom Vijaya slaughtered, an act they also note is being repeated by those who claim descent from

Vijaya. Even though in the tract from which I have quoted the common descent of Tamils and Sinhalese is recognized, it is nonetheless remarked that they are separate "nations." Also implicit in the argument is that as a nation, Tamils are properly subordinate to the Sinhalese conquerors.

In the same tract the "legitimate" fears that the Sinhalese have of Tamils—and therefore, by extension, the legitimacy of the Sinhalese response—are enumerated. The pamphlet cites liberally a lecture, "Sketches of Ceylon History," given in 1906 by Sir Ponnambalam Arunachalam. Arunachalam was a prominent member of the English-educated elite and an early Tamil nationalist.

> After the time of King Dutugemunu, that is after the defeat of the Tamil King Elara "the Tamils proved a never-failing source of harassment. They made frequent incursions into Ceylon, and Tamil Kings often sat on Vijaya's throne." In 104 B.C. they even took the most precious treasure in Ceylon, the begging bowl of the Buddha. "Sometimes the tide of invasion has rolled back into South India, as by King Gajabahu who in 113 A.D. brought back a multitude of Sinhala captives (Pannaseeha 1979, 3).

The same pamphleteer at one point lists among the causes of the anti-Tamil riots in 1977—shortly after the ascent to power of the present UNP government with a massive popular vote—"the cutting of Bo trees," "the maligning of the Sinhala people by calling Duttu Gamunu a murderer and the others as cads and the exaggeration of the incidents that took place," and "The constant degradation of the Sinhala people and the calling themselves [Tamils] a subject race when they have more privileges than any minority of any country in the world" (Pannaseeha 1979, 19).

Some of the fury of the pamphlet could be dismissed as merely the work of a deranged fanatic.[6] The pamphlet, however, is a published version of evidence given before the 1979 Sansoni Commission appointed to inquire into the circumstances surrounding the violent ethnic rioting of 1977. The evidence was compiled and written by a Buddhist monk of the Bhikku Training Centre at Maharagama near Colombo.

For their part Tamils are armed in their propaganda war with similar references but contradictory interpretation. Thus Paul Jayarajan (n.d.), who lists among his credentials his legal training and a period as senior scholar at Emmanuel College, Cambridge, attacks the Vijaya story in detail. He ridicules as simply fantasy the legend that Sihabahu had a lion father and that Lanka was inhabited by man-eating demons at the time of Vijaya's landing, but he asserts as reasonable fact that Vijaya was helped in his conquest by a woman of the people already living on the island. Jayarajan dissects the Vijaya myth with legal and scholarly skills. His great concern to separate "fact" from "fiction" underlines the enormous import of the Vijaya legend as a story of Sinhalese origins and territorial claims in modern Sri Lanka.

Satchi Ponnambalam (1983) likewise dismisses interpretations by the Sinhalese of their history. For him, the Vijaya myth is a "pure flight of fancy," as is "the account of 1,000 years of Tamil invasions and Sinhalese-Tamil wars, as presented by the chronicles and modern historians, false." Furthermore, referring to the ancient city sites (now part of a Unesco-financed Cultural Triangle Project and integral to Sinhalese Buddhist nationalist outpourings), "Nor was there a glorious Sinhalese-Buddhist civilization of Anuradhapura-Polonnaruwa-Sigiriya." Of Sigiriya (lion rock) Ponnambalam adds, "The map of Sigiriya . . . shows three caves and an audience hall. There are 21 oppressively sensuous half-figure portraits of celestial females [otherwise known as the Sigiri frescoes and often compared in style and beauty with the Ajanta paintings advancing singly and in pairs. One cannot conceive of any civilization in this rock and its maidens" (Ponnambalam 1983, 234).

Propaganda, serious reasoned scholarship, and political rhetoric, populist in style and character, commingle in the present situation of expanding hostilities, often in a single work. The political and social circumstances are now such that no one can remain impartial, and even someone who tries to do so will be drawn willy-nilly, into the discourse. Sri Lanka as much as any country deflates that pumped-up imperiousness of some academics, especially in the West, who claim to be above and outside the ideological world of their interpretation. History, so called, is the very stuff of politics in Sri Lanka, and few statements on the subject or references to historical myth and legend are independent of political argument.

The Vijaya myth is vital to the understanding of some Sinhalese that they are "Aryans" from North India.[7] Sinhalese are thus to be distinguished from the South Indian Dravidian Tamils. K. M. de Silva, professor of history at Peradeniya University, writes:

> Both legend and linguistic evidence indicate that the Sinhalese were a
> people of Aryan origin who came to the island from Northern India
> about 500 B.C. The exact location of their original home in India
> cannot be determined with any degree of certainty. The founding of
> the Sinhalese is treated in elaborate detail in the Mahavamsa with
> great emphasis on the arrival of Vijaya (Silva 1977, 3).

Gananath Obeyesekere powerfully criticizes such influential Sinhalese scholars as Senerat Paranavitana, the eminent epigraphist. It is in recognition of Paranavitana's scholarship that a statue stands to him in front of the archeological museum at Sigiriya. But Obeyesekere (1984a) points out Paranavitana's inaccurate interpretation of inscriptional evidence used to assert Sinhalese North Indian claims. Obeyesekere, however, is not immune to similar attack. Satchi Ponnambalam, describing Obeyesekere as a "discerning social anthropologist," accuses him of unconscious Sinhala chauvinism brought about by an overreliance on false history. At one point he runs in tandem a quotation from an article by Obeyesekere and an excerpt from the writings of Anagarika Dharmapala, an important ideologue of Sinhalese Buddhist nationalism and a central figure in the Buddhist revival beginning in the last century (Obeyesekere 1979; Kapferer 1983; Jayawardena 1985). Ponnambalam, in his distorted rhetoric, charges Obeyesekere with trying to "vindicate the chauvinist fanaticism of Dharmapala" (1983, 235).

It is clear that interpretations of myth and history are vital in the ethnic consciousness of both Sinhalese and Tamils. Such interpretations are not the stale meal of academic fare; they are alive in processes that can generate the suffering of homelessness and bring about sudden and violent death. Government leaders and politicians, who compose the important constituencies of mythic acceptance (Gunasinghe 1985), infuse their rhetoric with references to legends.[8] Their audience is culturally prepared for these references. The legends of the *Dipavamsa* and the *Mahavamsa,* their stories of origin, of armed struggle, of heroic resurgence, are woven into the fabric of Sinhalese religious and ritual life. The prime minister of Sri Lanka, who is popular among the urban and rural poor, has published a short novel in Sinhala and in English which presents the heroic progress of Dutugemunu (Premadasa 1986). The tone of the novel aligns the prime minister with widespread Sinhalese populist sentiment.

Public events are often the occasion of ideological recharging by politicians at all levels within the government. At the opening of a small deity shrine in Panadura, a town just south of Colombo, Cyril Mathew, then the minister of industries and scientific affairs, stated that "74 percent of the Sinhala race should not be dominated by the 12 percent minority community."[9] At the same time he announced that nationals of Sri Lanka, whatever their community had the right to live anywhere in Sri Lanka and that "300 Buddhist temples have been excavated by the Archaeological Department in the North and the East" (Colombo *Island,* 6 July 1984). These areas are dominated by the Tamil minority. The program of reclamation of temples was also announced on the radio and television. Such statements are completely consistent with Sinhalese claims to territorial hegemony that are supported by a reading of the ancient chronicles. They are also consistent with schemes of Sinhalese colonization and resettlement and with the practice of building replicas of ancient monuments, such as the Ruwanveliseya of Dutugemunu, around the island.[10]

Cyril Mathew is a noted ideologue who had published a number of inflammatory tracts. These expand on themes such as the following, spoken at a commemorative ceremony at a school for monks *(pirivena)* in the south of the island:

> Mr. Mathews said that the purest form of Buddhism prevailed in Sri Lanka due to the efforts of bhikkus who protected it. It was also the prime duty of the Buddhists to protect the Buddha Sasana. The smallest race in South Asia was the Sinhalese and as such the rights

and privileges of the Sinhalese . . . should be protected (Colombo *Sun*, 19 July 1985).

Other Sinhalese leaders pepper their public speeches with similar sentiments. Addressing a gathering at Pandulagama, near Anuradhapura, to celebrate the sixth anniversary of a government home building program, the prime minister made reference to the historical meaning of the area. It was in "the fields of Pandulagama—where eons ago Dutugemunu's warriors fought Elara" (Colombo *Sun*, 5 July 1985).

Public statements such as these can be expected at times of national tension, especially at a time of religious festival, when ethnic consciousness is high. Cyril Mathew and the prime miniser were making their speeches at that general period in the ritual calendar known as Asala. This falls chiefly in July but runs into August. An important religious period for Tamils, it is also of great significance for Sinhalese. It is the time of the Kandy (Asala) *perahera*, a ceremonial of kingship and the state (Seneviratne 1978.) This festival, which has many symbolic significances, is said by some Sinhalese to commemorate the victory of the legendary Sinhalese king Gajabahu I over the South Indian Colas and his release of 12,000 of their Sinhalese captives. According to tradition Dutugemunu laid the foundation stone for the Ruwanveliseya *dagaba*, the most revered monument in Anuradhapura, on the Asala *poya* (full moon). The principal festival of Kataragama occurs in Asala, in the southeastern region of the island. It is the region from which Dutugemunu rose against Elara, and some traditions are emphatic that God Kataragama supported Dutugemunu's triumph. Thousands of Sinhalese, largely from the heavily urbanized coastal areas, flock every year to this festival. Just before the Kataragama festival, at Dondra in the Southern Province, an important major festival to God Vishnu is held. Vishnu is the protector of Vijaya and his descendants and the guardian of Buddhism on the island. I have referred to only a few of the more famous festivals that take place throughout Sinhalese areas at the time of Asala—a period that also marks the onset of the rains (*vas*), a time when the Buddha first went into retreat. The Buddha and his teaching and the cultural heritage of the Sinhalese is at the forefront of consciousness at this time in the ritual calendar.

This ritual context gives the speeches of the ministers greater significance. Just possibly, too, some additional understanding is lent to the timing of the ethnic rioting. The worst riots ever erupted in 1983, just after the main festivities of Asala. The two anti-Tamil riots of 1977 and 1981 also occurred at the time of Asala.[11]

The Demystification of Myth: Rationality and Legitimation

The powerful ideological force of myth and other cultural interpretations of history have led Sri Lankan scholars, anguished by the present turn of events, to reveal their mystifying falsity. If the mists are blown away, then it is hoped that the clear vision of reason will prevail. If the myths are revealed for what they are, as the fantasies of religious cosmology rather than empirically valid history, then some of the ideological power of the inflammatory statements of politicians will be weakened. In an analysis by the Committee for Rational Development (1984) of the causes of the 1983 riots it is considered necessary to deny or qualify some of the "facts" of the chronicles and other traditional historical writings. Thus Vijaya and the Sinhalese are shown not to have been the first human inhabitants of the island, the Sinhalese are found to be the descendants of Indian immigrants to Sri Lanka before, during, and well after the Vijayan period, Dutugemunu is found to have fought Sinhalese kings as well as Tamil kings and, furthermore, to have allied with Tamil lords in his fight against Elara, and so on.

The foregoing reasoned corrections of popular Sri Lankan history are excellent examples of the responsible intellectual and scholarly concern to demystify the distortions of myth. While this exercise is essential, it fails to address some of the crucial ways in which myth and cosmic history achieve their emotional potency, for the critics of whatever kind adopt a mode of reasoning which is not that of the myths. The critics argue from positions outside the myths and the legends and I consider produce a radically incomplete understanding of the power of the myths in social and political action.

There are two main assumptions that guide the scholarly and political discourse of demystification in Sri Lanka. The first is that myth and reality can easily be distinguished. Myth is the elaboration of the fantastic. It will not stand the test of empirical evidence, of common sense, or of rational logic. A second, related assumption is that myth is epiphenomenal—that is, myth is born in a pragmatic social and political world and is a reflection of it. The specific distortions of myth, which take form through the particular interests of social actors, are ideological. Myth is shaped, often fantastically, to express the rights and claims of actors in particular social and political contexts. I shall discuss these two approaches to myth—myth as the fantastically irrational and myth as social and political pragmatics—as they appear in rhetorical and scholarly discourse in Sri Lanka.

Myth may indeed be fantastic. The marvelous and impossible events of myth, as Levi-Strauss and others have demonstrated, suspend the temporal reality of lived experience. This is the "method" of myth, a method whereby human beings can penetrate beneath the obscuring surface of everyday life and discover its ordering principles. Myth is the logic of the concrete. Its fantastic impossibilities contain the reasoning of a culturally arbitrary common sense. This is not the universalist common sense or rationalism of the kind often assumed in a Western pragmatic empiricism or analysis of a "scientific," positivist variety. The reduction of mythic reasoning to the terms of a rationalist universalism can do more to elaborate and perpetuate the sense of the fantastic than to demystify it.

Jayarajan's polemically extreme interpretation of the Vijaya myth is an example of the error that arises from exploring myth in terms of a universalizing rational common sense. To Jayarajan, the birth of Sihabahu from the union of a lion and a princess is undoubtedly fantastic, impossible, and therefore untrue. "A common feature of fables and legends," he says, "is the recounting of happenings which are obviously impossible in reality so as to boggle the imagination of the reader" (n.d., 3). Some events in the Vijaya myth are, by Jayarajan's standards, not impossible and hence acceptable. This is so for one moment in the Vijaya story, when the hero encounters a demoness, Kuveni, who gives food to Vijaya and his men.

> There is no reason to discount the story of Vijaya's meeting with
> Kuveni . . . because if a degrading fact is mentioned about Vijaya in the
> chronicles it is more likely to be true than a mythical glorification of
> him. There is no doubt whatsoever that the exiles suffered from
> hunger and thirst when they landed and were given food by Kuveni.
> Unless they were helped by the local inhabitants how could such a
> band of hapless refugees have had any chance of survival in an island
> reputed to be inhabited by demons and cannibals and who had for
> hundreds of years been able to prevent traders or marauders from
> settling in the island. (Jayarajan n.d., 25).

Jayarajan's main error is his assumption that events that fall within the terms of his own true-or-false common sense logic can be accepted as fact. He misses the obvious point that what may appear as plausible from his own standpoint may be no less impossible than the obviously fantastic. Within the structural logic of the Vijaya myth all events are constructions, whether they fit with common sense or not, and are ordered to the thematic and logic internal to the myth as a whole. Taken as a whole, the Vijaya legend essays a process whereby social relations are destroyed and reconstituted. The legend explicates a theme of rebirth. The feeding by Kuveni of Vijaya and his men symbolizes nurture following an event of rebirth. The rationalistic, common sense perspective of Jayarajan, determined by a logic external to the myth itself, radically distorts and obscures one of the central messages of the Vijaya legend.

Clearly, Jayarajan is led to his argument as a function of his own ideological commitment formed in the present political situation in Sri Lanka. Even so, the method of his discourse is one that he shares with many others in connection with Sri Lanka who would oppose him politically. This is a method which employs a rationalism born in the historical circumstances of social and scientific transformations largely centered in Europe that led to the emergence of the capitalist West, its colonial expansion, and Western industrial and technological domination. The logic of its rationality, its true-or-false, fact-or-fiction, real-or-ideal dualisms became integral to a culture of domination. It was such a rationalism that was part of the ideology of the legitimacy of colonial rule. A similar rationalism became vital to the ideology of ruling-class groups uniting opposed and conflicting class fractions in a "culture of class." Thus in Sri Lanka the proponents of rival ethnic nationalisms and their opponents, most of whom are from social and economically dominant class fractions, engage in intellectual and political struggle within the same ideological space. In this way class processes are a critical element in continually recreating rationalism as defining the terms of a political discourse centered on the religious chronicles and their myths and legends. It should be noted, in addition, that this rationalism was mediated through reinterpretations of Buddhist—and Hindu—religious thought and practice. Such rationalism tied to the nationalism of dominant groups was a factor in accentuating the import of the religious chronicles that are of similar importance in the ethnic struggle of today.

What I stress, however, is that this ideological rationalism is an important factor in reproducing the relevance of the myths and legends in the modern political situation. Empiricism is the handmaiden of such rationalism, and its cult of the fact gives greater authenticity to certain sources of information than to others. Written documents, as regarded by rationalists, even though they incorporate subjectivisms, false statements, and so on, nonetheless contain fact that can be sifted out according to rationalist canons. The chronicles as repositories of fact in a rationalist empiricist sense are not disputed. The rhetoric of argument merely revolves around what is "truly" fact or "really" fiction. In certain instances, as I have shown with reference to Jayarajan, events which are nothing more than metaphors of a greater cosmic argument are invested with a facticity they otherwise did not have. The rhetoric of argument can confirm more than it dispels and is committed to an endless cycle of conjectures and refutations. But I must underline two further points.

First, the rationalist valuation of the written texts and the connection of such a valuation to present ideological processes of class power is engaged in the authentication of precisely that which such rationalism may otherwise oppose. The chronicles are valued above the evidence of the so-called folk tradition, which is often regarded as the source of subjectivist irrationalism. So valued the chronicles become the instruments for the validation of the folk tradition. This is so despite the observation by scholars—such as Geiger (1984)—that the chronicles are constructions built upon the traditions of the folk.

The authenticating position of the chronicles can be seen as having import within modern Sri Lankan class processes. Thus, the ideas of the dominated—the folk—become hegemonically incorporated in the ideas of those who are in commanding positions in social and political life. The ruling and the ruled discover a common ideological ground. This is a theme to which I shall return in later chapters but, of course, is an argument that has been demonstrated repeatedly for diverse social and political situations throughout the world.

What I note here, and it is my second point, is that the process of ideological incorporation is a transformation in the structure of reasoning. Events which discover their facticity in world-generating cosmic principles revealed in that science of the concrete of folk myth are demonstrated as authentic according to rationalist canons. In other words, the events discover an authenticity in accordance with the different but no less cosmological arguments of a capitalist technological world. This transformation is a logic of a modern hegemonic process. It is a practice of ideological incorporation and a method of conjoining distinct cultural and ideological perspectives. I stress that one mode of understanding does not necessarily disappear in the other. Rather they are brought into conjunction and synergically interact, one increasing the force of the other through the logic and social circumstance of their combination. An understanding of this is important to my discussion as a whole relating to the issue of the motive and passionate emotive power of ideologies of ethnic nationalism in Sri Lanka.

Gananath Obeyesekere addresses this question. He, more than many modern anthropologists, has been consistently interested in the emotional forces of symbolic action. His work is highly significant in anthropology as a whole and is vital to an understanding of Sri Lanka. Nonetheless, it displays some of the faults of a kind of rationalism I have already discussed but one shared with important anthropological and sociological traditions. A consideration of certain aspects of his analysis will help to underline further the direction of my own.

I share with Obeyesekere his disagreement with the way much historical scholarship of Sri Lanka proceeds. He criticizes the practice of some historians of dismembering myths and legends, ignoring the totality of their structure, and constructing history on the basis of those bits that agree with their common sense. Historical processes "cannot be gathered by looking at parts of the myths literally, or by abstracting 'rational' or commonsense elements from the 'nonrational.' " (Obeyesekere 1984a, 378) Obeyesekere's critique is important, particularly so in a situation in which historians of ancient and medieval Sri Lanka rely on the ancient chronicles and other religious texts for reconstructing the past. The rationalist and fragmented approach of some historians leads them to "invent" a history that probably never happened. More critical, given the situation of modern Sri Lanka, history is made the servant and forceful component of ideologies engaged in the generation of human suffering.

But Obeyesekere's own arguments on myth and history suffer from the same rationalist twist as those he criticizes. This rationalism is fundamental to his view of myth as a legitimation of social and political interests. Obeyesekere's point of view is unabashedly Malinowskian, and he is committed to myth as a social and political charter.[12] Such a

Malinowskian position is one which indeed subjects myth to the interpretational logic of common sense but a common sense that is often the
analyst's own and not necessarily the logic of the people who are given
to engaging mythic argument pragmatically. Thus Obeyesekere discusses
the legend of King Gajabahu.

Gajabahu is the legendary Sinhalese folk hero who, as it is told, lived
in the second century B.C. and, waging war on the Colans in South India,
brought back many thousands of captives to Sri Lanka, where they were
settled largely in the Kandyan hill country. Applying common sense,
Obeyesekere argues that this action is incomprehensible.

> By contrast, the king of Cola who lived in Gajabahu's father's reign put
> his Sinhala captives to work raising the bunds of the Kaveri, a useful
> irrigation enterprise. It was singularly foolish of Gajabahu not to have
> used this human labor for similar construction purposes, for the hill
> country and coastal regions where he settled his captives were, in the
> second century, remote, inaccessible, and inhospitable. An
> anthropological analysis treating this episode as a myth yields a
> different set of conclusions. This version of the Gajabahu story is
> what I call a "colonization myth," functionally similar to the Moses
> myth of the Bible. As an origin myth it explains the existence of
> South Indian settlers in parts of the Kandyan provinces . . . probably
> justifying their "anomalous status," to use Malinowski's words
> (Obeyesekere 1984a, 366).

Obeyesekere forsakes one kind of commonsense rationality for another, but a rationality, nonetheless, constituted in the one logic. The
myth by itself declares an irrationality which is resolved when it is located
in its pragmatic context. Thus, for Obeyesekere, Gajabahu's action in
putting his captives to work, which when compared with other events of
myth is irrational, reveals a rational utility when it is seen, by the canons
of common sense, to legitimate alien presence. The fault of Obeyesekere's
analysis is the fault of Malinowski's reduction of myth to pragmatic
utilitarianism. It is a fault shared by Obeyesekere with the same historians
whom he admonishes and with nationalistically motivated rationalist
rhetoreticians of the like of Jayarajan.

All of the foregoing, moreover, including Obeyesekere, who asserts a
position to the contrary, reduce the myth or legend to terms that exist
apart from the myth taken as a whole. The legends are broken up into
selected components which are not related to each other in the form of
the myth as a whole. Rather they are subjected to a logic of scrutiny
which lies outside the structure of the myth in its entirety. By way of
comparison, it is the particular contribution of structuralist and semiotic
analyses of myth to have examined myth as a whole and to have pointed
to the inner significance of the logical structure of myth. I am critical,
however, of such approaches insofar as they demonstrate a tendency to
apply the analysts' own universalist methodological canons—based, for

example, on a universalist dualism of nature and culture—which may also be independent of the reasoning of myth. Even so, I stress the advance of structuralist approaches over the functionalist and pragmatic perspective on myth to be found in the work of Malinowski and still current in the modern scholarship of Obeyesekere and others.

Let me emphasize that while I am critical of Obeyesekere, his stress on the social and political context of myth and its relation to the meaning of myth is important. My point is, however, that by not attending sufficiently to the inner logic of the myth important connections between myth and encompassing political and social realities, as well as the vital force of myth in such situations, are lost or obscured. I wish also to clarify another issue: I am not opposed to common sense per se. As Feyerabend (1978) argues, common sense is sometimes to be preferred to the apparent insights of those who eschew common sense professionally. This is evident in many of the economic development programs which the advanced West presses on the Third World. The common sense of the peasantry has frequently been superior to the informed scientific and technical knowledge of well-paid advisors. What I am arguing against is that common sense which refuses to acknowledge its own cultural and ideological constitutive ground. As I have implied, the rationalism that I address is in itself a cosmology. More, it is ontological, constituting the being of persons in the world and vital to their orientation toward the horizons of their existential realities.

My argument with the Malinowskian point of view of Obeyesekere is ultimately directed toward its inability to grasp the legitimating and other powers of myth fully. The approach fails, in other words, in its principal analytical objective. This is so because it takes myth as epiphenomenal to material reality and because it does not acknowledge the possibility that myths and those who engage them may share in the one structure of reasoning or, as I shall demonstrate, ontology. It is the latter dimension, that human beings and their myths participate in common ontological ground, that I consider extends an understanding of the legitimating and other powers of myth.

The pragmatic, myth-as-charter view regards myth as having had effect because it endorses the political status quo or a present social order and the claims of persons or groups within it. The myth is harnessed to reality, is manipulated into a social situation, and is otherwise independent of that reality about which it speaks. Myth seen this way is passive, and its power lies outside the reasoning that weaves its events.

In seeing myth simply as an epiphenomenal function of a social and political order the scholar fails to comprehend the potency of the myth itself, the extent of the power it may bring to the situation in which it is engaged. The form of myth, the bare bones of its logic or structure of reasoning, whereby its content is organized and the "significance" of internal event is located, may already be part of the world it reflects. The myth, therefore, in its internal structure of reasoning is not epiphenomenal but integral. This is likely always to be so. Thus the interpretation, the selection of mythic events and their reconstruction according to rationalist principles recreates the myth as part of a rationalist cosmology. Made congruent with a rationalist world it achieves potency—a potency born of the world into which it is introduced and which is now inscribed within it. But I would add to this a further point: myths may be dormant, waiting to be activated, but they can constrain those who awaken them to a logic they declare independently. Myth can take part in its own interpretation. Human beings can be motivated in their interpretations through the form of the myth itself and may not make "free" selections according to independent social and political interests, which is the position of Malinowski and Obeyesekere. As Sahlins (1981) has argued, myths can provide a framework through which the experience of the world achieves significance. Thus the course of reality can be directed according to the logic of myth and vice versa. I shall return to a discussion of this point. For the moment I wish to draw attention to another aspect of my argument.

Myths have force and an emotional power in the spheres of human action because their logic or reasoning connects with the way human beings are already oriented within their realities. In this sense mythic event may be as much legitimated by the world as it legitimates lived reality. The fury of debate which surrounds mythic event recorded in the chronicles is undoubtedly derived from the symbolization by such events of relevant aspects of the present ethnic conflict and suffering. But some of the anger receives its impetus in the rationalism of the antagonists. This rationalism is integral to their person, their being, and disagreement—the suggestion that they have been irrational—is a personal onslaught potentially as threatening as an attack on their ethnic identity. Indeed, in this case ethnic standpoint and rationalism may be joined. The chronicles come to have specific import in the construction and significance of ethnic identity in some part through the structure of reasoning, through the rationalism, that is integral to the person of the interpreter of the chronicles. In the structure of interpretation the events of the chronicles merge with the identity of the person.

Broadly, the legitimating and emotional force of myth is not in the events as such but in the logic that conditions their significance. This is so when the logic is also vital in the way human actors are culturally given to constituting a self in the everyday routine world and move out toward others in that world. Mythic reality is mediated by human beings into the worlds in which they live. Where human beings recognize the argument of mythic reality as corresponding to their own personal constitutions—their orientation within and movement through reality— so myth gathers force and can come to be seen as embodying ultimate truth. Myth so enlivened, I suggest, can become imbued with commanding power, binding human actors to the logical movement of its scheme. In this sense, myth is not subordinated to the interests of the individual or the group but can itself have motive force. It comes to define significant experience in the world, experience which in its significance is also conceived of as intrinsic to the constitution of the person. By virtue of the fact that myth engages a reasoning which is also integral to everyday realities, part of the taken-for-granted or "habitus" (Bourdieu 1977) of the mundane world, myth can charge the emotions and fire the passions.

The Malinowskian charter view of myth explains the apparent strong emotional appeal of myths by some kind of descent into psychologism. The power of myth is in its fulfillment of needs that are taken as universal and fundamental to all humankind. Human psychology is rooted in the individual before any participation in a world that engages others. The psychological world is separated from the social, which varies in its resolutions of basic psychological urgency, producing distinct social and cultural orders accordingly. My position resists such an analytical dualism. The sociological and psychological are inseparable and simultaneous. One does not precede the other, as in the sociologism of Durkheim or the psychologism of Malinowski. Furthermore, their force over human action is in the total situation of human experience. Thus the emotions and the passions are of the world, not seated within the individual alone and emanating from the individual. They are produced, too, within the structures of life, in the cultural logic of its movement. And thus myth can create the emotional and passionate forces which are often responses to the events it presents. This is because, as I have said, myths can contain those principles whereby human beings engage their world and realize in experience their passage through the world.

Obeyesekere argues for the psychological reality of the events of myth for the popular imagination. In this understanding, the vast bulk of the politically significant masses, the relatively little educated peasantry and proletariat, are in effect regarded as being easily duped by mythic falsity. They are bound by their "folk knowledge," which presents the myth as real history. "Myths like that of . . . Gajabahu are the people's own view of their history, and hence psychologically more real than the actual events, which, even if they were presented or made available, would be strenuously denied" (Obeyesekere 1984a, 377). This is a view from the top, and it is consistent with an ideology of rationalist domination wherein the nature of knowledge—folk, scholarly, rational, or scientific—is engaged in the discourse of class relations and in the conflicts among class fractions. My principal difficulty with Obeyesekere's position, however, is that it fails, possibly because of its psychological reductionism, to locate sufficiently the strenuous attachment to a particular history in the cultural fabric and motivating logics of the social and historical structures of the everyday world. The mythic events are not so much real for the populace in the terms of an empiricist history but real by virtue of the cultural reasoning that guides their significance. Such a reasoning and the motivating forces of an encompassing historical and cultural world, moreover, may condition and direct even the action of those in possession of "legitimate" knowledge, the empiricists and rationalists. It is a solid tradition in much scholarship to regard the emotions and the passions as irrational and beyond reason. This too is the argument of Buddhism, whether presented in the learned texts of the monks or through popular myth and rite. I shall take a different course here, finding the roots of supposed irrationality to be grounded in cultural and social structures and in the logic of their inner reasoning.

The myths and legends of political rhetoric have emotional and legitimating power not simply because they are part of folk knowledge or folk history. They have force because they enshrine and incorporate a fundamental intentionality, an orientation toward the world of experience, which engages many Sinhalese in their everyday life. By this I do not mean that the myths comprise beliefs, value orientations, attitudes, norms, or the like in the senses often employed in functionalist sociologies. The myths are fundamental in a more active and vital sense. They carry ontological weight and derive their powerful potential accordingly. The myths of Sinhalese ethnic nationalism demonstrate this point and, further, they illustrate how modern social, economic, and political circumstances generate innovative meaning and force in the ontological schemes of the myths.

3

Evil, Power, and the State

Interpreters of the Vijaya and Dutugemunu legends, especially those commentators concerned with demystification of them, argue correctly that they are religious statements. The *Dipavamsa* and the *Mahavamsa*, the chronicles which give the principal versions of the legends I shall discuss—those most commonly referred to by scholars and ideologues alike—were written by monks in the fourth century and the late fifth century A.D., respectively (Geiger 1984).[1] Either the religious character of the texts is regarded unproblematically or, as often happens, their religious nature is taken as confirmation of their authenticity and authority. Sometimes the religious argument of the chronicles is given as the reason for dismissal of their facticity and denial of their import. Rarely is the religious form of the texts themselves, except in the work of Indologists or scholars of religion, subjected to deeper consideration. In the religious arguments of the *Dipavamsa* and the *Mahavamsa* cosmological issues are explored. Indeed, the logic of their cosmology also reveals an ontology. It is in their cosmology and a more fundamental ontology, particularly as regards the legends of Vijaya and Dutugemunu, that the *Dipavamsa* and *Mahavamsa* reveal vital connections with more popular, often oral traditions and find continual force in and relevance to modern social and political processes.

The cosmological structure of the chronicles is made clear at the outset. Both begin with enunciation of primordial cosmic statements. The *Dipavamsa* begins with the glorification of the Buddha, which is followed by an account of his mastery of Mara. This extends into an account of the three visits of Buddha to Lanka, his preparation of the island for human habitation—which involves the removal of the demons *(yakkas)* to a kind of parallel reality on the island of Giri[2]—the appearance of the first king, Mahasammata, and a listing of the twenty-eight kings following. This cosmogony is a prelude to the account of the Vijaya legend—as it is in the *Mahavamsa*—and in some ways includes themes explored through that legend and other stories. In the *Mahavamsa*, for example, the verses preparatory to the Vijaya legend raise the central theme of kingship. The ideal kings, Mahasammata, Asoka, and Dutugemunu, are referred to in relation to central principles of Buddhism. The chronicles make cosmology the paradigm of history, which in its syntagmatic unfolding reveals the cosmological principles that form history and that the events of history continually demonstrate. History is cosmology and cosmology is history.

Both Buddhism and Hinduism, regardless of sect or particular tradition, essay in effect a theory of history. Broadly, history constitutes an interwoven stream of events in which the results of actions at one moment are manifest in beneficence or suffering at another. This is the principle of karma, common to both Buddhism and Hinduism, which is the theory of the interconnection of events. The actions of Vijaya and Dutugemunu, the events surrounding them, and their consequences reflect karmic principles. Thus Vijaya's betrayal of the demoness Kuveni, who helped him conquer the yakkas, has unfortunate karmic consequences for his successor, Panduvasdeva. In the popular tradition outside the chronicles, Panduvasdeva suffers from an illness which is the vengeance of Kuveni. It is the karmic principle underlying the connection of the events of history, which might even be said to be the underlying force behind their relevance to modern events. The spirit and actions of Vijaya and Dutugemunu, in accordance with the karmic principle, are indeed being engaged in current lived realities. Through karma the past is always inextricably interwoven with the present, the experiences and events of which are to a degree determined by the karmic force of the past. The principle of karma connects Sinhalese and Tamils to their history in a vital and immediate way. Their history enters consciousness in a manner perhaps distinct from that of peoples elsewhere whose cosmology does not describe so complete a theory of history. In Sri Lanka history is never distant or past but present and immediate.

Karma is consistent with a religion which sees the cosmos as being in constant flux, running a continuous cycle of growth and decay; of birth, death, and rebirth; of unity, development, fragmentation, and reunification. The events of the *Dipavamsa* and the *Mahavamsa* constitute moments in such a process and, I suggest, are shaped, elaborated, magnified, and distorted to match the logic of the cosmic process. The Vijaya legend and the events leading to the heroic progress of Dutugemunu follow the cosmic course.

The Legend of Vijaya

In the *Mahavamsa* version of the Vijaya story, which is more elaborate than the *Dipavamsa* version, Vijaya is the elder of twin sons born of the incestuous union of twins, Sihabahu and his sister Sihasivali. Their twinship and incest signifies their unity of difference in identity and their identity through difference, the ideal form of closure in hierarchical totalities. This theme is established in the story of Sihabahu and elaborated in the legend of his son, Vijaya. The legend of Vijaya gains significance in the story of Sihabahu, the ultimate progenitor of the Sinhalese and their name-giver. I shall begin with the legend of Sihabahu.

Sihabahu: The Cosmogenesis of a People

Sihabahu and his sister were born of the union of a rampaging savaging lion and the errant Indian princess of Vanga, who was "very amorous and for shame the king and queen could not suffer her" (*Mahavamsa* 6:3). The princess, like the lion, stood outside the moral order of human society and wandered like the lion with a band of traders across various political territories. The lion attacks the caravan. The princess shares the quality of fearlessness with the lion and alone confronts him while the traders flee. Their likeness in quality and their position (one could say "individuality") external to society are associated, I interpret, with the lion's desire for the princess. They are united in their difference by the power of the lion who carries the princess off to his den. Sihabahu, as the child of this union, has the physical characteristics of both the lion and a human being. He symbolizes in his person his foundation upon nature and his essential unity with it. This is a recurrent theme in both Buddhism and Hinduism, in which the constitution of human beings and all modes of materiality in nature are seen as generating differentiation and fragmentation and producing suffering. I should add here that nature in Buddhist cosmological thought, for example, is potentially as unifying as it is fragmenting. Indeed, nature and culture are each potentially fragmenting and destructive of the other as they may be unifying or in harmony the one with the other. The essential unity and even the encompassing world of nature as against the divided realities of human orders is symbolized by the roaming lion and the traveling princess. In nature they cross and intersect the arbitrarily created boundaries of human political orders. The primordial creative unity of nature is also carried in the Vijaya myth. The Vanga princess as the genetrix of a new social order returns to nature, and it is from the womb of the earth that she and her children reemerge. The lion's den is a cave that he blocks daily with an enormous boulder that confines his growing family while he goes hunting.

Metaphorically the unity of lion and princess, and of the princess and her twins in the enclosing womb of the lion's cave, is broken in the entry of mother and children into the outside world. The differentiation and fragmentation of a unity in nature is effected by the son, Sihabahu. He opens the "womb" by removing the boulder, and he carries his mother and sister to the borderland of Vanga territory. In this act nature is brought into conflict with human society, at least as it is conceived by human beings. The *Mahavamsa* relates that the lion searches for his lost family. His search is seen as an attack on human settlements that disrupts their order. Against the pleading of his mother, Sihabahu agrees to kill the lion, his father, on behalf of his grandfather the Vanga king, who offers a rich reward. The lion, full of love for his son, moves unsuspectingly to his death. Sihabahu cuts off his father's head and returns to the Vanga city, where he is offered the kingship in gratitude.

The events that describe the escape from the cave and the death of the lion are open to many interpretations. They carry the Oedipal message of the son's desire to kill the father, the repudiation of ties of kinship, an act of sacrifice, the signifying of the separation of culture from nature, and the resolution of Sihabahu's own bodily contradiction. I propose that the events essay both a resolution of the fragmentation set in motion by the division and differentiation of birth and a transformation. Sihabahu's killing of his father is a metaphor of sacrificial encompassment. By his act he fully incorporates his father as his father once incorporated him by enclosing Sihabahu in his cave. Here also is the transformation, which is the inverse of the former order of things.

The events leading to the birth of Sihabahu are occasioned by his mother's flouting the conventions of parental authority and leaving the world of human beings to unite with nature. Nature, in effect, incorporates human beings and dominates them. Inversely, when Sihabahu goes to kill his father he acts on the authority of the state and is its agent. Indeed, he is worthy to be its embodiment, its king. When he ignores the pleading of his mother he does not deny the state and society as his mother once did. Rather he defies his mother, and in fact his kinship with his father, in the interest of the order of the state. Sihabahu's violent destruction of his father is the violent reassertion of the powerful order of the state. Further, human beings no longer find their unity incorporated within nature and dominated by it, and they are not fragmented by and in opposition to nature. Sihabahu brings about a new unity, this time once again of human beings in harmony with nature but with their society in a dominant, unthreatened position in relation to nature. When Sihabahu returns to Vanga he relinquishes the proffered kingship.[3] Instead, he returns to the land of his lion father, and in union with his sister he builds a city and rules wisely and well.[4]

A crucial feature of the argument of the Sihabahu legend should not be overlooked. This concerns the character and role of power in hierarchy. The lion and Sihabahu display the ambivalence of power, its unifying, fragmenting, creative, and destructive aspects. Although these opposing aspects of power are always united—the lion and Sihabahu both destroy as they unite—the dominance of one over the other depends on the presence of such virtues as compassion and love. It is the lion's love for the princess which transforms his rage into an act of creative generation and Sihabahu's refusal of compassion and the lion's anger which cause the lion's destruction. The ambivalence of power and the copresence of its opposed aspects is vital in the other myths that I shall discuss. Thus the myth of Sihabahu's son, Vijaya, elaborates the themes of unity.

The cosmological arguments of the Sihabahu myth recur in the legend of Sihabahu's son, Vijaya. Again the familiar themes appear, of unity, division, differentiation and fragmentation, the violence of transformation, and the movement to order and the reconstitution of the state through the metaphor of rebirth and sacrifice.

Vijaya and the Founding of the Sinhala State

The union of Sihabahu and Sihasivali produces sixteen pairs of twin sons.[5] The first pair of twins is Vijaya and Sumitta, Vijaya being the elder. Vijaya is an unruly prince; with his band of followers he disrupts the life of his father's kingdom. The prince, as did his grandmother and his grandfather, the lion, acts against the authority and the order of the state. Sihabahu, exercising his kingly authority in the interests of his subjects, who request his help, acts to curb his son. Sihabahu asserts once again the order of the state and rejects his son, as he did his father. Indeed, it can be said that he fragments his son as his son threatened to fragment the state. The social order of Vijaya and his dissolute following is smashed. The families of Vijaya's following are disunited. Vijaya and his men are put into one boat, the women into another, and the children into yet another. They are then cast adrift on the sea and subjected to the turbulent elements of nature. The destructive order of Vijaya and his band is metaphorically, perhaps, enclosed and determined by the power of nature. I see a parallel here between the lion's encompassment of the Vanga princess and her children and the encompassment of Vijaya and his following.

The fragmentation of the social order of Vijaya and his band is a prelude to a transformation that involves the founding of a new unified order. The process of transformation is contained in a metaphor of rebirth. Vijaya and his men cross the water and eventually make landfall on the shore of Lanka.[6] So exhausted they cannot walk, they crawl, and their hands are reddened by the earth. It is because of the color of the earth that they give the island its name, Tambapanni (copper-colored palms), but this color may also achieve significance, when the action is placed in context, as symbolic of the blood of birth. In the *Mahavamsa* this event concludes a series of important transformative events involving Vijaya and his following, the ultimate consequence of which is the establishment of cities and a new order of government, including the founding of Anuradhapura with Vijaya as the consecrated monarch, the creation of new social units based on marriage to women brought from India, and the conversion of Vijaya and his men from persons antagonistic to state and society to persons who protect and embody their order.

While the Vijaya myth repeats critical themes of the Sihabahu legend, other arguments which are at least implicit in the Sihabahu story are emphasized. In both the shorter *Dipavamsa* version and in the elaborate *Mahavamsa* account the theme of evil is introduced explicitly. Further, evil is linked to the structure of transformation, to the re-creation of order and the generation of the internal hierarchy of the state.

The Dipavamsa relates, "Prince Vijaya was daring and uneducated; he committed most wicked and fearful deeds, plundering the people" (Dipavamsa, 160). En route to Lanka, Vijaya and his band make landfall at the island of Supparaka. They return the hospitality of the inhabitants with "theft, adultery, falsehood, and slander, of an immoral, most dreadful, bad conduct" (Dipavamsa, 161). In the *Mahavamsa* is written, "Vijaya was of evil conduct and his followers were even (like himself), and many intolerable deeds of violence were done by them" (Mahavamsa 6:39). Brief mention is made in the Mahavamsa of the landfall of Vijaya's party on the way to Lanka. The chronicle states that Vijaya had to leave because he was "in danger by reason of the violence of his followers" (Mahavamsa 6:47).

Vijaya and his followers are demonic. Their action and treatment have much in common with present Sinhalese understandings of demonic evil, and their dispersal by Sihabahu equates well with the logic of demonic destruction in exoricsm ritual (Kapferer 1983). At the conclusion of some large-scale all-night exorcisms, detritus of the demonic food offerings, broken baskets, and the destroyed remnants of the ritual "buildings" are cast into streams or else the sea. The sea crossed by Vijaya is a deeply ambiguous symbol of death *and* rebirth; such ambiguity, of course, is consistent with Sinhala Buddhist cosmological thought. It may be added that in exorcism of demons the action of destroying the demon is simultaneously an act of reconsitituting the wholeness and the order of the body of the demon's victim.

This is most apparent in the principal Sinhalese antisorcery rite, the Suniyama.[7] In this ritual, the patient is initially placed in a position outside the main ritual edifice, the *atamagala*. This building is simultaneously a model of the palace of King Mahasammata, whose queen, Manikpala, was the first victim of sorcery, a model of the Buddhist state, and a model of the hierarchical order of the cosmos. In the healing or protective process the patient moves inside the building, is symbolically reborn, and is made whole again within the integrated and hierarchical order of the Buddhist cosmos-state. As a consequence of this progress of the patient, the destructive power of Suniyam, the being of evil, is reversed. In some exorcist interpretations the demon of sorcery is transformed into a divinely protective figure.

I should add that in current Sinhalese thought and practice, to be attacked and inhabited by the demon—a victim often assumes the identity and mien of his demonic tormentor—is to be imprisoned or bound by the demon. The object of most exorcist practice is to cut the demonic bond and so to bind the demon. This is a recurrent theme of the ritual practices of the antisorcery Suniyama. Immediately upon the patient's entering the cosmic palace, he or she is ritually bound by corded hoops of coconut palm—theoretically 108. These signify, among other things, the victim's total determination by Suniyam. The bonds are then cut and the patient is transformed into wholeness and released from Suniyam's hold.

I do not consider it farfetched to discern similarities between the foregoing ideas of important rites of exorcism and the events surrounding Vijaya. There are symbolic parallels in Sihabahu's punishment of Vijaya and his followers. Sihabahu causes "Vijaya and his followers . . . to be shaven over half the head" (Mahavamsa 6:43). This signifies loss of freedom, and the term used in the chronicle has an additional sense of "slave." In exorcism, to be tied or bound by the demon is to suffer a loss of personal autonomy.[8] Such personal autonomy or freedom is possible only within the encompassing order of the cosmic state.

The landing of Vijaya on the shores of Lanka marks the beginning of the main events of transformation, whereby Vijaya moves from being a demonic prince to being a benevolent and orderly king. This transformation occurs simultaneously with the creation of a new, original state order. In the *Mahavamsa* the moment when these transformations begin could be interpreted as taking the form of an exorcism. Vishnu, acting on the authority of Buddha and Sakra, appears as an old man before Vijaya and his men. He sprinkles them with water and ties a thread around their hands (Mahavamsa 7:8,9). There is a similarity here with the present practice of curative exorcism. This action is performed as a curative act in itself in the minor *tel matirima* rite, as an action (*apa nul, nul bandinava*) prior to a full night-long exorcism, as an action at Suniyama and at *mal bali* rites, during which the victim holds a thread throughout the dangerous passage to relief, and at curative spirit ceremonies among others.[9] Indeed, the action performed on Vijaya and his men is explicitly referred to by demon exorcists in their rites and by deity priests (*kapurala, Pattinihami*) in the main ceremonies (*gammaduva, devolmaduva*) addressed to the deities. I draw attention to the association of these mythic actions with present cultural practice because I consider that the Vijaya myth and present practice share the one logic of transformation.

This logic is one of movement or process in hierarchy. As I have already said, the various beings constituted in the cosmic hierarchy can be conceived of as moments in the process of hierarchy, a process of continual growth and decay, of fragmentation and reformation. In accordance with the hierarchical principle and the forces that condition its motion, low or demonic forms of being can be reconstituted as higher, nondemonic forms. But this is so only in accordance with the critical feature of hierarchy, that of encompassment.   In the hierarchical system to which I refer, dominant beings in the cosmos are dominant in the sense that they can encompass and incorporate other forms or manifest possibilities of the cosmic whole.   As a general rule Buddha and the gods are by definition encompassing.   They can express in themselves lower, less unified, fragmented, and demonic possibilities of themselves.   Their power is thus contained, for they can move down into the destructive and terrifying depths of a cosmic totality and become demonic.   But they can also move up, reconstituting themselves and the realities they can embody into an ordered, nonfragmented, benevolent, protective unity.

This logic of movement and transformation in and through hierarchy is that which directs the process of much ritual in Sri Lanka and underlies the transformation of Vijaya.   Further, in the abstract hierarchical conception I have outlined, evil as a materialization in manifest demonic form, is both a moment in a process and a force that generates transformation in the cosmic whole.   In ritual and in the Vijaya myth the manifestation of evil engenders other possibilities of the cosmic entirety and creates a new wholeness and order.   In an important sense the evil of Vijaya generates the state and its hierarchical unity.   A message contained in this observation, moreover, is that evil is overcome and negated in the order of the state.

Vijaya in his demonic evil is a fragmented and lower possibility of his higher potential as a king who is the embodiment of the cosmically ordered state.   His demon possibility of being engages him with the other evil, the demon inhabitants of the island, the yakkas.   But the struggle will demonstate the greater fragmenting power of kingship because it combines the power of order and the regenerative and transformational process set in motion by the struggle between the two forms of fragmenting power whereby the encompassment in hierarchy is produced.

Vijaya's men are hurled into a chasm and are thus imprisoned by the demoness Kuveni.[10]   But Vijaya, protected by Vishnu's thread, terrorizes her into submission and wins from her the release of his men.   In many ways he behaves like a modern exorcist who snares the demon in a noose as Vijaya did to Kuveni (Mahavamsa 7:20).[11]   Vijaya and his men are shown hospitality by Kuveni.   Evil and violence sup together.   Vijaya and Kuveni enter into a perfect reciprocal relation.   Vijaya nurtures Kuveni with the food that is provided by Kuveni but prepared by Vijaya's men.[12]   They transform together.   Kuveni changes from a demon into a sixteen-year-old maiden, the perfect age for marital and sexual union, and cohabits with Vijaya.   This union can be interpreted as a metaphor of creation or generation of the increased power of Vijaya, who through his union with Kuveni encompasses her destructive power.   As the power of Vijaya and Kuveni grows, so does the power of the demons whom they will destroy together.   Here is an example of the logic of transformational generation in hierarchy, whereby less powerful manifestations progressively give way to more powerful and encompassing manifestations or generate in parallel equally powerful ordering or disordering manifestations. Thus the yakkas gather at a wedding festivity, and at this gathering time of the demonic, Vijaya slaughters the yakkas, who are revealed to him by Kuveni.[13] In his slaughtering of the yakkas, Vijaya in effect encompasses them and moves higher in hierarchy. As in exorcism, where the overcoming of evil in its most powerful forms engenders a "pivoting of the sacred" and the emergence of divine ordering, a similar transformation occurs in Vijaya. He becomes creatively ordering and institutes the benevolent state within which evil is expunged or denied its disordering potency.

Vijaya regains the unity that was fragmented earlier by his father, Sihabahu, a new autonomous unity. Vijaya and his men establish the cities and institutions of their government. Vijaya reestablishes the family and the rules of marriage, instigating the marriage of his men to women from Madhura in South India. Through these ties the social hierarchy of the world order is also regained. The king of Madhura sends "maidens whom he had fitted out, according to their rank, elephants withal and horses and wagons, worthy of a king, and craftsmen and a thousand families of the eighteen guilds" (Mahavamsa 7:57).

With the emergence of the hierarchical order of the state, the union of Kuveni and Vijaya is broken. Kuveni attempts to return to the community of remaining yakkas but is killed as a spy. The children she has had by Vijaya run away to the wilds, where in incestuous union they engender the Vaddas (*pulinda*), who live in the forest and outside the state order created by Vijaya. Kuveni and her progeny, in effect, fall to the outer, marginal reaches of human society, whereas Vijaya assumes his position at the apex. He is consecrated king, and he consecrates as queen the daughter of the king of Pandi.

Dutugemunu and the Rebirth of the State

As the Vijaya story elaborates on themes present in the Sihabahu myth, the legend of Dutugemunu constitutes a further development, perhaps an apogee. The events of the Dutugemunu legend take place after the establishment of Buddhism in Sri Lanka. But the power centered on Anuradhapura is not a Buddhist power but Hindu, in the person of King Elara. Dutugemunu's conquest of Elara is a celebration of the restoration of a Buddhist king in Anuradhapura and the restoration of Sinhala Buddhist hegemony. Many of the events in the *Mahavamsa* surrounding Dutugemunu have to do with Dutugemunu's postconquest meritorious building program—his construction of works to the glory of the Buddha. This is integral to Dutugemunu's renunciation of the world following his violent restoration of the world order. Dutugemunu's building of monuments to Buddhism can be interpreted as action of cosmic stabilization whereby the inherent fragmenting possibility of the world order and of its kingly embodiment—inherent as a function of the logic of hierarchy and incorporating encompassment—is overcome by the affirmation of Buddhist cosmic unifying principles. I will restrict this discussion of the legend to the events leading to the death of Elara, which signifies the completion of the regeneration of a hierarchical world order dominated by a Sinhalese Buddhist king. The cosmic stability of kingdom and king is dependent on the assertion of unifying cosmic principles in the building of Buddhist monuments and in the renunciation of the king.

Dutugemunu's birth is generated out of evil action. His mother is Viharadevi, the daughter of the king of Kalyani, who in the unreasoning passion of anger kills a Buddhist monk, an *arahant*. The king discovers a secret love letter written by his younger brother to his queen and delivered by a man in the guise of a monk (*bhikkhu*). The false monk has entered the king's palace by subterfuge, in the company of an arahant who regularly took his meals at the palace. Finding the letter, which has fallen to the floor, the king slays both men and throws them into the sea. The passionate and disordered wrath of the king of Kalyani brings natural disaster. The sea overflows the land. Human society is subsumed by nature and destroyed, it is fragmented in the failure of the manifest principles of cosmic order.

The king's daughter, Viharadevi, is placed in a golden vessel and launched by the king into the same destructive sea. The *Mahavamsa* contains no comment on this act, but it could be interpreted as an offering of appeasement or as a sacrifice. Indeed, this is the interpretation given in the recounting of the same myth in the seventeenth-century chronicle of Sinhalese kings, the *Rajavaliya* (1954, 23–24). In the context of the story it is possible to extend the interpretation. Accepted by the gods, the princess is in effect a daughter of the gods, as well as the daughter of a king. Through the king's evil the princess rises even higher in the cosmic hierarchy.

Viharadevi is borne south to the area of the Sinhalese king "in retreat," Kakavannatissa, at Magama, near Kataragama. The princess reaches land near a Buddhist temple (*vihara*), hence her name, "goddess of the temple." Viharadevi is consecrated queen to King Kakavanna.

The moral opposite of her father, Viharadevi engages in meritorious acts. She lavishes gifts upon the Buddhist clergy. The chief monk of the community she supports considers her to have attained "great happiness" through such action. But Viharadevi responds that she is, in fact, unhappy because she has not conceived children. The queen is told to approach a dying novice (*samanera*), a pious man who has tended sick monks. She pleads with the novice, giving beautiful offerings of flowers, garments, and medicines to the monkhood, to be reborn as her son. The novice agrees and upon his death becomes a child in the queen's womb, the child who is to be Dutugemunu.

In the events leading to the conception of Dutugemunu, Viharadevi travels from the destructive fragmentation wrought by evil action to the heights of perfect and pious unity. Symbolically, it can be said, she passes from one situation in which action leads to the rejection of Buddhism—the king of Kalyani's reason is clouded by illusion, so he is incapable of distinguishing between true and false Buddhism—to another situation in which Buddhism is fully embraced and is unified perfectly with the kingship. Viharadevi embodies Buddhism and is a symbol of healing and unifying power. Her child was once a healer, a unifier. A feature of traditional healers in Sri Lanka is that they incorporate the disordering aspects of the illnesses they treat. Such an interpretation could be given to the mortal sickness of the *samanera*. As the vehicle of the *samanera's* rebirth Viharadevi makes the healer whole: fragmentation is once more unified. She signs the unifying potential of the child who grows in her womb.

Viharadevi is the embodiment of a unified hierarchical whole. As such she contains and expresses the powers—destructive, ordering, and benevolent—which are the moments of the cosmic process. These, of course, are also the aspects of the powers of kingship and of the state, which combine in dialectical complementarity the terrible destructive powers of the demonic with the ordering benevolence of the divine.

The pregnancy longings of Viharadevi manifest aspects of these powers. She desires a honeycomb of great length with which to feed 12,000 bhikkhus, she to eat what remains. She gives the purest of gifts and indexes her piety and subordination—by eating the remnants—to the Buddhist clergy.[14] Her benevolence is linked with her awful desire to drink the water used to purify the sword which strikes off the head of the "first among Elara's warriors" (*Mahavamsa* 22:44–45). The reordering of purification following a destructive act precedes the third longing, which is heavy with the symbolism of re-creation. Viharadevi longs to "adorn herself with the garlands of unfaded lotus-blossoms brought from the lotus marshes of Anuradhapura" (*Mahavamsa* 22:46).[15] The three longings are fulfilled.

The theme of the mythic events surrounding Viharadevi find greater elaboration in the marvelous acts of which her legendary son is at the center. Ten champions gather about Dutugemunu. Many of them have demonic, marginal characteristics, and indeed some of them are demons exorcised in modern healing rites. One of the champions, for example, is Mahasona, a demon greatly feared in the West and South of the island (Kapferer 1983). The first champion of the ten, Nandhimitta, is the son of the sister of one of Elara's own generals.[16] In this identity Nandhimitta is a symbolic condensation of potential weakness, of destruction, within Elara's own order. Nandhimitta tears apart those of his own people who desecrate Buddhist dagabas (*Mahavamsa* 23:9). He is the danger of negation within structure, and he embodies this demonic contradiction in his own physical being. As a boy he had the strength of ten elephants, possessed in conjunction with the anatomical peculiarity that his genitals were hidden within his body like those of a woman. Dutugemunu's second champion, Suranimala, is endowed with great strength and speed; he is urged to seek the protection of Dutugemunu's father and not to live near Tamil territory, lest he come under Elara's power (*Mahavamsa* 23:20–33). He is considered indolent by his kin, and in the popular tradition, as his name implies, he is regarded as a great drunkard.[17] Gothaimbara, the fourth champion, who comes after Mahasona in the *Mahavamsa* account, is dwarfish and is the subject of jests from his brothers (*Mahavamsa* 23:50).

Dutugemunu's eighth champion, Khanjadeva, limps, but despite his infirmity he is able to kill buffaloes by whirling them around his head and dashing them to the ground (*Mahavamsa* 23:78–81). The gathering of the champions is a building of destructive power, but a power to be directed at the state of Elara. It will protect Dutugemunu and his order, whereas it may destroy others. The champions mirror the ambiguity of kingly power. I am puzzled as to why Dutugemunu has ten champions. It is conceivable that they are the ten manifestations of Vishnu and thus constitute a link with the Vijaya myth, wherein Vishnu is charged with protecting Vijaya, whose descendants will establish the religion of the Buddha.[18] Dutugemunu's father commands the champions not to take sides in any internecine strife within his kingdom. They do not, even though Dutugemunu and his brother, Tissa, engage in a war of succession. In my interpretation, the ten champions as Vishnu are the protectors of the kingdom and collectively embody its encompassing and fragmenting power. Their nonalignment is consistent with the logic of their form and their import as symbols of the kingdom and not the kingship.

The demonic potential of the hierarch Dutugemunu is realized when the prince denies the authority of his father. He refuses to abstain from making war on the Tamils, as his father commands, and sends his father a woman's ornament. This action signs King Kakavanna as a king encompassed and not encompassing. In a manner similar to the violent but regenerative process of like actions—Sihabahu to the lion; Vijaya to Sihabahu—in the other myths discussed, Dutugemunu's action begins a process of ordering disorder. King Kakavanna threatens to bind his "angry" (*duttha*), demonic son with a golden chain. Dutugemunu flees to the margins, to the forest area of Malaya.[19] This occupation of the margins, of course, symbolizes that what is ultimately encompassing cannot be encompassed. Symbolically, Dutugemunu at the margins in fact encompasses his father.

Upon his father's death, Dutugemunu has himself consecrated king. But the primary symbols of power and the kingship are usurped by Tissa. The *Mahavamsa* presents a series of inversions that are open to interpretation as a symbolic representation of Dutugemunu's position at the base of a hierarchical order he should rightfully head and embody in his person.

I think that the inversions and the events that follow them point simultaneously to Dutugemunu's position outside, at the margin, or at the base of order and his central and dominant potential, which, when realized, will encompass the order that now subsumes and disorders him and that he concomitantly disorders.

Tissa takes possession of Viharadevi and the elephant Kandula, the marvelous vehicle of Dutugemunu. Tissa ignores Dutugemunu's command to return them to his care and routs Dutugemunu's army at Culanganiyapitthi, where "fell many thousands of the king's men" (*Mahavamsa* 24:19–20). Dutugemunu regathers his forces and defeats his brother Tissa in personal combat, but through the aid of his horse, a mare, and the elephant Kandula.[20] The latter throws Tissa, his rider, recognizing him as representing the weakness of the female (*Mahavamsa* 24:37–38), and goes to his true master, Dutugemunu. Tissa hides in a vihara under a bed for fear of his brother. Eventually Tissa, disguised as a monk, comes into the presence of Dutugemunu but is protected by Viharadevi. She had rejoined Dutugemunu earlier, and the *Mahavamsa* relates that Dutugemunu had great reverence for her. Dutugemunu does not demonstrate the unreason of his grandfather, who killed both the false monk and the true monk. He shows compassion, heals the breach between himself and his brother, and sends his brother to direct the work of the harvest.

My highly abbreviated recounting of these events as they are recorded in the *Mahavamsa* displays a series of inversions, which, in their reversal, lead to the reestablishment of order. Their reversal is also a transformation. Thus Dutugemunu, who was outside the state or at its margins or is its representative without power, comes inside the state and is reinstated as the embodiment of its possibilities. He moves from being demonic to being beneficent, incorporating within himself their dynamic ordering complementarity. The stage is set for Dutugemunu, having traversed the range of the hierarchical order he embodies, to achieve a higher encompassment.

While Dutugemunu moves from the outside in and becomes the controlling center of his state, he simultaneously moves the state he commands to a position outside and opposed to that encompassed by Elara. The kingdom at Magama ruled by Dutugemunu's father, Kakavanna, is a tributary state within Elara's wider realm. Dutugemunu's defiance of and subsequent succession to his father, without bending to his father's will, is a moment in the transition whereby Dutugemunu's state moves from inside Elara's kingdom to the outside. Here too is a further significance of Dutugemunu's war with his brother Tissa. Tissa stands in a relation to Dutugemunu virtually identical to that of Sumitta to Vijaya. Both Tissa and Sumitta are younger brothers, and I think that symbolically they encode continuity with the past, or the continuation of a transformation they did not occasion. Their connection, incidentally, with continuity receives further confirmation in their explicit link with fertility. The sons of Vijaya and Dutugemunu do not succeed to the kingships; their brothers and their brothers' sons do.[21] Tissa is told by Dutugemunu to direct the harvest, is protected by his fertile mother, and is identified with the female by Kandula.

That the ultimate figures of encompassment, unifying cosmic kings, are not succeeded by their progeny is consistent with the logic of hierarchy. The ultimate encompasser cannot be encompassed. For Dutugemunu or Vijaya to be succeeded by sons would be, I suggest, tantamount to their encompassment and a negation of what they represent. Continuity must take place through the one whom the encompasser has demonstrably encompassed. I contend, moreover, that it is this logic of encompassment and hierarchy that generates Vijaya's disordering action in relation to Sihabahu and demands that he must realize his encompassing power in another reality, a distant realm. Vijaya and Dutugemunu are the creations of the logic of hierarchy. It is such mythic reasoning which conditions their character and their action and quite apart from any basis in an empirical historical world. The argument of the hierarchy that they embody also conditions the cultural significance of the themes of the Sinhalese chronicles, which are replete with the struggles between fathers and sons and between brothers. Their conflict is not a manifestation of a universal Freudian Oedipal psyche, as some have claimed, but is significant above all in a cultural reasoning about the nature of power in hierarchy and the relation between the encompassed and the encompassing.

The violence of Dutugemunu—and of Vijaya—is the violence of the sacred. It is the violence of opposition, of birth, and of recreative transformation. Again such violence is not, as Girard (1977) argues, a manifestation by the religious of a universal psychology at the heart of humankind. It is a violence that takes shape and significance in the cultural principles of a cosmic hierarchy.[22] Dutugemunu's victory over Tissa moves his kingdom outside the orbit of Elara's and into conflict with it. His military campaign against Elara takes the form of a huge cosmic event, which joins progressive spatial encompassment with a movement up the vertical order of hierarchy. The divine cosmic progression of Dutugemunu's march is made clear in the earlier chronicle, the *Dipavamsa*, where, in one of its few fragmentary references to Dutugemunu, it records that he put "thirty-two kings to death and alone continued the royal succession" (18:54). The *Mahavamsa* makes similar mention. The number thirty-two is symbolic of the thirty-two marks of the Buddha that signifies the Buddha's own encompassment.

Like demons, Dutugemunu and his champions come from the outer margins of the political and social universe and gather greater and greater destructive force.[23] But also, unlike a demon and more like a god—which he in fact becomes upon his death, when he ascends into the Tusita heaven, the abode of the gods—Dutugemunu is able to overpower those whom he confronts and surmount them with the new order he brings. Again, like a god, Dutugemunu himself is transformed in the progression of his hierarchical encompassment, moving from the demonic to the divine. Dutugemunu's final encompassment and transformation in his movement through hierarchy finds symbolic condensation in his victory over Elara and the destruction of a potential successor, Bhalluka, the nephew of Elara's main champion.

Dutugemunu as the king embodies the order he heads. He is the incorporation of hierarchy and its powers. The personal combat with Elara recorded in the *Mahavamsa* (25:67–71) is cosmologically ordained, regardless of whether or not it occurred in fact. Like must engage with like in a cosmic duel in which two ideal embodiments of related but different forms of hierarchical encompassment must determine who is to be the encompassed and, therefore, the cosmic principles that are to be the conditions of hierarchical unity. The duel, I note, sets in train two forms of negation. The negation of Elara in personal destruction and fragmentation and the negation of Dutugemunu in transcendence of self. The duel incidentally defines the fragmenting and ordering powers of kingship, which are integral to modern Sinhalese ideas about sorcery.

The honor that Dutugemunu accords Elara upon his killing of him marks both Dutugemunu's incorporation of Elara's order and Dutugemunu's own transformation from the demonic to compassionate beneficence. Dutugemunu celebrates the funeral rites for Elara—which in both Buddhist and Hindu culture contain the symbolic meanings of sacrifice and rebirth—and "On the spot where his body had fallen he burned it with the catafalque, and there did he build a monument and ordain worship" (*Mahavamsa* 25:73–74). One possible interpretation of his action, given the structure of the Dutugemunu legend as a whole, is that it signs a death of an aspect of Dutugemunu's own self. A self which he possessed when his kingdom was part of Elara's overlordship. The failure of a hierarchical order united in Buddhism is refracted in Dutugemunu's demonic character and in his action. The reattainment of a Buddhist order negates his demon and cools his action, leading to personal transcendence.

The events that immediately follow Dutugemunu's victory further establish the argument. A message is sent to Bhalluka upon the king's death. He engages Dutugemunu's army in battle and attempts to commit Dutugemunu to personal combat. Dutugemunu's mount, Kandula, gives ground at Bhalluka's onslaught. This is not cowardice—Dutugemunu expresses surprise at his elephant's retreat—but is consistent with the logic of Dutugemunu's transformation and position of dominance in hierarchy. Bhalluka is not an encompasser like Elara and, therefore, is not Dutugemunu's equivalent. This, I think, accounts for the mythic significance of Kandula's backing away.

Dutugemunu does not strike a blow to destroy but raises his sword to cover his mouth as he exchanges verbal insults with Bhalluka—a war of words, not of arms. That Dutugemunu, in fact, does not engage in physical destructive combat against Bhalluka is consistent with Dutugemunu's transformation into encompassing Buddhist beneficence

Bhalluka is killed by the last of Dutugemunu's ten champions, Phussadeva. There are multiple cosmological significances surrounding this action. Phussadeva as a champion is the equivalent of Bhalluka, the protector of king and kingdom. In modern Sri Lanka he is considered to have been the vassal lord of a territory near Sankapala in the eastern corner of Sabaragamuva Province. Phussadeva, in the *Mahavamsa*, blows a conch with the terrifying sound of a "bursting thunderbolt." The conch is the principal symbol of Vishnu. Sankapala is an important Vishnu shrine. It is reasonable to assume that Phussadeva is a manifestation of Vishnu and that in killing Bhalluka he acts in his role as the protector of Sri Lanka and of Vijaya and his descendants. He is the fragmenting force of the kingdom now unified in encompassment.

When Dutugemunu raises his sword to his mouth he deflects an arrow aimed by Bhalluka. The latter is deluded into thinking he has struck the king, which exposes Bhalluka to an arrow from Phussadeva's bow. Phussadeva strikes twice so that Bhalluka falls dead in an attitude of submission before the king. I speculate that the circumstances of Bhalluka's death not only signify the end of the threatened continuity of the old order, but also the vitality and potency of the new Buddhist order.

Phussadeva's first arrow accidentally strikes the royal person, the earring of Dutugemunu (*Mahavamsa* 25:91–92). Phussadeva recognizes personal fault and cuts his own ear lobe to assuage his guilt and as self-enactment of the "royal justice." His blood streams down (*Mahavamsa* 25:94–101). These actions can be interpreted as simultaneously confirming the sanctity of Dutugemunu's person and as an example of reconstitutive blood sacrifice. In return for the sacrifice the king in his divinity purifies and negates the sense of guilt. The offending arrow is planted head down in the ground, by the king, cleansed with purified water, and returned to Phussadeva. In this act of divine reciprocity Dutugemunu signifies the end of hostilities, the germination of a new order, and his beneficence and righteousness.

I have by no means exhausted the symbolic richness of the foregoing events. For example, Phussadeva's killing of Bhalluka parallels Dutugemunu's slaying of Elara. As the king sacrificially incorporates, so does his kingdom, for both Bhalluka and Phussadeva can be interpreted as the symbolic representations of their respective kingdoms. Bhalluka's death signifies the weakness of the kingdom without a king and his submissive fall is indicative of the subordination in hierarchy of Elara's kingdom. Phussadeva's remorse at striking his king can be seen as a statement to the effect that king and kingdom must be united, not opposed. The divine act of Dutugemunu's reciprocity is an acknowledgment that his encompassing power acts as the life-giving force of the kingdom.[24]

There is much more of the Dutugemunu story than I have space to analyze here, but the subsequent events in the *Mahavamsa* are concerned largely with his erection of a number of famous Buddhist monuments. The account given of these works confirms and extends aspects of the argument already presented. But my analysis here of the Dutugemunu legend and of the other myths important in the Sinhalese historical consciousness, even though grossly incomplete, should be sufficient to demonstrate their progressive elaboration of a fundamental cosmological scheme and their vital interconnection. At a few points I have extended the analysis by making some reference to extant popular traditions. I now make the connection even stronger. The myths I have analyzed display a cosmological argument that is immediately comparable to a great variety of other myths that are active in the daily ritual life of ordinary Sinhalese Buddhists. In particular, they bear a strong resemblance to the Sinhalese sorcery myths discussed earlier and to more widespread Sinhalese Buddhist cultural ideas and practices concerning evil.

Myths of History, Myths of Evil

All the Sinhalese demon myths are myths about evil. In the popular traditions some of the legendary Sinhalese folk heroes are explicitly understood to have demon form and appear in the myths. Thus, according to some exorcists, Kalu Kumara, the Black Prince, the demon who lusts after women, devours their children, attacks the fetus in the womb, and renders women infertile, is a manifestation of Vijaya. Some ritual specialists recognize Kalu Kumara and Kalu Devatava as identical. The latter is understood by some to be located at the base of the sacred Bo tree in Anuradhapura. He is metaphorically, like Vijaya, the demonic deity at the root of Sinhalese Buddhism. Other exorcists claim that Kalu Kumara is the son of Vijaya and Kuveni. Certain of the events of his myth of origin accord nicely with the Vijaya story. Kalu Kumara sleeps with maidens at the cemetery gounds and is so unruly that the people complain to the king. The king banishes his son (Kapferer 1983).[25] But regardless of whether the figures of legend occur in the demon myths or not, the legends and the myths share a similar logical form. This is especially true of the stories of Suniyam and Oddi Raja of Vadiga.

I shall present two abbreviated versions of the main myths in what I call the Suniyam corpus. Both the myths were collected from exorcists in the Galle-Matara area in the south of the island. The first myth concerns the original evil inflicted upon the first queen, Manikpala.[26] This myth is the foundation myth of the principal sorcery rite, the Suniyama. The entire rite is, in effect, a reenactment of the myth, and the patient, whether male or female, is cast in the role of Queen Manikpala. I note that this contains events which are also recorded in the *Agganna Suttanta*, the Buddhist text which recounts the events of creation and the origin of kingship.

The First Act of Sorcery

The myth begins with an account of the creation of the world, the emergence of life, the development of the male and female human forms, their desire, and their reproductive proliferation as a function of their desire.

Eventually the population becomes so great that the people decide to elect a king. They make this decision on the basis of their observation of nature wherein they see that the animals, birds, and fish have kings.

At a great gathering of the people Mahasammata is elected king. He chooses as his wife Manikpala, who is the sister of Vishnu. Mahasammata is the child of the Sun and a former incarnation of the Buddha.

Mahasammata leaves his palace, where he had been making joyous love to Manikpala, to fight the Asuras. Unfortunately Devadatta, alias Vasavarti Maraya, lusts after Manikpala.

Vasavarti assumes the form of Mahasammata. But when he approaches the queen's bedchamber a servant girl smells him. He has the stench of a viper, not the scent of lotus blooms and sandalwood, as has Mahasammata.

The queen, warned, locks her room, but Vasavarti assumes the form of a fire viper. He breaks through the door and lodges in the queen's womb. The queen becomes incurably ill. The distraught Mahasammata sends for ten learned men led by Oddissa. They perform the ceremony of the seven steps and the queen is cured.

The second myth concerns the birth of Suniyam Yaka, who in most of the exorcist traditions is also known as Maha Oddi Raja, or Oddissa. Oddissa is the one who cured Manikpala and is variously understood as the more benign transformed aspect of Suniyam. In the myth from which I draw this account he is referred to as Madana Yaka, a lustful demonic form of Vishnu.

The Birth of Oddissa

The story opens with a description of the city of Vadiga, in India. This is followed by an account of the four main caste divisions. The queen of Vadiga is described as having been at her toilet in a pond, which contained seven different kinds of flower. From overhead, Vasavarti Maraya sees the queen. He desires her, possesses (*avesa*) her, and unbeknown to the queen, engages in sexual union with her. The queen becomes unconscious. Learned men are summoned and a special "cere-mony for the womb" (*gabe mangalla*) is recommended. But the queen's illness continues. Her body grows pale.

The queen has three different kinds of [pregnancy] craving. The third she declares to the king. To his horror she says that she desires to walk around the city naked, except for serpents coiled about her body. At first the king wants to execute her, but he relents.

Eventually the queen gives birth to a son. Wise men warn the king of the power of the prince, that he will overrun Vadiga and the neighboring kingdoms, devouring the inhabitants, but the king takes no action. When the prince turns sixteen he goes into the jungle. He pulls cobras from anthills and collects many other kinds of snake. He drapes them around his body and returns to Vadiga, slaughters the king, overrunning his kingdom and neighboring kingdoms as well.

Prince Oddissa then journeys across the sea to Lanka. Here he causes great havoc, cannibalizing the people. Ananda, a disciple of the Buddha, pleads with him, but he becomes more furious. Finally, the Buddha intervenes and has Oddissa bound in iron by Vishnu. Buddha has compassion for the prince and allows Oddissa to go free, provided he bows to the authority of the Buddha. This Oddissa says he will do, and he declares, furthermore, that he will cure disease and give protection to human beings.[27]

In the historical myths and the myths about the origin of sorcery, evil is synonymous with disorder and fragmentation. As a moment in the cosmic process and something productive of great suffering it is conceived of as coming from outside the state. It opposes and attacks the state, often gaining entry through the force of delusion. Evil and the agents of evil often bear intimate kinship with the agents and beings of order, nonsuffering, and compassion. Devadatta, the main disciple of the Buddha and the brother of the Buddha's wife, became his main adversary. Devadatta is often identified with Mara, the great being of evil, who in well-known legend and folk story attempted to sway the Buddha from his path to enlightenment. Exorcists (*adura*) and deity priests (*kapurala*) identify the main demonic aspect of Suniyam, Vasavarti Maraya, as Mara and as a form of Devadatta. In the comedy of the principal exorcism rites, exorcists will address Vasavarti Maraya and the demonic generally as *massina* (cross-cousin, in-law). Oddissa (Oddi Raja), the son of the king of Vadiga's queen, destroys and fragments his father's polity and the other surrounding kingdoms. All the Sinhalese heroes I have discussed attack their fathers, and Vijaya and Dutugemunu particularly lay waste around them, destroying neighboring kingdoms. Suniyam, or Oddi Raja, as the strongest Sinhalese manifestation of evil does likewise.[28]

I have said that in the myths of evil, disorder and fragmentation come from outside the state. This may seem to be contradicted by the fact that the agents of evil have close kinship with the agents of order. It can be argued, therefore, that evil comes from within the state, an analytic position that would not greatly affect my discussion. I suggest, however, that when evil manifests its power, the logic of the myths indicates that this power is external and in opposition to the state. In other words, what may have been inside moves to the outside and achieves its negating contradiction accordingly. Put another way, weakness in the internal structure of the state may give rise to the evil of fragmentation and allow its destructive intrusion, but such weakness is not evil per se. Thus Queen Manikpala carries the demon seed in her womb, but this illegitimate intrusion into her body was through no fault of her own.

In the Suniyam and Oddi Raja myths the demonic goes from inside the state to outside. It attacks from the margins. Vijaya and Dutugemunu in their disordering modes attack from the margins, or from the outside in.

In all the myths discussed, outside and inside are not absolutes. They are moments in the cosmic process at which hierarchy is progressively fragmented and torn apart or unified and re-created. Dutugemunu and Oddi Raja are beings of fragmentation and disorder when they descend the hierarchy of order and become beings of the outside. They become inside when they ascend hierarchy and assume its unifying principles. Oddi Raja and Suniyam, as well as Dutugemunu and Vijaya, transform from evil to good and from disordering and violent to beneficent and protective. This is apparent in their myths and in their rituals.

It is relevant that in some of the Suniyam myths, especially where Oddi Raja is concerned, evil is depicted as a foreigner, specifically one who is not a Buddhist. Oddi is avowed to be a Hindu but is converted in a confrontation with the Buddha, who reasons with him. Having caused great carnage in Lanka, Suniyam agrees to the Buddha's command that he relinquish his evil ways and protect against evil rather than cause it. Oddi becomes a creature of order through his agreement to subordinate himself to the Buddha. In some traditions, Suniyam, or Oddi Raja, in his benign form is a being of territorial integrity, a guardian of the village boundary.[29]

The assertion of the Buddha's authority in the transformation of Suniyam or Oddi Raja is the assertion of hierarchy, specifically the hierarchy of the beneficent Buddhist state. The opposition of Suniyam and Oddi Raja is not simply an opposition of disorder to order. The demonic, though it fragments and disorders the orders with which it is brought into conflict or which it attacks, is nonetheless an order, even of disorder. Demons are ordered one to the other in hierarchy (Kapferer 1983). The point is that they are disordering, as they themselves may become disordered, in conjunction with beings, forces, or orders whose organizing principles demons negate or who for a variety of reasons fail to encompass the demonic. The radical danger and evil-producing disorder of Suniyam or Oddi Raja is that their order is in accordance with principles which diametrically negate those of the Buddha. Suniyam is a reduction into terrifying oblivion consequent upon the total absence of knowledge and reason as opposed to the nothingness of the Buddha, a transcendence of perfect knowledge and enlightenment.[30] The horrible destructive force of a Suniyam and an Oddi Raja, for which Hindu is often a metaphor in the myths, is, nonetheless, capable of being tamed by or refashioned to the terms of Buddhist hierarchical principles, and converted, as indeed was Oddi Raja, to the interests, ideas, and practices of Buddhism.

The myths of evil, like the myths of history, are cosmological arguments about the nature of the state and of its relation to evil. In the myths of evil the state, specifically the state organized according to Buddhist principles, is the metaphor and the mechanism for the control and elimination of evil and suffering. In the myths of history, evil—and its attendant destructive fragmentation—is the metaphor for the process of the state and its decline, reformation, and re-creation in accordance with the laws of Buddhist cosmology. The myths of evil and the myths of the state in history essay a logic about the nature of power and the ambivalence of kingship, with its demonic and benign qualities. More specifically, the myths of evil and of the state are about the nature of the Buddhist state. They depict its hierarchical ordering as continually manifesting moments between the threat of complete annihilation in fragmentation and perfect unity in transcendence.

Evil is a possibility of the state. It is as much part of its vital power as it may be a sign of its destructive weakness. The myths of the chronicles and of the popular tradition display a cosmological argument which treats the demonic, violent, fragmenting power of the state—the king's evil—as integral to the creation or re-creation of a perfect, equanimous unity. In this sense, violence, destruction, disorder, and fragmentation are not contradictory to the formation of a harmoniously ordered state. But, perhaps, like Dutugemunu, the king as the state must realize his alternative demonic possibility, even move outside and against himself, to regain or achieve the ultimate harmony of the state. When Dutugemunu attacks Tissa he may be interpreted as metaphorically moving against himself. Tissa holds important aspects of Dutugemunu's kingly identity—which might underlie Dutugemunu's initial defeat—his mother, symbolic of his right to the throne, and the elephant, the symbol of state and the gift from his father.

Dutugemunu is a righteous Buddhist king, and like the great Asoka, the Buddhist king of India who sent the first envoys of Buddhism to Sri Lanka, a *cakravartin*. Like Asoka he is aware of the evil of the destruction he causes. Agonizing over the millions he has been caused to slaughter, Dutugemunu is comforted by the monks who declare that "only one and a half human beings had been slain. ... One had come into the [three] refuges, and the other had taken on himself the five precepts" (*Mahavamsa*

25:109–10). All the others are stated to be "not more esteemed than beasts" as they are not Buddhists. Dutugemunu realizes his own evil, even if a reduced evil. Dutugemunu's monument-building, merit-earning, postconquest activity can obviously be interpreted as the expunging of his own evil through the assertion of principles that govern unity at the apex of the cosmic hierarchy. The extent of the great works is equal to the slaughter. This action, part of Dutugemunu's self-sacrificing renunciation, can be compared with the actions of Viharadevi following the evil action of her father, the king of Kalyani.

Both the myths of evil and the legends of the state set the protostate and ideal Buddhist state in contrast to other political forms. In this contrast, the Buddhist king, or the proto-Buddhist king—Mahasammata or Vijaya, for example—is presented as united with his people and essentially their servant. Mahasammata is the original king, the king whose household was afflicted by the first evil, and he is a king by election. Sihabahu acts on the will of his people to exile Vijaya. Vijaya is consecrated king at the wish of his comrades and ministers. Dutugemunu is assuaged of his guilt by being told that his destruction was not of the Buddhist people, and he gives himself up to a life of compassion and good works. Under him, the *Mahavamsa* relates, the people live "happily." The Buddhist ideal king or proto-ideal king is good and righteous, not merely because he upholds Buddhist principles, but also because he acts in concert with and in the interests of the people. The ideal Buddhist king is virtually a "democratic" hierarch. Indeed I would go so far as to suggest that hierocracy and democracy exist in complementarity in Buddhist notions of the ideal king as exemplified in Sinhalese Buddhist myths. Hierocracy and democracy, therefore, are not contradictions in the Buddhist conception of kingship.

The relation between hierarchy and power is a theme of all the myths I have discussed. Power exercised in the interests of a hierarchy conditioned by Buddhist cosmic principles establishes order that functions for the welfare of the people. Their action is freed by incorporation within a hierarchical order wherein they are released from the confining and restrictive possibility of self and of the conflict between individual selves. Power which is antagonistic to the Buddhist hierarchy, the power of the demonic, is the destructive power of self and can imprison individuals, denying to them and to others the capacity to act. Kings or princes who exercise individual power and do not acknowledge encompassment are evil, and they manifest this evil by the denial to the people of their power to act. Like the consuming demon, Suniyam, they ingest others into their own individuality, rather than incorporating them within a unifying cosmic order. Such kings are evil because they are the absolute assertion of self. The good and righteous kings are those who acknowledge the encompassment of their power, who renounce their self and in such action release others from self-imprisonment and give them the freedom of action, the "democracy" of hierarchy.

Evil, as depicted in the myths, finds its chief metaphors in kings or princes whose actions are antagonistic to Buddhist principles. Hindu kings—or the kings of declining Buddhist states, those moving in a direction counter to Buddhist unifying principles—are the symbols of evil, of its causation in the rejection of knowledge and reason and its effect in suffering and violence. In the myths demons grow in the households of kings as a result of the kings' refusal to heed astrological advice and the wisdom of sages. Kings or princes as the powerful metaphors of evil characteristically attack their own people and act against their interests. The magnitude of their mythic horror is that they are the absolute negation of the ideal resolution of hierarchy and democracy. Such kings and princes act with powers founded in hierarchy but against the ultimate order of hierarchy. Born to hierarchical position, they defeat its ordering capacity and turn the power of position destructively against a wider embracing unity.

The metaphors of evil, evil kingship aside, are all metaphors of the destruction of hierarchy and of order hierarchically constituted. Correspondingly, the violent reassertion of hierarchy, and not the mere exertion of power—a demonic power which is individual and outside hierarchy or external to it—restores a harmonious order that overcomes suffering. An aspect of such suffering is the confinement, the absolute restriction, determination, and powerlessness of the person. Power in unity with hierarchy is creative, regenerative, and releases the person. In the Buddhist thought of the myths such power reproduces the purity and unity, the good, of the cosmic origin. Power in contradiction of hierarchy generates suffering in existence. It produces fragmentation and is manifest most clearly at the base of hierarchy which is overcome by unifying power. What is at base constitutes both the metaphors of fragmentation and of violent destructive power. Evil power is synonymous with the base as, too, is the greater potential for evil. Thus those who are at the bottom of the world, hierarchically conceived, have the possibility of manifesting destruction and violence in themselves, in their personal condition, and in their relation to others. Similarly, the manifestation in the person, king or otherwise, of destructive potency or indication of personal or existential fragmentation, for example, in illness, is tantamount to the constitution or reconstitution of the person at the base of hierarchy or in a position external to its protective order.

I have insisted that the arguments of the myths are present in ritual action. This is magnificently evident in the Suniyama, the anti sorcery ritual.[31] The Suniyama is commonly performed in the cities and villages of the western and southern coasts of Sri Lanka. In its enactment the Suniyama is virtually a hermeneutic of many of the myths to which I

The Cosmic Palace of Mahasammata. An exorcist purifies the palace preparatory to the Dance of the Seven Steps. (Photo by Bruce Kapferer)

The Dance of the Seven Steps. The patient dressed in the shawl of Queen Manikpala starts the step by step progression, from lotus bloom to lotus bloom, into Mahasammata's palace. The blooms are arranged on the ground in the form of a serpent, the serpent of the beginning of time, and also the fire viper that invaded Manikpala's bedchamber. (Photo by David Beatty)

have referred. A brief account of it provides additional demonstration for the kind of logic I have been presenting. Further, the following description indicates that the logic of the myths can also be engaged to the constitution of the very being of the person.

The Suniyama: From the Womb of the State

The Suniyama begins at dusk and continues until it reaches a climax around the middle of the following day. The patient seated in a chair, is covered in Queen Manikpala's shawl, and confronts the *atamagala*, or the cosmic palace of Mahasammata. This ritual building is, among other things a model of a traditional hierarchical order encompassed in the idea

In the Womb of State. The patient can be seen seated inside the cosmic palace. (Photo by David Beatty)

A Comedy of Brahmins: The Vadiga Patuna. Odissa and the nine other healing Brahmins—manifestations of Vishnu—come to cure the patient. The sexual metaphors of regeneration are explicit. (Photo by David Beatty)

of the Buddha. The cosmic hierarchy is ritually and progressively generated in the organization of music and dance, which reaches its height when the dancers appear in the form of the four guardian gods of Sinhalese Buddhism—Vishnu, Kataragama, Saman, and Natha. This concludes what the exorcists understand as the period of the evening watch (Kapferer 1983).

At approximately midnight a lengthy episode known as the Dance of the Seven Steps (*Hat Adiya*) is enacted. Ritual offerings in the form of seven lotus blooms are placed on the ground between the patient and the palace. They form the shape of a serpent. Some exorcists say it is Mahakala Naga, the great cosmic serpent at the beginning of time. The patient is moved slowly along the path of the lotuses, the lotus being a powerful symbol of the beginning of life. At each lotus, offerings are made and long poems are uttered. The poems recount stories (*jatakas*) from the previous lives of the Buddha. The episode is conceived by exorcists as a representation of the first seven steps of the Buddha following his birth. The entire sequence is understood as a reconstitution of the

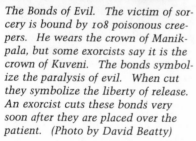

The Bonds of Evil.   The victim of sor-
cery is bound by 108 poisonous cree-
pers.   He wears the crown of Manik-
pala, but some exorcists say it is the
crown of Kuveni.   The bonds symbol-
ize the paralysis of evil.   When cut
they symbolize the liberty of release.
An exorcist cuts these bonds very
soon after they are placed over the
patient.   (Photo by David Beatty)

Out of the Chrysalis of the State.
The cosmic palace is broken down at
the end of the Suniyama.   This dra-
matic conclusion presents the tran-
scendent rebirth of the patient.   In
effect, too, the event shows the inti-
mate connection between unification
and fragmentation, life and death.
(Photo by Bruce Kapferer)

integrity of the patient.   The *Hat Adiya* concludes with the patient
crawling through a door into the palace.   The patient is now seated inside
the palace.   He or she sits on a mat under which has been drawn the
symbolic yantra of Cosmic Man, the original being (Mahakala Purushya).

The main period of transition has now been completed.   This
transition has followed a process whereby the patient moves from an
external, personally fragmented, subordinated, demonic and foreign condition to a position inside the cosmic palace.   In effect the patient is now
in a condition of originary reconstitution within the hierarchical order of
state and society.

The period of the morning watch now begins.   The first episode,
which ideally should start at 3.00 A.M. in the time scheme of the exorcism,
is the *Vadiga Patuna*.   It portrays the arrival of the Brahmins from India
who performed the first Suniyama to cure Manikpala and of whom the

chief is Oddissa. The episode is performed as marvelous comedy, consistent with the conversion of contradiction, which is the significant message of the episode. It marks the nature of the transformation that is taking place in the sorcery victim.

The comedy of the Vadiga Patuna as it is routinely enacted in all the performances I have witnessed plays on a Hindu India–Buddhist Sri Lanka contrast specifically, the hierarchy of India and the Buddhist hierarchy of Sri Lanka. The Brahmins cut ridiculous figures. They wear dark glasses and carry rolled umbrellas. They talk the gibberish of a foreign language and make all manner of verbal slips and obscenities when interpreted through the Sinhala language. Eventually they are converted. They become resocialized, speak Sinhala, and acknowledge the authority of the Buddha. Their transformation not only indicates the parallel transformation taking place in the patient; it also enables them in the logic of the rite as a whole, to give further effect to the curative course of the rite. Their dangerous foreign-derived magical practice is "domesticated" within the cosmic polity of the Buddhist order and becomes vital in the restructuring and reaffirmation of this order.

The ritual events following the Vadiga Patuna cut the demonic connection and complete the transformational process. As I described earlier the victim is quite literally released from the bonds of the antisocial, determining, and restrictive power of evil sorcery. The patient is made free within the life-giving Buddhist cosmic, political, and social order. In this process of reconstitution the victim is made whole and becomes the embodiment of the Buddhist cosmic order. Within the whole is re-created the part, and the person is restored to her or his former capacity for action in the world. The victim thus transformed can now reenter the ordinary world reempowered and without the external protection of the ritual buildings. The ordering essence symbolized in Mahasammata's palace is now united internally with the body of the erstwhile patient re-creating the patient's body as a reintegrated whole. No finer sense of this could be given than in the final episodes of the Suniyama. These take place over the midday period of the rite or some eighteen hours after the rite began.

I refer to the sequence known as the Destruction of the Palace (*Chedana Vidiya*). Exorcist-dancers appear carrying knives. They are led by the principal dancer brandishing the sword (*kuduva*) of Vasavarti Maraya, the great being of evil. He is usually presented as being in a furious, almost "drunken" rage; indeed in many performances the dancer has consumed quantities of arrack. Vasavarti and his companions attack the palace and tear it down. Amid the destruction and the fury of the falling debris the patient appears to rise up; merging whole as if from a chrysalis. Indeed, and in perfect consistency with the symbolic metaphors of the rite, the patient is reborn out of the very womb of the Cosmic State.

My brief description is intended to be self-explanatory. I stress, however, that in the Suniyama and in all traditional Sinhalese rites of healing the patient is reconstituted through being placed in the process of hierarchical regeneration (Kapferer 1983). The patient is transformed into health in the course of entering into the motion of cosmic regeneration conditioned by the ordering principles of the coherent Buddhist state and society. In this transformation the patient moves from outside to inside, from a being unencompassed, the subject of destruction, to a being encompassed, who finds renewed order within that which encloses.

In the conception just described the person as an ordered being achieves this only in the context of an ordered Buddhist state and society. Furthermore, the person as an integrated whole fuses with the ideal Buddhist cosmos and its polity and society. The cosmic state is made internal to the person, its principles vital to internal coherence. Such principles are those which conceive of the cosmic whole as internally hierarchically differentiated, and it is after such a conception that the body is remade. I add that the principles that condition the inner being of the person are also those that condition the social and political relations which extend around the person. Thus the cosmic totality that restores the inner being simultaneously reconstitutes the everyday social order as this centers on the patient. The Suniyama, and exorcism ritual generally, often take as patients people in some way central in a local order, in a household, in a neighborhood or larger community. Often prominent patrons in local political communities are at the center of Suniyam rituals. The reordering of a person by such rituals is also a reordering of the social and political world of patients and is so conceived by their families, clients and other associates.

The metaphors of cosmic rebuilding and personal restoration in the Suniyama, as in all exorcisms, are violent. Their violence is generated in the clash of the great forces of cosmic contradiction within which is caught the very fate of cosmos, state, and person. The violence of their destruction and reformation in the Suniyama, however, concludes with the achievement of an ultimately transcendent equanimity, harmony, and peace. This statement of the Suniyama is also that of the legend of Dutugemunu and of other stories that are part of a widespread Sinhalese Buddhist consciousness. Thus, in the Suniyama, enclosed and safe within the edifice of the cosmic state and manifesting the peace and harmony of one in unity with it, the erstwhile victim of evil sits calmly, like the Buddha before the furious Mara, or nonreactively, like Dutugemunu before Bhalluka, while the embodiment of perfect evil, barred outside and railing impotently to get in, marshalls all its venomous powers to no effect.

There is nothing surprising in the similarities of argument between the myths and practice of evil and sorcery and the legends of historical consciousness. All the myths discussed are variations within the one culturally and historically formed cosmological understanding. The myths are part of a single discourse in which different legends expand or deeply explore themes upon which others touch only briefly. This is not to ignore the fact that many of the myths have emerged at different historical moments and have taken their shape within a variety of social, economic, and political circumstances. Nor do I overlook the fact that the myths are continually achieving significance, often innovative and being refashioned. This is so even in the ritual contexts of their apparently atemporal repetition, for these ritual contexts are embraced by, as they arise from, the wider social and political realities of which they are a part. Rather, what I have directed attention to here is the form or logic of the myths. While I consider that the logic of myth can come to have force in context—that is, in situated practices—this is not so in any idealist determinist sense. I have discussed the meaning of the myths as it is apparent in ·the interpretation of the context which the myths form in themselves. This meaning, which I have outlined in only the barest terms, has no necessity or determination or even relevance for lived social and political realities. The approach I have adopted is cognate with structuralist approaches to myth. But it is not an approach that subscribes to the idealism of many such approaches; that is, in my perspective the "meaning" of the myths insofar as they are relevant in the everyday world is not in the myths alone. Neither is their meaning ultimatedly reducible to the pragmatics of everyday social and political realities, the myth as charter view of Malinowski. My perspective acknowledges the importance of the issues raised by such approaches. In my own understanding the meaning of myth can never be divorced from its practice. But this practice is not entirely separable from logic of the myth which is engaged in practical circumstance. Thus neither the logic of the myth nor the social and political circumstances in which myths come to be used is prior to the other. Myth and its context work in conjunction to produce their meaning. My rejection of structuralist idealism or a materialist and practical realism, such as that of Malinowski, in the consideration of the meaning of myth requires further explication.

Ricoeur (1963), in an important disagreement with Levi-Strauss's structuralism, denies the method its claim of having discovered a way of determining the meaning of myth. If structuralists have discovered meaning, says Ricoeur, then it is the meaning of nonmeaning ("*le sens du non-sens*"), syntax without lived significance. Given the terms of his argument, he is right. For myth examined as a unity in itself, divorced from history and outside any context other than that which it provides, is not part of any action or experience of human beings in their everyday social and political worlds. The actors on the mythic stage of structuralist analysis are pawns and counters in a series of logical moves, a logic which may not inhabit the consciousness of those real, living personages for whom the myths have meaning and who confer meaning upon the mythic action. Structuralism derives a logic from its method, which as many of its critics have noted is not unmotivated. The motivation of the method is in the culture, or the ideological commitment of the analyst. Thus the structuralist method can ignore the lived significances of mythic event and simultaneously impose a logic of its own, which is not of the making of the myth. Dumont (1986:223–33) makes these points strongly when he notes that structuralism is ideologically given to treat certain oppositions such as nature/culture, man/woman as equivalents when they are not (a propensity of egalitarianism, which will be discussed in part 2) and conflates contexts that may otherwise be distinguished in the ideology under study or vice versa. These criticisms are valid, though I do not consider that they necessarily negate the value of a structuralist approach. I hasten to add, however, that my analysis of the legends of history is not structuralist in the sense I have discussed, though I do share some of the objectives of structuralism.

A primary objective has been to demonstrate that the myths of evil and of history articulate a definite logic, a logic not tied to a method of analysis. It is not necessarily derived from my own cultural or ideological position in history either. The logic I describe is basic in much Hindu and, especially, Buddhist theological or philosophical texts of ancient and modern lineage. It is also central to the way Sinhalese traditional ritual practitioners understand the structuring of event and action in rituals, especially those of demon exorcism and the larger ceremonies to the deities. The myths and legends I have discussed are often part of these rites. Furthermore, these rites in the hermeneutics of their performance suggest the type of analysis I have applied to the myths here, independent of ritual context.

The cosmic logic I have outlined is a scheme without any necessary significance in lived realities. Insofar as the scheme is filled with potential force, however, especially in a modern context of ethnic nationalism, it is as well to stress some of the central parameters of the logic, a logic within which the modern Sri Lankan state and a personal identity within the state can take form.

I have shown that in the myths and rites of evil, as in the legends of history, the order of the body is identified with and produced within the order of the state. More important, as in the Suniyama, the person is reborn, reconstituted, from the womb of the state, a state rebuilt as an ordered hierarchy. There are parallels here in the legends of Vijaya and Dutugemunu, both of whom are reconstituted as benign, encompassing instruments of state, in the process of the establishment or regeneration of state order. Their violence, as the violent metaphors and acts of the Suniyama rite, is an ordering violence engaged to the formation or reformation of the wholeness and health of the state, the person of the state, and of the person within the state. In the argument of the myths and rites of evil and of the state, violence is not a contradiction either of the person of the Sinhalese Buddhist or of the Buddhist state. Indeed, it may be integral to the continuity of the person and of the state and integral to their reformation. Violence is appropriate in the expunging of evil, an evil which by definition defies the unified order of the Buddhist state.[32]

The foregoing scheme is filled with potential and ominous import once it is made a foundation of the being of person and state in lived realities. This is so in one important sense at least. I refer to a central argument which treats person and state as one and that furthermore regards the integrity of the person as dependent on the encompassing unity of the state. It is an argument which in specific circumstances can give rise to the conception, outside ritual contexts, of an attack upon the state as also an attack upon the person and vice versa. This ontological potency of the cosmic logic I have outlined can be realized in an ethnic consciousness formed in the ideology of modern state nationalism.

I shall conclude this chapter with a general discussion of the relation between ontology and ideology as I use the two words. This is critical to my argument as a whole concerning the import of the cosmic logic of the myths, legends, and rites of Sinhalese Buddhists in extending an understanding of the present tragedy of ethnic hostilities in Sri Lanka.

Ideology and Ontology

The cosmic logic which I have outlined constitutes an ontology; that is, it describes the fundamental principles of a being in the world and the orientation of such a being toward the horizons of its experience. It is an ontology confined within the structure of events of certain myths and, as I have shown, it is an ontology which governs the constitution and reconstitution of being in some rituals. I stress two points. First, the ontology I have outlined is not the only ontology in accordance with which Sinhalese Buddhists in Sri Lanka can discover or realize the significance of their everyday experiences. Second, the logic or the reasoning of the ontology I have discussed is capable of realizing a variety of meanings in context without breaking the links in the chain of its reasoning. As a result it can unify diverse meanings, making them appear as different instances of the same thing.

There are many ontologies or modes of being in the Sinhalese Buddhist cultural universe, both within Buddhist historical tradition and formed external to it. Thus, Sri Lanka's long history of articulation into a wider political world order has ingrained—through the force of arms and other powerful forms of domination—ontologies relevant to the modern capitalist world. I refer, for example, to an individual ontology wherein the individual realizes his or her value in the possession of commodities which have worth in a capitalist economy. One has worth in oneself and is oriented to others through material possessions. The scientific attitude toward the legends of history discussed in the preceding chapter is ontological. The extreme rationalism displayed by this attitude is integral to the very being of its protagonists, a being, an ontological orientation, formed in the process of modern historical and cultural changes. This ontology is the ground upon which some people build their notions of the obvious, of the taken-for-granted, and of incontestable commonsense.

Certain ontologies can come to be of overriding import. This can be a consequence of what I understand as ideological processes, whereby certain interpretations within culture are made in the circumstances of political and social action. Ideology in my usage is a selective cultural construction whereby certain significances relevant to experience are systematically organized into a relatively coherent scheme. The ideas that are brought into ideological relation may have a grounding in a variety of different ontologies. But there is always the potential, I suggest, for one ontology to become dominant in the historical ideological process and to provide the inherent logic for ideological coherence. This is especially so when certain mythic traditions are engaged to the formation of ideology, for such traditions, as exemplified by the ones discussed, are likely to beat out a systematic logical theme. In this situation the logic or the ontology of the myth made relevant in the motion of a historical world and once subservient to such a world can come to have a more determining force. It can turn the tables on those who use it, becoming the master and no longer the servant. This is so, moreover, if the logic, but, I insist, not necessarily the meaning, is already integral to the constitution or reconstitution of person and the orientation of persons to the world in a variety of contexts.

I emphasise that ontology realizes its meanings, and exerts the force of its logic, only through the ideological action of human beings in a social and political world. In an important sense, ontology awaits its meaning and perhaps never exhausts its meaningful potential. This is so, for the meaning of the logic must always be emergent, emergent through its active conjunction with lived realities. Ontologies may be heavy with significant potential, as I believe are the Sinhalese Buddhist ontologies of evil, power, and the state. But this potency of import is realized through the ideological engagement of the logic of ontology within social and political realities. In such contexts ontologies give rise to possibilities which cannot be discerned through a reduction to the logic of ontology alone or to the mythic or ritual context in which the logic of ontologies discover their "purest" manifestation. Ideology, in the conception essayed here, does not merely manifest an ontology. Rather ideology is active in a more vital sense and generates a meaning in ontology and also conditions for its practical force. Through ideology the terms and relations of an ontological scheme receive valuation, a valuation laden with import in a historically lived reality.

The chronicles of Sinhalese Buddhist history demonstrate the role of ontology in ideology. Numerous scholars have drawn attention to the chronicles as ideology (Mendis 1946; Bechert 1977; Gunawardana 1978, 1982, 1984; Obeyesekere 1984a; Siriweera 1984). Gunawardana states that the monk who wrote the *Mahavamsa* was influenced by his position within a predominantly Buddhist social order, which he perceived to be threatened by South Indian invasions. "In relating heroic tales of Buddhist rulers who struggled to 'reestablish the sasana,' whenever the ideal order had been disrupted, the chronicler was presenting what he thought to be an inspiring model for contemporaries for future generations" (Gunawardana 1984, 1). Siriweera compares the events relating the deeds of Dutugemunu in the *Mahavamsa* with the record of the same events in the thirteenth century *Pujavaliya* (Liyanagamage 1978). The *Pujavaliya* was written by the monk Mayurapada, who was the contemporary of the South Indian invader Magha. Magha is infamous in the Sinhalese imagination for the ravages he committed upon the island. It is the experience of Magha that Siriweera uses to account for Elara's change from being the righteous king of the *Mahavamsa* to being an unrighteous ruler who destroyed monasteries in the *Pujavaliya* (Siriweera 1984, 64). A similar argument can be presented for the seventeenth-century *Rajavaliya*, where the evil of Elara and his followers receives even stronger elaboration, and Elara's army is equated with the hordes of Mara. Dighajantu, Elara's standardbearer, is taunted by Dutugemunu's champion, Nirmalaya (Suranimala in the *Mahavamsa*): "Where goest thou, worthless Tamil?" (*Rajavaliya* 1954, 35). The *Rajavaliya* was written at a time of considerable social and political dislocation. The island had been penetrated by the colonial powers and the Dutch had just ousted the Portuguese. Neither the Portuguese nor the Dutch were particularly sympathetic to Buddhism, and this, coupled with the presence of new foreign powers fragmenting the Sinhalese, may have stimulated an elaboration of the glories of a Sinhalese past. Indeed, the more rounded characterization of the Tamils as evil may be a metaphor of the disruptions and changes taking place as a result of the colonial presence.[33]

If the chronicles are filled with the meaning of the times in which they were written, they also display a systematic logic. Certain significant possibilities of the logic become more apparent in successive versions of the mythic events. That Elara changes from righteous to unrighteous is consistent within the terms of the logic I have discussed. Dutugemunu's rise to dominance, given the logic of transformation through hierarchy and the principle of encompassment, should be coincident with a decline of Elara into fragmented subordination, a move to the demonic. If anything the later texts reveal, through their ideological activation in specific historical contexts, interpretational possibilities latent in their logic but not so clearly evident in earlier versions such as the *Mahavamsa*.

The changes or elaborations evident from text to text do not occur haphazardly. The continuities from one chronicle to the next, moreover, are not merely continuities born of the fact that the texts deal with broadly the same legendary occurrences. Their continuity is a continuity of logical scheme. The texts cannot be reduced merely to the context in which they were written or to the ontological principles underlying mythic construction. They are ideological in the sense in which I use the word; that is, the events of a lived social and political reality are selected to achieve their significance in accordance with an ontology which, in its turn, gains force and meaning in a world of flesh and blood.

If ideology is a distortion of the realities upon which it reflects, this distortion is not produced merely by the particular social and political position of the ideological producers in the world. That many of the chronicles were written by monks undoubtedly accounts for the recurrent theme of the relation of power, the kingship, and the state to Buddhism. The ideological distortions are also produced in the ontological commitments of the monks as monks who are proponents of a cosmological attitude that has deep implications for their orientation in the world. Insofar as the chronicles are important references in the political discourse of modern Sri Lanka, the ideological distortions of the past become the foundation of the ideological distortions of the present.

If ontology is empowered through ideology, so is ideology empowered by its engagement of an ontology. To return to an earlier example, the designation of Elara and his Tamil followers as evil grows in ideological significance through its relevant ontology. The epithets *evil* and *wicked* carry the additional metaphoric load of *demonic*, *outside*, and *subordinate*. Jointly they signify not just a threat to order but a lesser claim to rights in a Sinhalese-dominated political order. Ontologically, in other words, the alignment of Tamils with the demonic can have dreadful consequences. The association of Tamils with evil and vice versa is not simply ethnic prejudice or racism defined sociologically, often in reference to a range of conceptually dubious criteria. It is perhaps more radical. Tamils are not just a separate category, subordinated and discriminated against. They are threateningly evil, striking at the very core of Sinhalese Buddhist identity and existence. This is so especially in political resistance.

I have described the reasoning of the texts as also integral to the routine world of daily experience. It is the logic of healing rites, of deity ceremonies, of rites at the temple, and of rituals in the household. The nature of this cultural life varies among different traditions and areas of historical settlement, between town and country, and according to caste and class. The organization of temple worship in an elite neighborhood in Colombo is likely to be very different from the organization of worship at a temple in an impoverished shanty area, and the outer cultural form of weddings, puberty ceremonies, curing rites, and so on, will differ greatly. Nevertheless the logic of the ontology of such practices is strikingly similar. Because the ontology I describe is present in a vast array of routine cultural practices, any ideology that engages such ontology can reach immediately into the ordinary consciousness of daily life. More than this, it can reach into the consciousness of people in vastly different social and political circumstances. Here, in my view, are the roots of what some have identified as the hegemonic properties (Gramsci 1971) and hence motivating power of certain ideologies throughout large and diverse populations. The organizing and integrating potential of ideology, the propensity of certain ideological formations to unify, to embrace persons of varying and perhaps opposed political and social interests, and to engage them in concerted, directed action, may owe much to the logic of an ontology that the ideology inscribes.

A politically ideological statement grounded in a widespread ontology has the potential for immediate acceptance. This is so even if the ideologically clothed ontology is made to resound with a message for its context which is a distortion of the significance it achieves in other more routine practices. Ideology formed on such ontological ground gathers force because it shares the same taken-for-grantedness of habitual experience.

It is the ontology of ideology which contributes to the angry interchanges in the press and elsewhere over statements of ideological import. An article in the Sinhala newspaper *Divaina* (Colombo, 26 June 1985) written by a monk, Kelaniya Siriniwassa, strongly disavows an earlier assertion by a Mirando Obeyesekera that Dutugemunu's champions, Nandhimitta and Velusumana, were Tamils.[34] The monk rejects statements such as Obeyesekera's on the assertion that the reading of the *Mahavamsa* and not the interpretation of names would prove otherwise. He adds that if identity is to be determined through the study of names then "Mirando" would suggest that Obeyesekera is a burgher (*landesi jatika*—Dutch race). Given Sinhalese suspicions of the burgher ethnic minority, this is a loaded comment. Kelaniya Siriniwassa associates Obeyesekera with other Sinhalese "traitors against the nation [race]" (*jati drohi*), strongly linking them with alleged Tamil interests. Some of the fury of the argument is generated in its ontology. Obeyesekera challenged taken-for-granted assumptions germane to a specific orientation within the world. Opposition to the Buddhist state is to be Tamil or to be outside and against the nation. Nandhimitta and Velusumana are "of course" Sinhalese because they are with Dutugemunu and the nation.

The logic of ontology as part of routine cultural practice is both vital in the self-constitution of the person and active in the significant interpretation of lived experience. Such vitality is intensified when it is harnessed to a nationalist political ideology. To challenge assumptions integral to the being of the nation also attacks the person at his or her ontological depth, at the very source of being and existence in the world. Here is a further understanding of the force of ideology structured through ontology. Ideology can engage the person in a fundamental and what may be experienced as a "primodial" way. And so the passions are fired and people may burn.

Attention to the ontological dimensions of ideology and to the embeddedness of ontology in a wide array of cultural practices may also extend an understanding of the power of ideological rhetoric. In the context of Sri Lanka many of the influential ideologues, politicians, priests, and others share common ontological ground with their audiences. Accordingly, they are not necessarily manipulating what they understand to be the world of their audiences from a position outside it. Further, the power and passionate intensity of their speech-mongering or written propaganda is not a cynical manipulation of the emotions and attitudes of others. The ontology that may underlie the ideology they develop may also be a vital dimension of the self-identity of the ideological producers. In other words, there is self-commitment in their passion. Inherent in such commitment is dreadful and violent possibility, for, committed to their passions, such leaders and other politically important influencers of popular opinion may be led to pursue to conclusion the inner logic of their course, a logic that is simultaneously in them and in the world of their action.

Ontology as I use the word is beneath the level of conscious reflection, is prereflective. Ideology, in contrast, is overt in the reflected world, active as assertion about, and interpretation of, reality. In Geerztian terms ideology is both a model of reality and a model for it. Ontology exists in reflective consciousness as a moment of ideology and always as only a possibility or as a limited realization of ontological potential. Occasionally it may spring before reflective consciousness as that reve-latory but only momentarily grasped flash of insight or understanding about the nature of the world. I have in mind here what Heidegger has to say about the aesthetic experience, particularly the poetic experience, or what others call the religious or numinous experience. While not part of conscious reflection, ontology is nonetheless as integral to consciousness as its logic is ingrained in the habituated practices of the everyday realities of human beings.

This discussion of the relation between ontology and ideology neither reduces their force in conjunction to the psychological or subjective nor to an objective social world that somehow stands apart from the human subject. Ontology is as assuredly part of the realities through which human beings move as it may be ingrained in their person, in their being, and is vital in their self-constitution. Ontology is neither subjective nor objective but both. Ideology formed with the logic of ontology and realizing some of its potential is simultaneously part of the historical world toward which human beings move and potentially vital in their person. Thus the human passions of hatred and violence, like compassion and love, are at once of the world, of its instituted orders and practices, and of the individuals who inhabit that world.

4

Ideological Practice, Ethnic Nationalism, and the Passions

The ontology of ideology is most evident at times of crisis. The reflections of influential Sinhalese Buddhists virtually in a state of civil war repeatedly echo the logic of the myths. President Jayawardene, speaking on the new Sri Lankan constitution and its institution of an elected president, established his own continuity with the legendary Vijaya: "We have had an unbroken line of monarchs from Vijaya to Elizabeth II for over 2,500 years.[1] They were replaced by Presidents when we became a republic . . . and now myself, the 306th head of state from Vijaya in unbroken line" (Colombo *Daily News* 12 March 1985).

In the same speech President Jayawardene had occasion to mention an unjust, "wicked and corrupt" king, Sri Wickrama Rajasingha, who, Jayawardene pointed out, was of the Nayakkar dynasty, a foreign dynasty of South Indian extraction, and Hindu, who reigned at Kandy. The dictatorship of this king ended in a rebellion by Sinhalese lords, a fact to which President Jayawardene also drew significant attention as he elaborated on the nature of modern Sri Lankan democracy.

The serious fighting against the various Tamil separatist movements is occurring in the main areas of Tamil habitation, the Northern and Eastern provinces. The training camps for the separatist organizations are chiefly in Tamil Nadu, in South India. Located in India, the separatist fighters have gone from inside the state to a position outside it. This reality gains further significance through the ontology of evil and the state, in which destructive and violent demonic forces gather outside the state. Spatial metaphors which have the sense of outside and foreign are simultaneously metaphors of hierarchy, of a demonic base ranged against the principles of order, which concentrate at the apex. The full meaning of this is achieved in the following statement by President Jayawardene, especially in the light of the current political situation. Opening the new session of Parliament in February 1985, the President had this to say:

> The borders of Sri Lanka are Point Pedro and Devinuwara (Dondra) in
> the North and South; Batticaloa and Colombo in the East and West.
> The terrorists are attempting to shoot their way into the heart of Sri
> Lanka to the borders of what they call the State of Eelam. If we do not
> occupy the border the border will come to us (Colombo *Island,* 11
> February 1985).

Threatened by terrors from without that were producing division within,
it follows ontologically that the unifying metaphor of Dutugemunu should
be evoked. This was excellently achieved by Sri Lankan Prime Minister
Premadasa a few weeks later. He was speaking on the occasion of the
opening of a new housing project near Tangalle, on the south coast east
of Dondra, in the homeland of the legendary Dutugemenu (Ruhunu).
Premadasa denies any Sinhala "racist" connection in the symbolism of
Dutugemunu—a charge made by many concerned Sri Lankans, Tamils,
and Sinhalese in the present deteriorating situation. Rather, Premadasa
draws the significance of Dutugemunu's unifying, encompassing, and
rational power. Speaking on the disruption and violence in the land
Premadasa had the following to say:

> Leaders had arisen in the south as in other parts of the country to lead
> the battle against them, and King Kawanatissa was one such leader.
> The great Dutugemunu was another.
>   Some people held the wrong belief that King Dutugemunu was a
> racial warrior. He was actually a rational leader, whose object was to
> preserve the freedom and integrity of the country. He was also a
> leader who realized from where the danger to the nation came: the
> north and the east. That was why he went from the Ruhunu which
> had given his faithful elephant, to Anuradhapura to establish his
> kingdom (Colombo *Daily News,* 5 March 1985).

Dutugemunu, as a just and righteous king, is, of course, an important
metaphor of a just and righteous Buddhist state. He embodies ontologically the legitimate destructive but reconstitutive violence of the state.
This meaning is fully implicit within the ideological interpretation of
myth given by the prime minister. The violence of Dutugemunu is not
the thoroughly evil and ultimately fragmenting destructive force of
nonreason. Rather it is rational violence ultimately leading to the
reestablishment of the ordered state unified in reason. As I have explained,
this is not inconsistent with Buddhist thought—at least not that of the
principal historical texts written by monks. It is also not inconsistent
with the logic of ritual to rid human beings of affliction to engage
metaphors of extreme violence, a violence of the Buddha and of reconstitution as well as the violence of the demonic and of fragmentation.
    Modern Buddhist priests also see a positive relation between violence
and the state. They are not, I think, acting outside a possibility of
Buddhism or being non-Buddhist. The abandonment of the doctrine of
nonviolence (*ahimsa*), while not desirable, may nonetheless be necessary

for the survival of the Buddhist state.[2] The chief monk at the Dutugemunu Vihara at Baddegama, near Galle on the south coast, declared to a group of monks and laity who had gathered to pray for an end to terrorism that if they were not successful then the monks should disrobe and fight to preserve the glory of Buddhism. When terrorism is swept away, said the chief monk, then the warrior-priests can be reordained. One of the sutras chanted by the monks was that alleged to have been used by the Buddha to dispel demons (Colombo *Divaina*, 21 June 1985). Statements by Buddhist priests along similar lines are by no means uncommon. Thus another Buddhist priest, the director of a Buddhist school (*pirivena*) near Kalutara (a town south of Colombo), declared before a meeting of local government officials that the slogan of the Sinhala people should be "Death or Motherland" (*Mawbima Nathnam Maranaya*) (Colombo *Daily News* 2 February 1985).

In the ontology of myth and ritual practice evil is expunged and the restoration of the order of the state is achieved through the assertion of the cosmic hierarchy and of the powers that are constituted within the hierarchy. This logic could not have been more evident than on the occasion of the visit by the newly appointed commander of the Sri Lankan army to the chief priests of the Asgiriya and Malwatte chapters in Kandy. These chapters are the most significant centers of opinion of the Buddhist clergy on the island. The occasion was in itself forcefully symbolic of the association of Buddhism with the righteous, ordering, and violent arm of state power. The reported interchange between the chief incumbent (*mahanayake*) of the Asgiriya chapter and the commander is worth repeating at length: "Ven, Palipane Chandananda Mahanayake Thera said that he was personally happy to see a good Buddhist from a good family chosen for one of the most responsible high posts in the country such as the Commander of the Army."

The commander then stated that Sri Lanka was faced with the most critical period of its 2,500-year history, "threatened by terrorists who were being aided and abetted by foreign countries and organizations."

The mahanayake responded that "not only the Government but also the people in general and the Maha Sangha in particular have built up hopes that (the Commander) would deal with all enemy forces in the country with the blessings of the Triple Gem and all the protective deities of Sri Lanka" (Colombo *Daily News*, 27 February 1985).

The ontology of evil and of the state embedded in the myths and legends is strongly present in current realities. Its logic frames much of the political ideology of the modern Sri Lankan state, a Sinhalese Buddhist nation-state. Engaged in ideology, the ontology of the cosmic state is also part, therefore, of the structure of ideological practice. It is also poignantly evident in Sinhalese political humor.

In July 1985 the Indian government succeeded in bringing the Sri Lankan government and the Tamil liberationist organizations to the

From the Colombo Sun, *July 29, 1985. The caption reads, "Send Vadigapatunas for Thimpu talks."*

LANKA ASKED TO FOLLOW PUNJAB EXAMPLE

negotiating table. The discussions were to take place in Thimpu, the capital of Bhutan. The announcement of the talks—which were intended to follow the model of Gandhi's "resolution" of the Sikh crisis in the Punjab—gave rise to a political cartoon in the English-language *Sun* newspaper. The "Vadigapatunas" are drawn as the Brahmins of the Vadiga Patuna episode of the Suniyama antisorcery rite described in chapter 3. The Brahmins, who are invariably presented in performances of the rite as wearing Punjabi dress, are the curing and protective wizards of transformation from India, who restore Queen Manikpala to health. In the Suniyama they appear at that point in the transformation of the cosmic axis when the patient is set on the course of rebirth from within the womb of the state.

The cosmic logic lying at the interpretive heart of the cartoon did not, of course, realize its potential. The Thimpu talks failed to achieve any political resolution. In the ensuing months pressure on Sri Lanka's political leaders mounted and there was growing discontent at the government's handling of the crisis, particularly among Sinhalese in the strongly nationalist south of the island. President Jayawardene found himself juggling a variety of oppositional forces from within the Sinhalese

From Divaina, *February 1986.*

population as well as outside it.   In early February 1986 another political
cartoon appeared in the Sinhala newspaper *Divaina*.

The cartoon shows President Jayawardene twisting and turning within,
in effect, the process of a Sinhalese Buddhist cosmic hierarchy.   The
metaphors of the political commentary are drawn from the Sanni Yakuma.
This is an exorcism commonly performed along the western and southern
coasts of Sri Lanka (Kapferer 1983).   It is often enacted at the conclusion
of the Suniyama, although it is an exorcism in its own right, organized
to ward off illnesses caused by the eighteen disease-spreading *(sanni)*
demons.   In Jayawardene's right hand is held the mask of Deva Sanniya,
a collective representation of the eighteen demons, whose appearance in
the exorcism signs the restoration of the integrated order of the cosmic
hierarchy.   In the basket—a basket in which exorcists traditionally carry
their clothing—is the mask of Kola Sanniya.   He is the destructive demon
of the threshold, of the margins, and is at the base of hierarchy.   Deva
Sanniya in my interpretation of the logic of the exorcism is a benign
transformation of Kola Sanniya.   In the myth of Kola Sanniya's origin,
the demon is born the son of the king of Visalamahanuwara, the legendary
city of the Licchavis of Nepal.   In dreadful revenge for his father's slaying
of his mother, Kola Sanniya moves outside the state and, assuming
demonic form furiously destroys his father's city.   His horror is only
ended, as in the case of Oddi Raja or Suniyam, through the intervention
of the Buddha.   In the Sanni Yakuma ritual Kola Sanniya is not only

depicted as devouring and fragmenting evil at the base of hierarchy but also as threatening from the outside in.

The cartoon demonstrates excellently the role of Sinhalese Buddhist cosmology in the interpretation of modern political process. Accordingly, the cartoon can be seen as presenting President Jayawardene as the supreme exorcist of state caught in a violent transformational struggle to restore the encompassing equanimity of an ordered hierarchy threatened by a demonic possibility at its base.

The political rhetoric and humor engage the logic of a cosmic hierarchy, also integral to an ontology of life in the modern world; it is charged with the meaning and import of present historical circumstances, giving them particular shape and itself achieving new import. Thus "tradition" gathers original and potentially terrible import, especially where this logic is also part of the way some are oriented to the horizons of their existence within specific situations. Sinhalese notions of the demonic have broken free from their mythic and ritual containment. So, too, have the ideas and logic that surround the legendary heroes of the nation.

Ethnic Nationalism and New Meaning

Statements to the effect that the meanings of the past continue into the present are likely to be ideological in that they are born of current realities; that is, they are arguments about the past or interpretations of it which are motivated from within the structural conditions and processes of the historical present. The establishment of a telling link between the conditions of the present and the situation of the past is an important tool of political legitimation. It is such dangerous and inflammatory legitimating practice, densely evident in modern Sri Lanka, against which many Sinhalese and Tamil intellectuals are strenuously arguing. Much valuable evidence concerning the nature of past political conditions and its transformations, entirely contradictory to popular and ideological opinion, is thus being presented. Gunawardana (1984) argues convincingly that the Sinhala people of the times of the Vijaya legend were from small ruling groups and not coterminous with a larger linguistic category.

> It is only about the twelfth century that the Sinhala grouping could
> have been considered identical with the linguistic grouping. The
> relationship between the Sinhala and the Buddhist identities was even
> more complex. There is no close association between the two
> identities, but at no period do they appear to have coincided exactly to
> denote the self-same group of people (Gunawardana 1984, 43).

One significance of Gunawardana's evidence is that the linkage between language, religion, and nation defining a distinct ethnic group, the Sinhalese, aligned in opposition to Tamils, very much part of the modern ethnic nationalism of both Sinhalese and Tamils, developed well after the period of Dutugemunu. Indeed, as Gunawardana and other scholars have shown, internal evidence can be sifted out of the cosmology of the *Mahavamsa* to indicate that Dutugemunu achieved the leadership of a complex political alliance that cut across the ethnic divisions of modern meaning.

Modern nationalist ideology that fuels and supports the present tragic situation of interethnic hostility and warfare was formed in the colonial and postcolonial situations of the emergence of the modern nation-state. Among many other well-documented factors that created the current situation were the system of colonial rule, which was instrumental in contributing to the drawing of ethnic boundaries, territorial and social; a colonially introduced system of ethnic representation in the political process that preceded and led to independence; and the formation of political parties that established their bases on principles of the representation of ethnic interests; the struggle between dominant class fractions for political control, which exacerbated the historically created structural tendency to seek mass support with reference to such ethnic issues as language and religion. Ethnic political boundaries and cleavages were created in the nationalist struggle for independence, which turned in on itself increasingly in the postindependence situation. This situation was one in which old and newly emerging dominant class fractions, in their struggle to reproduce their positions or claims to dominance, engaged ethnic issues in addition to others. Those who shaped the modern nation-state and its ideologies were intimately part of an indigenous cultural world, as many were intimately part of wider worlds, part of an international bourgeoisie, sharing in its ontologically based ideologies. I stress this because the nationalist ideologies of modern Sri Lanka were integral to a wider process of world capitalism. Concomitantly, some Sri Lankan nationalists incorporated aspects of nationalist movements in Europe and elsewhere.

At a meeting in the southern town of Balapitiya in 1939, S. W. R. D. Bandaranaike, a figure prominent in the nationalist struggle and instrumental in making Sinhala the dominant national language during the 1950s against significant Tamil protest, stated: "I am prepared to sacrifice my life for the sake of my community, the Sinhalese. If anybody were to try to hinder our progress, I am determined to see that he is taught a lesson he will never forget" (Jaffna *Hindu Organ* 26 January 1939, cited in Russell 1982, 157).

When the meeting ended, one woman, a Mrs. Srimathie Abeygunawardena, "likened Mr. Bandaranaike to Hitler and appealed to the Sinhalese community to give him every possible assistance to reach the goal of freedom" (Russell 1982, 157). The Aryan myths of racial superiority developed in Europe, particularly in the nineteenth century, and part of scholarship and of politics in these countries became ingrained to some extent within the politics and scholarship centered on Sri Lanka. They became part of the language of Sinhalese Buddhist nationalist domination and influenced some of the scholarly interpretations by foreigners and Sinhalese alike of the origins of the Sinhalese and their ethnic distinction.

The social and political forces that gave rise to ethnic nationalism in Sri Lanka are what give nationalist ideology its principal power. The political and social structural processes and the ideology that arose within them are constituted in the one order. Thus, nationalism grew in the conditions of class transformations and contradictions and in the expansion of bureaucratic state power. As ideology took form in these processes, resolving contradiction at one level by distortion—by asserting, for example, that all Sinhalese were united in common interest, even though they were fragmented by class and other cultural forces, such as caste—and generating contradiction at another, in the form of increased inter-ethnic tension.

Kumari Jayawardena (1984a, 1984b) discusses the linked class and ideological processes leading to the anti-Tamil rioting in 1956. She examines the variations in ethnic consciousness among class fractions and the dominant political interests served by ethnic consciousness. Jayawardena argues, for example, that the "Sinhala Only" language issue was not crucial to the Sinhala working class, although they supported it as being in their interests for easier communication at work and with officialdom (Jayawardena 1984a, 164–65). Gunasinghe (1984) focuses specifically on the conditions that fomented the marked increase in the regularity of anti-Tamil rioting following the return to power of the UNP under the leadership of President Jayawardene. The year 1977 saw the return to an open economy. Various welfare services important for the survival of many in the working class were withdrawn. The subsidized rice ration was discontinued and the free health scheme subverted. Of greater importance in the argument was the ending of government protection of higher industry and middle-range entrepreneurial activity in which Sinhalese were particularly favored. Government protection and its expansion of the state sector during the period 1956–77 created jobs for Sinhalese youth. Paradoxically, the freeing of the market after 1977 and the consequent placing of Sinhalese business on a nearly equal footing with others in the economy, rapid inflation, and the contraction of the state sector opened up class contradictions that were felt especially by the previously favored Sinhalese population. Factors such as these, and also the potency of the ideology of Sinhala dominance, which had flourished among previously protected Sinhala business interests, precipitated the 1983 riots. This is important, for some of the gangs noticeable in the destruction of Tamils (Obeyesekere 1984b) were linked into the patronage system controlled by what Gunasinghe calls middle-range enterpreneurs.

An entrepreneurial stratum that accumulates and rises up due to state patronage acquires a social and ideological character distinct from an entrepreneurial group that emerges in a society subject to the free play of market forces. Such an entrepreneurial stratum expects the state to step in and protect them if it faces a difficult situation (Gunasinghe 1984, 213).

The aforementioned class processes in the development of ethnic nationalism and in the structuring of its conflict are critical to any understanding of the situation in Sri Lanka. I stress, too, that the ethnic ideology that is a feature of both Sinhalese and Tamil consciousness is also a phenomenon of class formation. But other processes not reducible to class are also involved especially with regard to the belief that ethnic unity is forged in the conditions of a common culture. Sinhalese nationalism, like all nationalisms, fetishizes culture. This fetishism and its attendant emotional intensity are developments upon transformations in the modern world of Sri Lanka. The traditionalism often revealed by Sinhalese in their stress on culture and history is born of recent changes. I shall discuss especially those changes that led to the nationalist valuation and revaluation of culture as an autonomous and socially and politically determining entity.

Ethnic Unity and the Fetishism of Culture

In chapter 2 I drew attention to the debates over the historical value of the legends recorded in the chronicles. One of the dangers, it is said, of regarding the mythic tales as if they were records of events that actually happened is that they are indeed the real history of "folk" knowledge. This is the argument of Obeyesekere, who adds that those who take the folk history as real—the relatively little educated mass, I assume—would be unlikely to alter such a conception because it is "more psychologically real than the actual events." Obeyesekere is right when he states that the myths comprise a folk history. Their "psychological reality," however, I regard as more problematic. Their force as an attitude of mind is achieved through certain social and political transformations that have to do with the current Sri Lankan situation. More immediately, implicit within Obeyesekere's argument is the notion that the poorly educated population prone to folk interpretation is at the mercy of more cynical interests that dominate the social order. So manipulated, working class and peasantry can be provoked into great violence. This may be so. The argument ignores the possibility, however, that leaders as well as followers are fully committed to mythic history. When President Jayawardene speaks of himself as the 306th leader of the nation in unbroken line from

Vijaya he is probably making a statement that he honestly believes. Folk history is not the privilege of the subordinated classes alone.

Further, the power of folk history and its modern significance *as history*, together with its particular form of ethnic nationalism, is part of the political and social transformations out of which modern Sri Lanka was created. What Anderson (1983) calls "print capitalism"—the rapid publication and dissemination of knowledge in the vernacular and in English—liberated the folk tradition from its local or regional base and distributed it widely. No longer spatially restricted, it became available to larger sections of the population. Indeed, insofar as it became part of learned debate and written discourse, the knowledge of the folk became common and diffuse.

I refer to the making of folk knowledge into common knowledge because this is exactly what happened. Before the advent of print capitalism in Sri Lanka, the effect of which accelerated after the arrival of the British in the late eighteenth century, much folk knowledge was in the hands of ritual and religious specialists. This, of course, was also true of the knowledge contained in the so-called great tradition, which was also made common knowledge. The information contained in such chronicles as the *Mahavamsa*, *Dipavamsa*, and *Rajavaliya*, for example, as well as in numerous other commentaries and theological argument written by priests, often highly relevant to localized folk traditions and drawing substantive content from them, owed its wide dissemination to the advent of print capitalism. As the knowledge of the clergy was opened up—often energetically through the activity of such religious and nationalist ideologues as the Anagarika Dharmapala (Obeyesekere 1979; Jayawardena 1985)—so the confinement of the folk tradition in the hands of individual specialists or, more typically, small bodies of extended kin was broken. With the advent of print capitalism folk knowledge gained commodity value and became widely disseminated, beyond the bounds of its traditional locale. Many so-called traditional specialists have gained their knowledge from written texts easily available in small shops throughout the island. The dissemination of folk knowledge, its conversion into common knowledge, was and is of course a nationalist enterprise. The folk traditions are repeated in school texts. Rituals such as the *gammaduva* and *devol maduva* for the deities Pattini and Devol, once part of declining rural traditions, have been revitalized under government sponsorship. They are staged in public parks and before mass audiences and cater to a marked renewal of popular interest in the supposed cultural practices of the past.[3]

Print capitalism is not the only mechanism whereby a restricted and specialist knowledge—folk knowledge in my usage—has achieved wide currency. There are few totally isolated communities in Sri Lanka that are beyond the reach of a day's run in a bus from any part of the island. The population often seems to be continuously on the move, going to work, visiting relatives, attending ceremonies, on pilgrimage.   Among the population as a whole this movement generates knowledge of different traditions.   To some extent the movement itself was and is generated by the capitalist, nation-building process, in the development of an effective transport network, in the promotion of economic development and resettlement programs, in the nationalist encouragement of Buddhist worship, and in the expression of Sinhalese identity through such worship. The government has continually opened archeological sites to the public. These have become popular areas of Buddhist pilgrimage.   Ten years ago the remains of the ancient civilization at Sigiriya did not attract the crowds of pilgrims it does now.

My point is straightforward.   The folk tradition has to a large extent achieved common currency, and its histories have been generalized into the history of a nation.   A popular tradition, forged in the processes of nationalism, is continually being created in this generalization of folk knowledge and folk history.   What is often called folk history is the transformation into popular history.   It is not specific within a local area or ingrained deeply in its special structural processes, tied to local hierarchy and differences in prestige of lineage and underlying the pattern of marriage practice.   These seem to be strong aspects of the folk accounts of the events surrounding Dutugemunu, as recounted to Marguerite Robinson (1968) for the village of Morapitiya in the Kandyan province.   She relates that she stayed in a house owned by the same family that sheltered Dutugemunu when he fled the boundaries of his father's kingdom.   Popular history, having none of the specificity of folk history, refracts the political nationalist processes of which it is a part.   It is vital in the special conditions and structures of the nation-state, taking form in the politics of ethnicity and in the conflicts born of the contradictions of class.

Popular tradition, that transformation of folk history and tradition, does not stand outside the events of recent history.   It may appear to do so, and this appearance is implicit in much scholarly discussion of the seeming emotional power of such tradition.   Thus the symbols of popular tradition are analyzed as evocative reference points, resources, as it were, waiting to be tapped.   In such argument they gain their power both from their remoteness in history—which establishes their objective facticity— and the ability of political leaders to establish a continuity with their meaning.   It is mainly the delusion of popular history as objective fact which concerned Sri Lankan scholars are engaged in exposing.   Their task is all the more difficult if it is also accepted that the masses are psychologically committed to false history as objective truth.   My argument here is a slight revision of what I see to be the argument not only with reference to Sri Lanka but in the wider discussion of ethnic nationalism (Nairn 1977; Gellner 1983; Smith 1981, 1986; Anderson 1983).

The power of popular history is located in the structural and institutional processes that generate and form popular history. Paradoxically, the political situation in which modern nationalism is shaped and which creates the false history of ideologial distortion is the selfsame situation which renders that false history objectively true. The history of ideology is not an interpretational subjectivism, a construction upon and against the "facts" of reality. It is part of the reality that is interpreted through constructed history, formed within such a reality, and to some extent constituting it. When the politician speaks his view of the past he acts reflexively, he speaks the world which he and others live. The legitimating power of ideological references to history lies not so much in the character of a remote past as in the present social and political situation of their speaking. The dangerous potential of such ideological references is in their production in the present and in the fact that the logic of their ontological ground discovers its meaning and import in the lived realities of the present.

If the imagined reality of the past achieves its force through its construction in the present, a similar argument could be made for arguments concerning the psychological power of attachment to certain versions of history.[4] The psychological force of the symbols of constructed history may not be the individual inheritance of a "false consciousness" from the past, a clinging to old psychological ways, but a psychology formed and reformed in the structures and practices of the current political reality. If the psychology of ethnic nationalism is to be comprehended— the insistence upon a particular conception of history, the emotive power of mythic symbol, the passion of its commitment and of its violence— this can be achieved by exploring the world through which an ethnic nationalism is formed.

The generation of a popular tradition, the breaking of the social, linguistic, and locality restrictions on knowledge, and the attendant homogenization of this knowledge and its dispersal, was fundamental in the formation of state ideology. In a sense the restricted knowledge of the "great tradition" and the "folk tradition" expanded out of the monastery and out of the village and, transforming in their combination, encompassed and defined the new "imaginary community" of the emerging nation-state. Through the creation of the popular tradition diverse regions were brought into a cultural conjunction within Sri Lanka and, I suggest, recognized increasingly a common ethnic identity and a single shared tradition, which they did not possess earlier. This emergent national culture also articulated different class interests, even as these class interests were manifesting a gathering opposition and conflict (Jayawardena 1972). Different class fractions—dominant, educated, often English-speaking elites—were articulated with subordinate fractions—the growing urban poor and a struggling peasantry—through the mediation of a popular tradition.[5]

The articulation was at the level of ideas and was complex. As the emergence of a popular tradition articulated different class fractions, so there also emerged differences within the created tradition produced in the same dynamics of class relations. Within the unifying popular tradition what I call a differentiated culture of class was also developing. The forms of life displayed in domestic and religious situations, and in leisure, for example, are quite distinct among certain fractions of the middle class from those found among the working classes. The formation of a popular tradition enabled the promotion of both unity and difference simultaneously in a way perfectly consistent with the underlying class forces that produced the popular tradition. This aspect of the simultaneous production of unifying and differentiating properties of the development of popular culture established its powerful potential as an ideological agency for the emergence of the recognition by Sinhalese of a solidary ethnic identity.

I am not underrating other factors such as Buddhist revivalism and a political opposition to colonial rulers. These processes were part and parcel of the form taken by the growth of a popular tradition and integral to its momentum. Nor am I overlooking the fact that in the creation of a popular tradition modes of restricted and specialist knowledge persisted and, indeed, still persist.

The general significance of what I am arguing should not be lost. The Sinhalese recognition of a strong ethnic identity is not merely because Sinhalese inhabit the one historical, cultural world. Rather, the powerful ethnic solidarity recognized by a great many Sinhalese and their belief in a cultural unity, both of which can override the conflicts of class and caste, were generated together. Sinhalese are not ethnically unified because they are from the one culture. One is not prior to the other, for these two aspects of their consciousness of reality were produced simultaneously and reinforce one another.

A critical feature of the formation of a popular culture is its process of symbolic disarticulation or decontextualization that removes ideas embedded in the fabric of social practices and symbolically idealizes them. Joined with the formation of a unified ethnic consciousness these symbols—customs, rites, language—are made emblematic of a unifying ethnic identity. Their idea comes to function in a new way, constituting relations rather than constituted within relationships. And so the Sinhalese Buddhist imagined community, a community which recognizes an overriding cultural unity despite internal social division, takes form. Sinhalese Buddhists come to recognize a kinship and solidarity as a function of their unique ethnic bond, a belief which grew in the conditions of the generalization and decontextualization of local and folk traditions and their formation into a popular culture.[6]

I have described a process of the reification of culture, the production of culture as an object in itself. As an object, a thing, culture became vital in the consciousness and realization of ethnic identity and to an ethnic unity. The belief is established that the Sinhalese are a community in identity *because* of their culture and that the one will be destroyed without the other. In this conception culture is imbued with determining qualities. It is an orientation to the object culture which became increasingly accentuated in the circumstances of nationalist politics based in ethnicity and in the promotion of ethnic unity. The religion of nationalism, as the recent history of Sri Lanka demonstrates, makes a fetish of culture. The nationalist sacralization of culture, its cult of culture, asserts the determining and unifying function of culture, culture as magical. Such a property of culture may indeed be so in Sri Lanka, where culture reified receives the full backing of state political and bureaucratic machinery in an effort to realize what is ideologically valued as the unifying potency of culture. This underlines my point. Culture in Sri Lanka is unifying not because of any natural intrinsic properties but because of the way it is fashioned as an object and made to stand in a dominant and determining relation to its context.

Critical to an understanding of the determining function of culture in Sinhalese nationalism is that culture and religion are coterminous. In the conception of Sinhalese, their culture is Buddhist, a culture of Buddhism. Culture, however, decontextualized and reified is already religious in quality and in potential. Culture, its artifacts, texts, or ideas, separated from any concrete situation of social interaction, made freely abstract, is placed beyond or outside any specific social contextual limitation on its meaning. Culture, thereby, like the ideas and icons of religious abstraction, is free to unite with any and every concrete circumstance and to fuse with their meanings. In this, specific situated meanings are generalized and abstract meaning is concretized. Each establishes its validity in the other. Here is one power of reified culture to apparently unify populations and for human beings to experience a sense, an emotional feeling of unity in it. But the religious quality of abstracted and reified culture is intensified in its unity with Buddhism. In the Buddhism of culture, culture objectified as everything Sinhalese see themselves doing as Sinhalese, culture becomes firmly the object of contemplation, devotion and worship.

The ideological value placed by Sinhalese nationalists in recent history upon their culture as Buddhist—a value often fundamentalist in practice seen in a concern by some Sinhalese to root out Hindu and Christian impurities—is important for several related reasons. A Sinhalese culture that is asserted in nationalism to be Buddhist is enshrined as encompassing and as determinant in its encompassment. The stress on the Buddhism of culture also defines the order of that unity which Sinhalese ideally form in their relations with each other. This unity is not the flat categorical association, a composition of equivalent units as in the nationalism of Australian egalitarianism or in much sociological description of the ethnic phenomenon (Mitchell 1956, 1987; Barth 1969; Gluckman 1958). It is rather a unity in hierarchy, wherein state, society, and person are placed in cosmically determined relations of incorporation and differentiation and are ordered and made whole accordingly. The Buddhism of Sinhalese cultural unity, a Buddhism defined in the politics of modern nationalism and in its class processes, gives particular value to the kinds of ontology of state and person I have discussed with reference to the chronicles. The devotional relation that Sinhalese are enjoined in nationalism to establish with their culture of Buddhism, moreover, effects the constitutive and determining force of nationalist culture at the level of personal inner being.

This is so both for those who are socially and politically dominant and for those who are subordinated in the social and political society of Sri Lanka. A feature of the religious, of the relation of contemplation and worship of idea and image the religious encourages, is that the devotee unites in essence with the object of devotion. This is the direction of religious action, it seems to me, of all the world's civilizing religions. Thus the logic of the ontology of nationalist tradition and myths and of the rites and ceremonies appropriated to the politics of nationalism can be made integral to the very constitution of being in the world. This is so quite apart from the fact that the logic of the ontology may be part of a great variety of everyday practices in which many Sinhalese may routinely engage. What the religion of the culture of nationalism does is to assert the overriding significance of a particular ontology for all contexts. Its power, furthermore, is to make it constitutive and orienting of the person even when such a person was formed in ontological realities outside that integral to nationalist argument. I refer to many of the leaders in Sri Lanka today whose orientation in reality was often very different from the people they now command in rhetoric and action. Their own nationalist devotion and practice in terms of the ideology they espouse opens them up to a reconstitution of their inner selves that can direct their action in the world, often in a way disastrous for those whose fate they dictate.

Ethnicity and the Violence of the People

The significance of Sinhalese nationalism as a particular ideology of the state gains force through the foregoing observations. The potential is great in the ontology of ideology for persons not merely to accept the legitimacy of the state but to recognize their personal integrity and the quality of their social relations and experience as being dependent on the order of the state. If the official violence of the state can be understood through the logic of the cosmic state appropriated to the ideology of the modern nationalist state of Sri Lanka, so too may the voluntary violence of the people in ethnic rioting be similarly comprehended.[7]

In the ideology of Sinhalese nationalism, the state, its bureaucratic apparatuses, and its agents are both the custodians of Sinhalese Buddhist culture and, in their cosmically ordained duty, responsible for the order of society and of the person. The integrity of the person and of his or her social relations are founded in a principle of hierarchical incorporation. The acceptance of this logic of domination, of power, and of personal constitution does not make a citizenry the blind followers of government. Indeed, such logic has a double edge. A failure in state order or in the hierarchializing power of the agents of state can produce a conflict of the people with the agents of state. It can give rise to a recognition that these agents have reduced themselves to a demonic possibility of their being and act against the interests of the citizenry. This can bring the citizenry to action designed to restore state order and thereby their own integrity of person.

I note, for example, that the argument of the myths is quite clear about righteous and unrighteous kings, good and evil instruments of the state. As President Jayawardene said, in agreement with the mythic ontology I explored, it was appropriate that Sinhala lords should rebel against the foreign, Hindu, and evil Wikrama Rajasinghe.

When I wrote this, rumors were rife in Colombo in the shanties and in the middle-class neighborhoods, that Jayawardene was masterminding a sellout to Tamil demands. On a street sign "Jayawardene Mawatta," the name *Elara* had been scrawled. It was being openly discussed that Jayawardene had kinship with Tamils and therefore sympathy with their cause. The bravado of street talk was that Jayawardene as the instrument of the Sinhalese Buddhist state was not killing enough. Jayawardene was moving from righteous to unrighteous, from good to evil, and even from being Sinhalese to Tamil. Old political memories were being revived. In a political contest for the seat of Kelaniya in 1950 he was nicknamed J. R. Nana (*nana* is the word for a Muslim man) after the alleged fact that his grandfather was Muslim. For some today he is Muslim no more, but Tamil (the Muslims are Tamil-speaking).

I have drawn attention to the fact that in myth and ritual the powerful metaphors and symbolism of the state, a state in mythic time, are engaged to return to a condition of healthy wholeness, the fragmented body attacked by the demons. The body and self of the patient as a healthy unity is reformed through the mythical metaphor of the state. In the modern context of Sinhalese Buddhist state nationalism, the metaphor of myth has become the reality of the politics of ethnicity.

My suggestion is plain. The Sri Lankan Buddhist state and the Sinhalese people are obviously in dangerous and reciprocal conjunction. An attack on Sinhalese is an attack on the state, and an attack on the organs or apparatuses of the state is an attack on the person. There is every reason, given the ontology I have discussed, for Sinhalese to take very personally indeed any opposition to the state by persons who are ontologically foreign and threatening to the hierarchical and encompassing unity of the state. Here is a reason, extraordinary as it may seem, for the sudden, almost inexplicable, transformation of a normally peaceful people into violent and murderously rampaging mobs. In their violence they are oriented to the reassertion and restoration of the hierarchy of the state, of their power, and of the integrity and wholeness of their persons. The rioting, in other words, may be likened to a gigantic exorcism. Tamils, the agents of evil, set to break the overarching unity of the Sinhalese state, are rooted out. Acting with the force of their own cosmic incorporation, the Sinhalese rioters fragment their demonic victims, as the Tamils threatened to fragment them, and by so doing resubordinate and reincorporate the Tamil demon in hierarchy.

The violence of the self is no less than the violence of the routine social world in which many Sinhalese must live. It is in this world, particularly within the strongly working-class areas of the major cities, among rural laborers and landless peasantry, that the ethnic violence found some of its greatest intensity. The killing of Tamil tea-estate laborers in the Matale, Kandy, and Nuwara Eliya areas of the central highland districts and the burning of Tamil shops was savage and impassioned. I have one account of an anguished Sinhalese member of Parliament trying to prevent the burning of a Tamil house and the murder of its occupants by a mob in the midst of its explosive rage. But the MP was forced to flee as the rioters turned on the intruder. Sinhalese rural poor likewise attacked Tamil workers in the estate areas of the south, in the tea-growing centers of Deniyaya and Morawaka. A year later the Hindu temples were still barred and shut.

But the major cities, especially Colombo, with a dominant Sinhalese population and a significant Tamil minority, saw the worst of the rioting. The destruction was widely covered in the world news media. Tamils of all social classes were discriminantly attacked in their homes and shops and were pulled from buses and cars. People who had lived peacefully for years and as close neighbors of Sinhalese were suddenly attacked brutally. I must stress, however, that I have a number of stories of Sinhalese who attempted to protect Tamil neighbors and friends from the savagery of others. In one predominantly working-class and shanty neighborhood of Colombo, Sinhalese youths blocked the access to a cluster of Tamil-owned houses to protect them from attack by outside gangs of Sinhalese youths. A Sinhalese gang leader (*ganang karaya*) in another large shanty area used his power to prevent attacks on Tamils. But equally, Sinhalese gangs made up largely of impoverished and unemployed youth (*rastiyadu karayo,* "aimless troublemakers") attacked Tamils in their houses and shops, settling old scores and looting. Ordinary Sinhalese pointed out individual Tamils to nearby police and members of the army who, from many accounts, encouraged atrocity. I know of one instance in which local Sinhalese pointed out two Tamil youths in their neighborhood as "Tigers" (*koti*) to passing soldiers, who immediately shot them.

A horror of the 1983 riots was that they were directed by Sinhalese toward Tamils whom they knew socially as well as toward many whom they did not know. The violence was turned inward among neighbors as well as outward to people known only as Tamils. Furthermore, the active rioters, looters, and killers were most often from the subordinated classes within the political and economic order. They turned upon themselves, human beings subject to the same conditions of life, as well as upon those more politically and economically powerful. This is not to vindicate those Sinhalese who are socially and politically dominant, for many of these, as I have said, have fanned the flames of ethnic nationalism and are active in that order which produces ethnic death. My concern is not to apportion blame; it is rather to demonstrate the destructive force of the creation of what Gluckman called a dominant social and political cleavage based in the ideology of ethnicity—a cleavage which in its dominance overrides all other forms of human association and can turn the most depressed and subordinated sections of a population destructively against themselves.[8]

Much of the fury over the division of ethnic nationalism is driven within the processes of class relations. These processes, in the capitalist circumstances of Sri Lanka, generate anguish, conflict, fear, and suffering at all points in the motion of the social and political order of Sri Lanka as a whole. Thus, it is processes integral to class relations that are critical in the abject destitution of the shanty dwellers in Colombo city; in the terror of the small trader that his business will fail in the competition of the market, reducing him to the impoverished circumstances from which he has escaped; and in the fear of the wealthy and politically powerful who worry that their riches will be plundered or that their disadvantaged political supporters will desert them for others in the apparently fickle world of Sri Lankan party politics.

It is obvious that far from all the fear and suffering which may beset human beings in Sri Lanka can be comprehended through an understanding of class relations. There are doubtless numerous other factors within the highly complex cultural universe of Sri Lankans that may focus on individuals and help explain their plight. What I stress, however, is that the ethnic consciousness generated in the nationalism of the modern nation-state of Sri Lanka creates a sense of unity in experience even when this experience is formed under vastly different, even opposed, circumstances of a class character or otherwise. Indeed, the various forces rooted in the social, political, and other material conditions of lived historical realities in Sri Lanka intensify an experiential unity in national ethnic identity. This is effected in one way because ingrained within the emergence of an ideology of ethnic nationalism is a particular ontology of the person and the state. Through the logic of this ontology, the condition of the person is synonymous with the condition of the state. The state in such a conception unites its internally differentiated population in a logic of hierarchy. As the state finds its coherence in this hierarchical order so does the person. The person discovers his or her internal unity as an essential hierarchical condition which, in turn, is dependent on the hierarchical encompassing unity of the Buddhist state. Personal suffering in the ethnic nationalism of Sinhalese becomes a particular suffering of the state. And so rich and poor and the powerful and the weak can unite as one, as a hierarchical combination of strength, and crush the fragmenting forces that have removed themselves from a controlled subordinate condition at the base and are ranged demonically against the coherence of Buddhist state and Buddhist person.

I began this analysis of the tragedy of ethnic nationalism in Sri Lanka by drawing attention to the similarity between the violence of ethnic destruction and the violence of sorcery. This thematic relation has been pursued throughout my development of the argument. Some of the foregoing points will be sharpened by a brief consideration of further aspects of sorcery practice in Sri Lanka. I shall limit this discussion mainly to the action that can be witnessed at some of the main shrines in Colombo city.

The Anguish at the Shrines and the Anger of the State

The immediately striking aspect of Sinhalese practice before the demonic deities of evil and sorcery is that people from all walks of life attend them. Some of the principal shrines to Suniyam are endowed by people as powerful as cabinet ministers, high government officials, and business directors. Obeyesekere (1975) gives evidence of the large numbers of urban and rural bourgeoisie—ranging from professionals and people in small business to poorly paid, lowly clerical workers—who visit the shrines. Numerous urban poor, persons in menial government jobs, factory workers, and unemployed can be seen calling upon the destructive and protective power of the demonic deities.

Those who come to the shrines come for reasons as diverse as their social circumstances. They come, for example, to seek the aid of Suniyam in finding a job, to punish a deserting husband, to ensure safe passage through the dangers of a surgical operation, to reverse failing business fortunes, to affect the outcome of litigation, to influence bureaucratic decisions in the award of government loans or the securing of government houses, to safeguard political position, to combat the personally threatening competition of others, and so on. The simultaneous protective and destructive, reversible transformational powers of Suniyam or his alter ego, the princely wizard Oddissa or Oddi Raja, are appropriate to such concerns. They symbolize in the dualism of their iconography and mythic representation—as creatures of the margins, as traders or masters of conversion—the particular powers they command. Suniyam par excellence inverts experience—poverty into wealth, the inner turbulence of personal fear and terror into equanimity and peace, and causes that destruction which is directed from the outside to rebound ruinously.

It is impossible not to be moved by the deep anguish expressed by many Sinhalese before Suniyam and other similar demonic deities. At the shrines, just before the final ritual act—typically the smashing of a coconut—supplicants may pause and, perfectly quiet and still, whisper a small prayer relating their suffering (dukganavilla).[9] In effect, they infuse the object used in their last act with the very essence of their deepest concern, and thus their desire fuses, through the object of their offering, with the powers of the being whom they invoke.

I shall give an example of one such prayer. It was uttered by an old woman of seventy who with her retired husband, a former dock worker, had been earning enough money for daily survival by taking in paying lodgers. She had sold some village land and her husband had added his retirement pension to secure a small house in a working-class area of Colombo. The woman would wash the clothes of her four youthful lodgers every weekend as a small service and hang them out to dry at the rear of her dwelling. The clothes were stolen off the line and the old woman and her husband were frightened lest the lodgers find alternative accommodations.

> Oh God Suniyam! If you help me may you become a future Buddha.
> I have no one to help me.
> My husband is now too old to earn money. We have only one son and
> he earns very little. This is why we have a boarding house. People in
> our neighborhood are envious [irishiyava]. Someone has stolen the
> clothes. They want us to lose our lodgers. I always think of the
> powerful heat of your victory. I know about your power. I have heard
> that you even fought with the asuras. O god who has ten forms, look
> from each one. Punish the thieves!
> I observe the eight precepts [ata sil] every poya.
> I cannot ask you to kill any living being. But with your divine
> wisdom, punish the thieves.
> Then they will stop their stealing.
> O god Suniyam, I cannot order you. I am a lowly human worm [nara].
> O lord Suniyam King! If I have any wrong thoughts [varadi situvili],
> forgive me.
> O god! I dwell on the life of my son. I am burning up thinking about
> him. He has no steady job, though he has been working for more than
> a year. You helped us buy our house. You are always with us. I

know you will guard us. This is why I come to worship before your
lotus feet [*padapatme*].
May you become a Buddha.

Such anguish is common before the shrines. It is equal to the furious
powers of the demonic gods addressed by the supplicants and to the
violent utterances and other sentiments expressed before the gods by their
priests (see chapter 2) and by laymen. At the shrine to the Hindu goddess
of divine destruction, Bhadrakali, the predominantly Sinhalese Buddhist
supplicants have the priests—Sinhalese men and women—inscribe eggs
with the names of their enemies, sometimes in the blood of the plaintiff.
These eggs, the most powerful symbols of cosmic origin, indicative of the
very root of being, are then smashed as will be the life essence of the
enemies.

Class forces contribute to the personal intensity of the anguish and
fury at the shrines as they assume a cultural meaning and recognition in
the continually developing beliefs and metaphors of the practice of sorcery.
What some have seen as an increase in the popularity of sorcery (Obeyesekere 1975), an observation that is far from unproblematic, can be
accounted for, partly at least, by Sri Lanka's dominant capitalist order in
which class forces are of expanding importance.

A distinctive feature of the everyday culture of class conceptions in
Sri Lanka is that they are formed within Sinhalese Buddhist hierarchical
ideology. The poor and the unemployed are not merely wretched, the
meritworthy foci of Buddhist compassion by the better-off, a compassion
that most often takes the form of public charitable displays. The destitute
and impoverished are frequently regarded as dangerous in their reduced
circumstances, fragmented and fragmenting, almost demonic. This meaning, constituted as it is within hierarchical logic, motivates, I suggest, the
common understanding among the well-to-do that poor neighborhoods
and shanty areas are infested with crime, violence, and all other modes
of social degradation. My point is not to dispute the likely facticity of
this claim. It is, rather, to argue that regardless of the truth of the
assertion it is an opinion that is consistent with hierarchical conception
and to a degree receives impetus through it.

In support of the foregoing I note that many of the main mediators
or acolytes of the beings of vengeance and destruction are from impoverished backgrounds, some living in shanty areas. This is true of the six
female attendants (*maniyo*) at the main Bhadrakali shrine in Colombo.
A woman soothsayer (*sastrakaraya*), widely renowned in the south of the
island (just outside Ahangama) is the daughter of a poverty-stricken ox-
cart driver. She manifests demonic powers, the destructive violence of
the demonic Black Prince, Kalu Yaka. These powers, consistent with her
lowly origins, are the powers at the base of a cosmic hierarchy, powers
upon which her clients frequently call.

One of the most important shrines to Suniyam, where I collected much of my sorcery material, is located in an extensive shanty area of Colombo. A violent god is given a violent home, and some of those who address the shrine at this place understand the god to draw some of his power from his situation.[10] The fear (*baya*) of sorcery has some foundation in the class processes of a capitalist order but is brought to consciousness through hierarchical interpretation. Politicians and especially people in business and trade express a great fear of sorcery. Undoubtedly the uncertainty of their occupational practice bears on their anxiety. It is an anxiety, however, that is more specifically motivated in cultural ideas of hierarchy. For as I have explained, the Sinhalese Buddhist conception of hierarchical process is one that recognizes change and transformation as vital within it: what at one time is dominant can reduce, can descend to levels which it once incorporated in its ascendancy. This is the logic of the motion of deities and demons and their transformation in the cosmic hierarchy. Transposed to the social and political world of everyday experience, it enlivens a consciousness of the high possibility of a similar transformational inversion in the fortune of life. In hierarchical thought the luck of circumstance is cosmically determined. This I shall discuss in chapter 7 as being in marked contrast to certain egalitarian thought where "the luck of the draw" is often interpreted as outside the order of the system and a manifestation of an ideal negated by the system.

The fear of sorcery is congruent with a system of hierarchy and its motion. Insofar as a capitalist order manifests the dynamism enthusiastically declared by its ideologies of competitiveness, individualism, progress, and success, such an order and its class process conceived through the interpretive framework of hierarchy is indeed likely to exacerbate the practice of sorcery.

Envy (*irishiyava*) is the most common cause of sorcery that the Sinhalese recognize. It is believed to come from the weak to the powerful, from the poor to the rich, to flow between competitors, bringing about the failure of those who would otherwise succeed and vice versa. Broadly, envy comes from the bottom up, attacking persons who in themselves and in their relations are constituted at a higher and encompassingly dominant level in hierarchy. Those who repeatedly interpret their misfortune as envy are routinely of some social or political dominance and prominence, as they understand themselves, in their various fields of action. But this does not exclude those who are in reduced circumstances from engaging the sorcery of envy as explanation for their condition.[11]

Destructive sorcery, motivated in the passions of envy, desire—love magic is an archetypal form of sorcery in Sri Lanka—hatred, and jealousy, attacks hierarchy and flows in its motion. It is most potent—as is demonic attack generally—at the margins, at moments of transition, at points of hierarchical reordering, when the cosmic unity is momentarily out of joint. Thus, as Dumont (1977, 1980) has pointed out for hierarchical systems, the various parts of the system are ideally only determinate through the system as a whole. They do not have independent determination. That which separates from an embeddedness within a cosmic, hierarchically ordered totality is potentially dangerous and evil and is directed against the system as a whole. In Dumont's argument this is why movable property, rather than fixed property—property subordinated within the hierarchical order and integral to social relations—is conceived of as dangerous in so-called traditional hierarchical orders. This notion is ingrained in the mythic symbolism of many of the demonic deities of Sri Lanka. Suniyam or Oddi Raja is often represented as a trader in movable goods and wealth, as is Devol Deviyo. I consider such a conception, and others linked to a logic of hierarchical motion, to have relevance for an understanding of the fear of envy expressed by traders and business people in Sri Lanka today. I have encountered many traders who take Suniyam as a personal protective god. The dangers inherent in movable wealth—and a consciousness of their threat to established local hierarchies—also contributes to an understanding of the fear that labor migrants returning to Sri Lanka from the various Middle Eastern and Arab oil states have of sorcery and of the routine antisorcery measures that they take.

The returning migrants bring back wealth. Indeed, they have become a major source of foreign revenue for Sri Lanka. Many invest their wealth in business and land, and their fortunes are often responsible for their social mobility in relation to their circumstances at departure and the mobility of their kin. The social order is made dynamic and the social and political arrangements of their localities undergo change and realignment. Interpreted hierarchically, independent foreign wealth attacks established local orders. The returning migrants may be likened to the sorcerer-traders of myth, and they fear the destructiveness that they embody and project. This can be part of the consciousness of even their close relatives. I encountered a young woman who experienced a series of fainting fits accompanied by frightening visions of her brother in the act of being killed. The woman's brother was shortly to return from the Middle East. She recovered when a small antisorcery rite (*kapuma*) was held by her family.

It is a feature of the practice of returning migrants to perform important rituals. Frequently these are Buddha danes, involving the chanting of protective *pirit* by local temple Buddhist monks, and sometimes the principal antisorcery Suniyama ritual. They guard against evil and can appropriately be regarded in the context as rites of transition. I stress here the aspect of these rituals as events of cosmic reaffirmation and of conversion. In accordance with hierarchical logic they incorporate dangerous movable foreign wealth and domesticate it, embedding it in the social and political relations of the local order, an order cosmically surmounted and encompassed in the idea of the Buddha. The rites are typically large community events in which food and other gifts are distributed and thus is the demon reintegrated and protectively subsumed in the hierarchical order. In these ritual occasions, too, new position and the reordering of relations around it are actively constituted within a ritually formed Buddhist cosmic encompassment (see the description of Suniyama in chapter 3).

The sorcery of envy is vital in the hierarchical process. But it is the dangerous instrument of human agency working against the cosmic order. Protective sorcery functions in perfect consistency with such a logic. In the instances of the returning migrants and their families, the antisorcery rites enclose them within the cosmic whole. Thereby the destructive envious passion is made impotent, for such envy is defined as thoroughly evil, opposed to the Buddhist cosmic hierarchy, and itself made the worthy object of destruction. The returning migrants in effect, like Suniyam, transform from destructive beings of the outside to beings in harmony with the cosmic hierarchy and reconstitutive of the context they have entered.

Buddhism, Sorcery, and State Hegemony

Buddhist cosmological ideas are engaged in the modern discourse on social relations formed in the conditions of a class society. Buddhism has never stood outside the dynamics of power in society. In the transformations into the present capitalist and increasingly commodity-oriented world of today's Sri Lanka, Buddhism, as the various studies of Buddhist revivalism show (Ames 1963; Roberts 1979; Obeyesekere 1979; Jayawardena 1985), is intimately engaged in the motion of class relations and at all levels of society. Its cosmic and hierarchical ideas have become, in numerous ways, the language of class, and Buddhism has constituted the particular meaning of class and its force, often at marked variance to that which may be observed in Western situations, in the everyday consciousness of Sinhalese.

The differences in social and material circumstances, often vast, in present-day Sri Lanka, the gap between rich and poor, the differences in social and economic and political influence which mark out the fine-grained distinctions between persons, the despair and hardship of daily existence, can all be comprehended and given expression in Buddhism. Buddhist ideas and the principles of hierarchy which permeate all spheres of life are ingredients in an ideology of class power. They are hegemonic in force, encouraging a unity of difference in circumstance and position as these are formed in class and other social relations. In this ideology there is no statement that differences in existence should be obliterated in the interests of unity, an argument in Australian egalitarianism. A Buddhist ideology of class power focuses directly upon the differences in the world, grasps them, and asserts them as the very principle of unity in the world. In this unity the suffering of all may be overcome.

The ideology is one which, in effect, encourages all in diverse circumstances to participate in their own domination, the ultimate being their domination and dependence on the power of the forces of the state. I outline the ideological argument as I interpret it. But I consider it to be a structure of reasoning which is ingrained in everyday practices. It extends an understanding of the fear of the powerful in relation to the weak, of the desperate anger and protest of the subordinate before their superiors or, most often, indirectly before the sorcery shrines. Most of all it may extend some insight into the occasional manifestation of the Sinhalese as a "community" of violence.

Broadly, in a Buddhism integral to the interpretation of class processes, social, economic, and political difference and circumstance is an aspect of differentiation as a universal principle in existence. Differentiation, in itself, is a continual entropic process fundamental within the movement of the cosmic whole. The process of differentiation produces conflict, social breakdown, and the suffering of all. This is the argument, it may be recalled, of the Mahasammata myth of the origin of the state and of evil. The inevitability of this suffering in existence can be overcome or reduced, however, by asserting a hierarchical order upon difference. By this, the destructive and fragmenting consequence of differentiation is transformed into an integrating force. Differentiation becomes a unifying principle. This is manifest in the institution of reciprocity, which binds society together in its differences. Hierarchy, I emphasise, acts on difference to generate reciprocity. In other words, power in hierarchy and difference is the spirit of the gift, which ultimately is the ordering power of the cosmos and of its embodiment, the state. A comparison can be drawn here with the spirit of the gift in egalitarian Australia. There the spirit of the gift is the natural essence of the individual, independent of any social and cosmic order. It manifests the purity of its form between individuals who are not different. It is the expression of pure self, independent of a social identity, and the spirit of the gift is in the exchange of self. To return to Sri Lanka, with the institution of reciprocity suffering within society is reduced, the rich give to the poor and vice versa, their acts of giving being the worship of the order of hierarchy in itself. This is a meaning of religious and ritual practice, of course, throughout Buddhist Sri Lanka, and it is integral to a comprehension of the Sinhalese commitment to the efficacy of such acts.

Over all, a Buddhist conception current in modern Sri Lanka that differentiation is disruptive can account for conflict and can attribute this conflict quite thoroughly to the complexities of present social, political, and economic circumstances. It resolves them—paradoxically perhaps if regarded from a position outside Sinhalese Buddhist society—by the affirmation of such difference but one ordered in hierarchical integration.

In this resolution of material contradictions, a resolution in power and in the incorporation of the weak in the powerful, all come to act in mutual benefit and the suffering of all is reduced. The wider significance of this in the situation of ethnic strife is that Buddhism, as a key element of Sinhalese ethnic identity, can operate ideologically to unify persons differently located and in potential social and political opposition within modern class processes. It can motivate them to call on the powers which contribute to this ideal unity and simultaneously align them against other forms of identified difference in the population, the Tamils. Such motivations may build in the circumstances of increasing differentiation and suffering, which is the situation of modern Sri Lanka.

Ideologically, therefore, Sinhalese Buddhists, both weak and strong, are motivated to join in cooperative action. The weak seek the benefits of incorporation in the powerful. This is encouraged by the strong, not merely because they may want to dominate the weak, but because such separation can contribute to their own suffering and anguish in a deeply personal sense. The submission of the weak to the strong is not mere submission, but a positive and forceful submission which demands the ordering reciprocity of hierarchy. It is a demand which may increase in intensity under present economic and political conditions in Sri Lanka. The force of such demand, motivated and organized in ideolgy, is further demonstrated in everyday practice and especially in sorcery.

One submits to superiors, in the conceptions of hierarchical ideology, not just because they are powerful but because they order one's person. Submission is a form of personal incorporation and embodiment in the other. This, in a minor sense, is the ideologically produced meaning behind submissive action displayed by many Sinhalese before officials in bureaucracies and before persons of social and political standing. Through such incorporative submission in hierarchy, moreover, the benefit of its favors in reciprocity is engendered. Here is an understanding of the violence of sorcery used to gain bureaucratic and other official help or support. By sorcery one forces entry into the body of the dominant, and its violence is that of breaking through those barriers in a socially and politically differentiated world that prevent the embodiment in hierarchy. This is a meaning behind the sexual metaphors of sorcery, of the mythic rape of Queen Manikpala by Vasavarti Maraya. Through embodiment one enters and can turn the will of the other, but, too, one can insist on the reciprocity of hierarchical power.

My discussion expands an understanding of patron-client relations in Sri Lanka. In its cultural universe, a client is not merely connected to another, as is the interpretation of similar phenomena in the West and elsewhere (Bailey 1969; Mayer 1966). A client is or may become a *part* of that other, is *embodied* in the patron, and achieves personal integrity and influence accordingly.[12]

I have described the antisorcery Suniyama rite as often performed by prominent local patrons. The Suniyama is performed to protect them against the fragmenting effects of sorcery upon their persons, households, and businesses. They often suspect someone close to them of sorcery— a person who is destroying from within. In the Suniyama rite the body of the patron is reintegrated, and clients are reincorporated with the person of the patron. I add, more generally, that people who fear and suspect sorcery routinely suspect people who are close, in some kind of intimate relation with them. They fear those who are so close that they are part of one's person, of one's body, but frequently a person who is a lower, inferior part of it. In such a hierarchical world one fears not only the outsider or stranger, one also fears those who are deeply part of one's self but who have moved outside and thereby fragment.

The practice of sorcery exerts the logic of the state and its hierarchy in the overcoming of anguish and suffering and in the restoration of personal integrity. The flames of fear which in another interpretation and in other ideological understanding may be fanned by class processes and other forces within the cultural universe of Sri Lanka achieve their extinction in the idea and power of the state. The passionate suffering of individuals is conceived as also the suffering of the state, to be assuaged through the assertion of its constitutive principles. One sorcery shrine in Colombo makes this explicit in its architecture. Supplicants must enter its premises through the jaws of a lion; the lion of the ancient fortress kingdom of Sigiriya, the lion of Sinhala, the lion of state.

People from all social backgrounds crowd the more important shrines. Their action takes the form of a mutual suffering, a collective suffering within the community of the state. Their appeal to the gods of sorcery is an appeal to the power of state, and in the logic of their ritual action, in their pleas, offerings, and violent sentiment, they become active in the restoration of the idea of the state as also integral to their own restoration. If class forces are manifest, among other things, by the personal suffering at the shrines—if class processes exacerbate the anguish—the forces of class become harnessed in the energy of state affirmation and in the power of the internal order it institutes and maintains. In another understanding, outside the hierarchical logic I have described, Sinhalese worship an idea that may be vital in their very destruction, an idea that is carried in Suniyam, who symbolizes both the violence of the state order and the violence of the state destroyed.

Sinhalese ethnic nationalism and sorcery, their "fearful symmetry," are founded within the one historically formed set of social and political circumstances. They achieve their meaning in the one setting and participate in the one ontologically inscribed ideology. The ideas of the Buddhist state at risk and in powerful regeneration are integral to both sorcery and nationalism. They resound, moreover, with the message that both the anguish of the person and the anguish of the nation are to be overcome in the power of hierarchy, in the union of the weak with the strong, and that within such an order person and nation can move out singly, explosively, and shatteringly against those who offend against equanimity and the integrity of the whole.

I stress that in the hierarchical unity of identity of Sinhalese Buddhist nationalist ideology, the powerful are enjoined to be powerful, to act as they ideally should in a cosmic and social universe the harmony of which is dependent on their strength. In a language born in the heat of capitalist transformations, class and other forms of social distinction are called upon to become thoroughly manifest and to exert their harmonious and integrative powers. How different from the egalitarian ideological world of Australian nationalism, which has no less oppressive potential. There the socially produced distinctions of modern reality must be suppressed in the overcoming of anguish and suffering.

Nationalism, Hierarchy, and the Passions

I have explored aspects of the development of ethnic nationalism in Sri Lanka: its mythic symbolism, the ontology of myth and its empowering in modern political ideology, the formation of this political ideology, and the circumstances which give this ideology force. All these have been directed toward one concern, the understanding of the escalating murderous ethnic violence in Sri Lanka. This violence includes both the killing of Tamils by rioting Sinhalese Buddhists and the organized violence of the state. I have not discussed the important contribution of Tamil rage and resistance to the present conflict. My knowledge is limited regarding the details of the Tamil situation. I note, however, that their action is largely determined within a political order commanded by Sinhalese. It is the Sinhalese who are the dominant and determining factor and it is the ideological processes engaged in their action that are most relevant to an understanding of the current situation.

Within Sri Lanka the function of myth and legend in national politics is hotly debated. It is not an idle intellectualism, an academic game play, but pregnant with serious practical import. My own contribution to the discussion is a variation on important scholarly opinion. I see the myths and legends as embodying a logic of the state and nation that is also vital in everyday practices and integral to the constitution of person. The logic of the myths is also central to the ideological formation of Sinhalese ethnic identity. A nationalist Sinhalese consciousness of unity in identity, I have argued, takes hierarchical shape. The present situation to some extent appears to be unfolding in accordance with such a logic; it seems to be part of the motive force behind events and an aspect of the emotion and passion of these events. Much of my analysis, ultimately concerned with the culture of political action, has been an exploration of the conditions and the processes that seem to give the argument of the myths and legends an awful potency.

Sahlins's analysis (1981, 1985) of the emergence of Hawaii from the cold into the heat of Western colonial expansion bears comparison with my argument. Some similarities are intended, for I find Sahlins's account theoretically compelling. But I stress a contrast in perspective. Broadly, he weds an evolutionism turned historicism with structuralist semiotics. Accordingly Sahlins declares his object to be "simply to show some ways that history is organized by structures of significance." But, of course the motive of his analysis is more than this. "From a structuralist perspective nothing is simpler than the discovery of continuities of cultural categories as modes of interpretation and action." Sahlins wishes to lay the groundwork for a more ambitious project which is to show how "culture is reordered" in the process of the cultural ordering of historical events (Sahlins 1981, 8). And so his account of the transformations of Hawaii unfold as a continuous stream of interconnected events with few disjunctions or radical breaks. What seems to be possible for an analysis of Hawaii would, I think, be impossible for an analysis of Sri Lanka. Numerous cultural and political forces have molded modern Sri Lanka, and there have been radical breaks and discontinuities in its development.

The Sinhalese Buddhist nationalist assertion of cultural and historical continuity is an ideological assertion born in modern politics. There are continuities in logic with the past, but the meaning of this logic is formed in present social and political processes. The force that the reasoning of the *Mahavamsa* appears to have in the current events of ethnic strife is forged in conditions which have given the arguments of the *Mahavamsa* dominant and totalizing position in the political order of Sri Lanka. Indeed, I suggest that the potency of the cultural reasoning is a property of the political order of nationalism, of the reification of culture in nationalism, and of its creation as a thing of worship. What is now called Sinhalese Buddhist culture is more coherent and systematic than it may ever have been in the past. It is such encompassing reified coherence which is a critical factor in its force, the capacity of persons acting within Sinhalese Buddhist culture, apparently to structure events in accordance with the logic of the myths of history. The force of cultural categories in Sahlins's account of Hawaiian historical transformations no doubt has something to do with the totalizing form of the Hawaiian religio-political system.

The power of cultural ideas in Sinhalese nationalism is intimately connected with the value placed on community in identity by Sinhalese. To some extent this and the universalization of cultural ideas developed together in the social and political transformations into modern Sri Lanka. My analysis of Sinhalese ethnicity builds upon the work of scholars (Gluckman 1958; Mitchell 1956, 1987; Epstein 1958) in the entirely different setting of Central Africa. They recognized the ethnicity they studied as a cultural form of capitalist industrial realities. They noted the reified nature of culture in the formation of ethnic groups and the original constitutive function of culture, that the object culture was the principle of the creation of social relations as it was not in tribal situations. Culture, in some ways like Sahlins' structuralism, was made prior to society, not integral to it. These aspects of ethnicity are marked in Sri Lanka. Cultural identity is a principle of association into collectivities of persons of like identity. In Sri Lanka other identities work in a similar categorical way. Thus persons who share the same caste identity or village area identity will engage such identity in the formation of social relations. This is especially noticeable in urban centers such as Colombo.

Identity bounds a set of relations but does not specify the organizational character of their internal or external relations. The bounds of identity are defined in relations of contrast or opposition, an aspect I shall discuss with reference to Australian nationalism. Identity as an associating principle, therefore, is highly situational; that is, the significance of identity as a principle of association is relevant or irrelevant in social situations according to the presence of other contrasting identities. The political order of nationalism and, especially, the link between identity and the state stabilizes identity, in this instance Sinhalese identity, and reduces its labile, situational character. Sinhalese identity is made socially and politically significant across numerous situations. This is further complicated when the character of these relations constituted in the identity of Sinhalese is further characterized in the ideology of hierarchy.

The Sinhalese state defines ethnic identity and hierarchy as the dominant principles of the social and political order. The Sinhalese ethnic category is filled with hierarchical content, which becomes the principle of internal ethnic coherence and is simultaneously placed in hierarchical relation to other ethnic categories within the political whole. The dreadful possibility and import of this dominating combination of identity and hierarchy in the political order of the Sri Lanka state should be clear from my analysis.

A solution to the current strife in Sri Lanka is self-evident from the analysis. Quite simply, it is the removal of ethnic identity and hierarchy as dominant state-sanctified principles of political and social order. This would involve a radical change in the ideological form of Sri Lankan state nationalism. The agents of the state would have to surrender critical ideological bases of their power. But as I have indicated, these ideological bases manifest their own internal contradictions, which can generate more strife and suffering for Sinhalese, let alone for others, instead of producing Buddhist equanimity. This should be clear, not just in the escalating war between Tamils and Sinhalese, but in the mounting civil strife within the Sinhalese population. This is assuming the very hierarchical violent form that structures the devastating conflict between Sinhalese and Tamils. But the commitment to the present course may be hard to break as for apartheid in South Africa, where the ideological form of relations is cognate, in my opinion, with egalitarian ideological principles. This is so not merely for the most critical reasons of power and class, for example, but because of the ideological forming of such processes. In this forming, the roots of state power in nationalism have been firmly set within cultural ground that is also ontological. This is so through the affirmation by the state of certain traditions and this is a reason for their danger when engaged to nationalism.

It is in its logic that tradition can force its message into the inner being of the person and achieve a validity for its message by virtue of such a union. The logic of an argument is made integral to the person and, correspondingly, the person is drawn into the scheme and process of things as these are shaped in the logic of nationalist tradition. Cultural categories do not have force merely because they organize significance in the world, although I certainly do not discount this fact. But they are further empowered in their unity with the person, in their assimilation to the constitution of the being of the person. It is when this occurs that persons are directed out to the horizons of their existence in committed acts and can change the world through such commitment. It is through a union with the ontology of person that the logic of mythic history can be manifested as existentially real. Here, in my view, is a key to understanding how the meaning of history that is constituted in the present is experienced as if it flowed from the past. The experiential unity that people feel in identity and in the culture of their identity can be ontologically motivated. This is so when the ideology of cultural unity, for example, contains a fundamental logic which is also that of the ontology that constitutes personal being in a variety of everyday practices. In any social and political world there may be a variety of ontologies, ways in which the being of person is formed and so directed out upon the world. The meaning of such ontology, furthermore, is also likely to be varied, engaged as it is in many different situated practices. But through the logic of ideology made dominant, for instance, in the mythic traditions of the nation, not only may a particular mode of being be brought to prominence but a diversity of meaning may be drawn into the systematic interpretation of nationalist tradition. Human beings in vastly different social and economic circumstance can be made to experience an existential unity with others. Not all ideologies necessarily have great ontological potential. But they may achieve it in the political and social transformations of history as I have shown with regard to Sri Lanka.

The emotions and passions of a nationalist ethnic consciousness are vital to its political force and violence. So critical are the emotions in nationalism that any understanding of nationalism that does not address them must be impoverished. I developed my argument on ontology and ideology in order to examine this issue and in such a way as not to reduce an understanding of nationalism to factors independent of nationalism itself. The roots of a nationalist passion are not external to it. The racism and violent destruction of other that it may manifest are not universal in human nature and have no necessity in their manifestation independent of nationalism itself. Similarly the emotions and passions which are integral to nationalism are not, in my analysis, given within a particular psychology—the psychology of the folk, for instance—and are not given in the symbolism of culture that somehow exists independent of its nationalist practice. Cultural symbols and language are not of themselves naturally evocative of ethnic feelings; they achieve such force in an ethnic consciousness, for instance, not independent of it. The emotions and passions of ethnic and nationalist consciousness receive direction through an ontology, an ontology given new, expanded, and potentially devastating meaning in the ideology of nationalism and in the history of its formation.

In the present situation the ideology of the state, ethnic consciousness, and the ontology of the person are in such combination as to make Tamils powerful metaphors of state and personal destruction.

Such metaphors and their rhetoric are not of themselves motivating or powerful or constitutive, as seems to be the implication of much recent anthropology that is strongly influenced by the arguments of linguistic philosophy. In academia and in philosophy, of course, the word is powerful: words are the form of life. This is not to diminish the significance of that anthropology which has demonstrated the importance of the metaphor and the trope in cultural analysis. My concern, rather, is to indicate that the dictates of fashionable analysis can sometimes lead to outright absurdity. Thus Paine (1981) heads an article on the nature of political rhetoric with a quotation from Hall (1972; 51), "The basic element of politics is, quite simply, talk." The worlds of lived experience, of political and social realities, cannot be reduced to the dialectics of discourse or of a conversation. Metaphors have force in the world through the ontology they engage and through the political and social realities of oppression, of inequality, of poverty, and so on. Bertrand Russell, anticipating some of the dangers of Wittgenstein's new school of linguistic philosophy, states, "We are now told that it is not the world that we are to try to understand but only sentences." (Russell 1959, 217).

There is a marvelous sequence of events in Dutugemunu's encounter with Bhalluka after the death of Elara. Bhalluka tries to shoot an arrow into Dutugemunu's mouth, but Dutugemunu parries it with his sword. The king's champion, Phussadeva, fires an arrow in response and with similar aim. Bhalluka is struck in the mouth and falls mortally wounded.

One possible interpretation of these events is that they sign the power of the king's speech. Dutugemunu and Bhalluka have been hurling insults at each other, and it is Bhalluka, the Tamil champion, who is silenced. Tamils are now fighting for a greater voice in a country which is also their own. It is to be hoped that Buddhist reason will ultimately prevail and that a final dreadful potential of the legend will not be realized.

Part 2

People against the State

Australian Nationalism and Egalitarian Individualism

War

Out in the dust he lies;
Flies in his mouth,
Ants in his eyes. . . .

I stood at the door
    Where he went out;
Full-grown man,
    Ruddy and stout;

I heard the march
    Of the trampling feet,
        Slow and steady
    Come down the street;

The beat of the drum
    Was clods on the heart,
For all that the regiment
    Looked so smart!

I heard the crackle
    Of hasty cheers
Run like the breaking
    Of unshed tears

And just for a moment
    As he went by,
I had sight of his face,
And the flash of his eye.

He died a hero's death,
    They said,
        When they came to tell me
    My boy was dead;

But out in the street
    A dead dog lies;
Flies in his mouth,
    Ants in his eyes.

Mary Gilmore

The Pool of Reflection, Australian War Memorial, Canberra. Visitors throw money into the pool. In the cloisters on either side are engraved the names of Australia's war dead. The names are arranged alphabetically and without wartime rank. This is in strict accord with the egalitarian ideal. (Photo courtesy Australian War Memorial)

5

When the World Crumbles and the Heavens Fall In

War, Death, and the Creation of Nation

On April 25, 1915, at 4.30 A.M., soldiers of the Australian Imperial Forces and New Zealand troops, to be known as the Australian and New Zealand Army Corps, the Anzacs, landed on the shores of Gallipoli in the Dardanelles.[1] Before they struck shore they began to die in numbers in their boats. Their slaughter and that of the defending Turkish forces continued through the ensuing eight months as the Anzacs grimly held on to the tiny piece of Turkish territory. The battle was probably lost before it began. The main body of Anzacs were withdrawn during two nights in mid December 1915. Only six men were lost during the withdrawal, a fact often commented upon as miraculously light, especially compared to the carnage of the months before. During the Gallipoli campaign more than ten thousand Australian and New Zealand dead were left on Turkish soil and some twenty thousand were wounded.

In the violence, horror, and suffering of the men of Anzac crystallized the nationalist imagination of Australia.[2] Inglis (1985) has remarked perceptively that the Australian accounts, rites, temples, and icons of Anzac—and other traditions of Australian fighting in other battles and wars—approach closely what Rousseau had in mind as "secular religion." There is hardly a town or city in Australia that does not have an Anzac memorial. Typically it occupies central public space and is the focus of the Anzac Day ceremonies, held on the day of the Gallipoli landings, in remembrance of all those Australians who have fallen or served in theaters of war. Anzac Day is arguably more important as a day of national commemoration than Australia Day, which falls on 26 January, marking the landing of the First Fleet and its cargo of convicts at Botany Bay in 1788. The two days indicate the direction of this analysis, for in my interpretation Australia Day is the day of the state, whereas Anzac Day is the day of the nation. In Australian nationalism there is a fundamental tension between the state and the nation, and it is this relation that I shall explore.

The central symbol of the Australian nation is the Australian War Memorial, located at Canberra, the national capital. It is the most visited place of national symbolic importance in Australia. The exploits of the Anzacs in the Dardanelles and in later acts of war are retold in the classrooms of the country. They reach a heightened point in consciousness in the newspapers and in national television during the festival of Anzac Day and on the days immediately surrounding it. The Anzac legend could be regarded as being almost on a par with the significance of the Vijaya and Dutugemunu legends of Sri Lanka—though Australians might demur at such a suggestion.

For one thing, the "facts" of Anzac, it can be said, are beyond dispute. Unlike the events of Dutugemunu and Vijaya they occurred within living memory and the evidence is available for all to see in the archives and museum displays of the War Memorial. C. E. W. Bean, the official chronicler of Anzac and the inspiration for the establishment of the War Memorial, was concerned that the facts of Anzac be beyond dispute.[3] His empiricism cannot be reduced to "scientific rationalist" empiricism, although like the Sinhalese and Tamil disclaimers of the "truth" of the Vijaya and Dutugemunu legends, he was no doubt oriented within the scholarly demands of a rationalist objectivity. Bean was obsessed with accuracy and the "facts," but it was not merely "the facts for themselves" that drove him. His prodigious energy was generated within an overt awareness, present from the very moment he left Australia with the troops, that he was witnessing the stuff of myth at the moment of its creation.[4] Bean's passion for detail was that of the ritualist. It can be likened to that of Sinhalese exorcists or Balinese ritual specialists as described by Geertz (1979), whose concern with the exactness of their work and the minuteness of detail flows from a knowledge that it is in their extreme care and precision that ideas become reality, that the cosmological processes they conjure achieve constitutive and reconstitutive power. Like Sinhalese and Balinese ritual workers, Bean made a fetish of detail from an understanding that a lack of observance or an inaccuracy of fact could lead to a failure of his mythic-ritual purpose. The world of Anzac, made to live in its recorded details, would enable later generations of Australians to enter its mythic reality, to reembody the Anzac ideals, and thereby to regenerate the nation established by the Anzacs.

Bean's relation to the facts of Anzac is fully commensurate with the commitment of many Sinhalese scholars and laymen to the facticity of the events in the Vijaya and Dutugemunu stories. The "truth" of the actual events depends on the interpretation. But more than this, a whole ontology, a logic of being and orientation in the world, is ingrained in the facts qua facts. For the facts to be denied is tantamount to denying the vital grounds of existence itself.

The nature of the Australian existence, of being in identity, fills the facts of Bean's documentation and interpretation of the events in the Dardanelles and elsewhere. The Anzac tradition expounds the doctrine of the Australian male egalitarian virtue of mateship. Bean outlines the spirit that sustained the Australian and New Zealand troops through the hell of the first few days of the Gallipoli landing:

> What motive sustained them? At the end of the second or third day of the Landing, when they had fought without sleep until the whole world seemed a dream, and they scarcely knew whether it was a world of reality or of delirium—and often, no doubt, it held something of both; when half of each battalion had been annihilated, and there seemed no prospect before any man except that of wounds or death in the most vile of surroundings; when the dead lay three deep in the rifle-pits under the blue sky and the place was filled with stench and sickness, and reason had almost vanished—what was it then that carried each man on? (Bean 1981:1, 606).

Bean argues that the Australian "love of a fight," hatred of the Turks for their ill-treatment of the wounded, patriotic loyalty to Australia or New Zealand, sentiment for Great Britain, and desire for fame were not the principal factors in the spiritual sustenance of the troops. Of paramount importance was that which lay

> in the mettle of the men themselves. To be the sort of man who would give way when his mates were trusting to his firmness; to be the sort of man who would fail when the line, the whole force, and the allied cause required his endurance . . . was the prospect which these men could not face. Life was very dear, but life was not worth living unless they could be true to their idea of Australian manhood. Standing upon that alone, when help failed and hope faded, when the end loomed clear in front of them, when the whole world seemed to crumble and the heaven fall in, they faced its ruin undismayed (Bean 1981:1, 607).

Bean describes the Anzac as the ideal male representative of the Australian nation to be a "natural" leader. This is a vital element of the autonomy of the individual in Australian egalitarianism in which the qualities of both leader and follower, dominant and subordinate, are inscribed within the individual. Bean repeatedly contrasts Australians with the soldier bearers of the characteristics of other nations. To Bean the Australian, "was more a child of nature even than the New Zealanders" (Bean 1981:1, 48). The Americans succumbed to the Australian's natural capacity for leadership: "When the Americans foregathered with him at the end of the war, he led them also" (Bean 1981:1, 48).

But the main contrast in Bean's accounts is always with the British. He states that the British "Tommies" "instinctively looked up to the Australian private as leader." The Tommies are described as "extraordinarily guileless, humble-minded to a degree, never boastful" (Bean 1981:1, 48). These are not the qualities of Australians valorized in Bean's nationalism and in the Australian nationalist culture of today, as will be seen. The Australian Anzac or "digger" in cultural self-conception is often depicted as filled with natural intelligence or cunning and full of self-pride—the repeated theme of folk poetry—which is reflected in boasting.[5] When Bean presents his depiction of the Tommy he is implicitly valuing the autonomy of Australian males, which is a transformation on the perceived British scheme of things.

In the autonomy of the Anzac are embedded such ideas of Australian egalitarianism as the distrust of social convention based in artificially created social and political orders, orders not founded in nature. Thus Bean describes British traditional military order as inappropriate to Australia's citizen army:[6]

> The fact that a man had received a good education, dressed well, spoke
> English faultlessly and belonged to the "officer" class, would merely
> incline them at first sight to laugh at him, or at least suspect that he
> was guilty of affectation—in their own language, "putting on dog."
> But they were seriously intent upon learning and were readily
> controlled by anyone really competent to teach them. They were hero-
> worshippers to the backbone. There was a difficulty in reconciling
> them to any sort of irksome rule. . . . At first there . . . existed . . .
> suppressed resentfulness of the whole system of "officers" (Bean: 1, 48).

The meaning implicit in Bean's phrase "really competent" and the Australian as "hero-worshipper" in the context of his chronicles and of Australian nationalism, lies in the Australian individualist valuation of natural, intrinsic qualities. Only as an individual expressing natural qualities of competence and leadership can such a person exert authority and control. This is the essence of Australian egalitarian thought, which I will discuss later. It is through the presence of such natural qualities that egalitarianism functions to bridge the distance between Australians of unequal rank. Bean focuses on the unity that developed between officers and men toward the end of the first three days on Gallipoli. He also notes the significance of men of different rank assuming each other's roles under fire. Both are evidence of the equality of men in nature and its importance in overcoming the suffering and destruction of artificial, imposed social orders.

> [A result] of the landing was that it fixed once and for all the relation
> of the Australian men to their officers. . . . Most of the men since
> their childhood had never known a direct command unqualified by
> "You might" or "if you please." . . . the shooting of officers was said to
> have been not unknown in Continental wars and even in South
> Africa. . . . Major Swannell of the 1st Battalion knew when he landed
> that there had been some such talk [of shooting him because of his
> severity during training in Egypt before the landing] about himself.
> From the moment they saw his bearing under fire, he became a hero of
> his men. . . .

"By God," said an Australian private to a war correspondent—"By God, our officers are splendid!" . . . Under the instant imminence of death there was room only for swift and single command by brave and determined leaders. Noncommissioned officers and privates constantly filled that need where the officers were lost. It was the deliberate policy of the Force that Australian officers should live largely among their troops. . . . They conversed with them as freely as a manager with the old hands on an Australian sheep-station, and the men talked equally naturally with them (Bean: 1, 549–50).

Bean's chronicles of Anzac are as ideological and inscribe an equivalent ontology as potentially powerful as any of the Sinhalese Buddhist myths and legends I have discussed. As in those myths, the ideas that are present within Bean's presentation and interpretation of the facts are current in Australian nationalist political culture. They also have force in the production of intolerance and suffering in the ideological activation of their logical potential. My immediate concern, however, is to explore some additional mythic qualities of Anzac which extend an understanding of its centrality within Australian nationalist thought, even among those who for various reasons may be embarrassed by aspects of the Anzac tradition or see it as a figment of the distant past and themselves as outside or apart from it.

The centrality of the Anzac tradition in Australian nationalism owes much to the efforts of agents of the state and to men of the stature of Bean. Their degree of success is undoubtedly related to the fact that the events leading to and following the disasters at Gallipoli occurred so soon after Australia's formal independence from England in 1901. The occurrences at the Dardanelles especially provided a wealth of symbolic opportunities, many of which have already been referred to, around which a nationalist ideology could form. But more, I stress that they were open to an interpretation of cosmogenic significance.

Anzac and the Cosmogenesis of a Nation

A greater understanding of the significance of Gallipoli and of the Anzac tradition in the Australian imagination can be achieved by placing Gallipoli in the context of some of the other major events of the war. My schematic outline is influenced by an anthropologist's interest in myth. I note, however, that my concentration is reflected in the focus of recent Australian film and television series and in popular books that continue to celebrate the national significance of Anzac.

1. October 1914. Troops leave Australia in transport ships. Australian naval vessel, HMAS *Sydney*, escorting the convoy, sinks a German ship, the *Emden*, "threatening" the convoy.
2. December 1914. Troops arrive at Alexandria, Egypt, and journey down the Nile to camps within sight of the pyramids outside Cairo.

Bean describes the train journey to the camps as one in which the troops moved "all day . . . up the green Nile flats crowded with a population which might have stepped out of the Old Testament" (Bean 1981:1, 115).
Australian troops are described as unruly, undisciplined, almost chaotic.
On Good Friday, 1915, Australian troops riot in a brothel area of Cairo. This is after some units have been ordered to get ready for the front. "British military police arrive on horseback and attempt to disperse the rioters by firing revolvers at them. . . . [In return they] are bombarded with rocks, beer bottles, lengths of fire hose, and abuse, and wisely withdrew" (Gammage 1975, 39).
3. 25 April 1915. Gallipoli Landing.
Losses great, requiring reinforcement. Units of the elite Australian Light Horse, who have to fight unmounted, brought in.
4. December 1915. Retreat and return to Egypt.
Bean describes the returned Anzacs thus: "[They] were a different force from the adventurous body that had left Egypt eight months before. They were a military force with strongly established military traditions." (Bean 1946, 183).
5. March 1916. Units of Anzac embark for Europe, where they distinguish themselves.
Anzac Light Horse and Camel corps (now all mounted) fight in the Middle East. Jerusalem captured from Turks in December 1917. By October 1918 these units are fighting through Damascus and into Lebanon.
6. War ends—in Middle East at the end of October, in Europe in November, 1918.

Taken as a whole, and examined as one might a Sinhalese Buddhist myth, the events involving the Anzacs essay a series of transformations, one involving a process of rebirth (resurrection?) which is virtually biblical. Gallipoli itself is often taken merely as a terrible defeat. But in the story as a whole it is a key event in the discovery and reformation of a coherent identity. A movement out of chaos, one which is almost demonic but which obscures the real character of Australians, is revealed in the suffering of Gallipoli. Reborn, the Australians become conquering heroes.

The events involving the Anzacs in the Mediterranean and Palestine, especially, were open to interpretation as a representation of the mythic occurrences vital to Western Christian civilization. This is important, for the Anzacs were not the first Australian troops to engage in foreign conflict. Units of Australian soldiers had fought in German-occupied New Guinea. The British had used Australian soldiers in the Boer War, a conflict which had bridged Australia's transition to national independence.[7] But this engagement has only limited significance in the nationalist imagination. The Anzacs are vital symbolic embodiments of the Australian nationalist imagination because they established an identity for Australia in the context of the very ideological and ontological roots of Western Judeo-Christian civilization. They did so in a situation in which the very basis of Western European Christian civilization was ideologically conceived as threatened by anti-Christian forces from within (the Germans) and by traditional enemies of Christianity and the West from without (the Turks).

Undoubtedly the cataclysmic magnitude of the destruction and the scale of the human suffering of the First World War underlies much of the importance gained by the tradition of the Anzacs in the imagination of Australians. But such world-shattering events, as the war propaganda drummed, achieved their significance in the image of a Western Christian world brought to the brink of annihilation. The Anzacs constituted their identity, and the identity of the nation, in violent action whereby they were seen to be engaged at the heart of Western civilization, reconstituting it as they reformed themselves. In so doing they symbolized their ontological unity and, too, the unity of the nation they represented with the Western European world. The Anzacs in their action symbolically tightened, their tradition intensified, the bonds between Australia and the European nations. The sentiments of this identity fueled the initial enthusiasms of the Australians for the war. The actions of the Anzacs brought these sentiments to fruition, within the ideological understanding that Australia was united with Western Christian civilization at its very foundations. This symbolic significance of the Anzac tradition continues to the present day in the structure of national politics and in such issues as the debate on ethnicity.

The journey of the Anzacs to the Dardanelles took them to the source of Western civilization, where, in the ideological imagination of the Anzac chroniclers, both of the time and in the more popular accounts of today, political democracy began, rational thought took root, and great literature flowered. I stress this because too often in the traditional association of the Anzacs with Greek heroes the interpretations stop at the athleticism, youth, and vigor of the Anzacs without dwelling on the deeper symbolic potential. The Anzacs symbolize in their youth the rebirth of the very soul of Western civilization and their embodiment of its fundamental ideals. It is this more complete idea that is present in the work of men such as Bean and reproduced in more recent popular studies of Anzac, which are, of course, vital in the generation of the Anzac tradition. Thus Patsy Adam-Smith describes the movement of the Anzacs toward their destiny at Gallipoli:

> They sailed to Mudros, the harbour of Lemnos Island. On the island's peaks Agamemnon, King of Mycenae, had lit a chain of fires to signal to Clytaemnestra, his queen, that he had taken nearby Troy. Here, to the one place consecrated by poets to the conflicts of heroes, to the forces and passions personified by the Olympian gods and goddesses,

half Europe, half Asia, came the new men, bred beneath a cross of stars
that Herodotus had not known of when he portrayed the localised war
at Thermopylae as global conflict. It is the most famous arena of the
world, the birth-place of the Iliad. Men had tried their mettle here
before Australia was dreamt of (Adam-Smith 1978, 58).

Not only do the Anzacs symbolize the Greek ideal of civilization
they are its defenders against the Turks. The Turks in Western romantic
conceptions of the time were until recently the oppressive dominators of
the Greeks and thus the enemies of Western Christian civilization. The
fight against the Turks gains some of its meaning in this context. Not
only is a revitalized Western civilization pitted against the Moslem, but
also, in the Anzac participation in the liberation of Jerusalem, the center
of the Judeo-Christian world is restored.

Such ideas of civilization and the cosmic and religious were probably
far from the overt thoughts of the Anzacs engaged in the fighting. This
was perhaps less true for the officers and certainly for the army chaplains
and padres. The latter gave lectures to the men on the historical
importance of the areas in which they fought and, of course, filled their
sermons with appropriate biblical references.[8]

Many of the soldiers, however, were irreligious virtually by intention.
Christian religion was part of the disciplinary framework of the military,
and the officers of religion were part of that structure of domination
which denied to the men a self-determining autonomy valued in egalitarian
thought.

Gammage stresses the antireligious sentiment—or at least the indif-
ference—of members of the Light Horse in Palestine. "They followed
the Crusaders, and they helped liberate the Holy land, but they never
admitted a serious zeal, they were not religious" (Gammage 1975, 140).
Gammage cites the verbatim comment of one trooper: "Had a good look
round Jerusalem. . . . Don't think much of the crib, of course the old
historical sites & buildings are interesting & beautiful in cases, but the
yarns about a lot of em are guesswork & some all balls." Casual and
touristlike, as Gammage states, this soldier nonetheless displays the
marked commonsense rationalism that is a marked aspect of Australian
egalitarian nationalism, possibly of egalitarianism more widely. Gammage cites examples of antireligious Australian humor as common now
as then. Australians objecting to the boatmens' prices at the Sea of
Galilee observed "that it was 'no wonder the other bloke' walked."
Gammage cites the well-known and wonderfully sacrilegious action of a
light horseman shown the tomb of St. Jerome at Bethlehem. He had been
"told that the oil lamp on top had been burning for 500 years. 'Well, its
high time it had a rest,' he exclaimed, and blew it out." (Gammage 1975,
140).

While such Australian humor may be seen to act against religion, it
nonetheless discovers its appreciation on a play of inversions within a

consciousness steeped in Christian ideas. Australian nationalist egalitarianism, as I have already said, discovers its metaphors in Christianity and in those religious views that can be seen as opposing Christianity. This is exemplified in the following, recounted by a New Zealand camelier in the desert campaign. It is a story about the gambling game of two-up, which is integral to the Anzac tradition and performed as a sacred act by many celebrants on Anzac Day.[9]

> The New Zealanders are very religious men. Their priests lead them out to a quiet spot where they can pray. The priest spreads out a holy mat with marks on it which means something they have great faith in. He kneels down beside the mat, then a row of worshippers kneel all round him, with another row bending over them, and another row standing behind them. The worshippers throw their offerings on to the holy mat, and the priest places two coins on a short piece of polished wood which he calls a kip, and raising his eyes to the sky, he throws up the coins as an offering to Allah. All the worshippers raise their eyes also to the sky, and then bow solemnly over the mat, and say together, "God Almighty," and the priest answers, "A pair of Micks," which means that the offerings are not accepted, or he may say, "Oh Lord, he has done 'em again," and the joyful cries of some of the worshippers show that Allah is pleased, and so they, too, are glad (Robertson 1938, 198).

This account of two-up indicates a measure of Christian prejudice toward Islam. Of more importance here, it suggests a deeper understanding of the nature of the irreligion of the Anzacs. Not only does it manifest a practice of egalitarianism, the "attack" on religion reflected in the attitudes of the Anzacs is in itself the religion of Anzac. The valorized irreligion of the Anzacs, which many of their historians celebrate, is nothing other than a manifestation at an individual level of the secular religion of the Anzac tradition. The irreverence is its very religiosity. Furthermore, this "religion" of the common man is formed within Judeo-Christian ideology even as it inverts and rejects it.

Regardless, however, of whether the Anzacs were aware of the symbolic possibilities that could be woven around their violent work, it was just as much the chroniclers, the official and unofficial historians of their acts, and the numerous other writers at home in Australia and abroad who made the Anzac legend. The official chronicler of the campaign in Sinai and Palestine, H. S. Gullett, is thoroughly aware of the significant potential of a war that engaged Christian and Muslim even as he discounts such a significance. The following excerpt illustrates this point and shows further aspects of the ideology of interpretation that are integral to the development of the Anzac tradition. The metaphors of youth and renewal can be noted.

> There is something unreal and incongruous in the thought of the young Christian Australian Commonwealth engaged in a fight to the

finish with the old Moslem Ottoman Empire. Before the war it is improbable that there were a hundred Turks in Australia or a hundred Australians in Turkey. . . .

Australian and Turk fought therefore as strangers, impelled by no racial antagonism or spirit of revenge, and the struggle, although wholehearted and bloody, was always strangely free from bitterness. The one people waging a "holy war" in preservation of its very life, the other battling for the defence of its motherland and its own place among the nations—no two armies ever fought with less personal animosity a protracted and decisive campaign. . . .

The Australians, who always referred to the Turk affectionately as "Old Jacko," regarded him with sincere respect, touched, as was natural in a manhood, conscious of race superiority, with pity. They found him a clean, chivalrous fighter, and thought of him, it may almost be said, as a temporarily misguided friend. (Gullett 1938: 37–38).

Gullett's shining account is to some extent clouded by the evident racism of the time, present in this excerpt and elsewhere in the text. There is much evidence that the Australian respect for the Turk was in practice not as high as the ideals asserted.[10] Certainly a lot of this can be explained away by the very savagery of war itself. Such would account for what Gammage describes as the "ferocious exultation" of this young Australian at the Gallipoli landing,

I had the good fortune of trying my nice shinny [sic] bayonet on a big fat Turk, he yelled out Allah, then on again we went & I came across a sniper when he saw me coming straight at him with cold steal [sic] he got up & started to run but my nimble feet caught him in two strides I stuck it right through his back. (Gammage 1975, 96)

Without discounting the facts of Australian respect for the Turks, I note its powerful mythic qualities. There is similarity here to the Buddhist chronicles of Dutugemunu, where the Sinhalese king demonstrates "respect" for the Tamil Hindu king, Elara. This respect is a sign of mythic equivalence, which it *must* be in the logical context of the myth. So too, I suggest, is it in the Australian relationship with the Turks. It is symbolically demanded for the Turks to be valorized for the full significance of the acts of the Anzacs to be realized. The import of Dutugemunu's victory for Sinhalese Buddhist identity, moreover, is that it is the transformational encompassment of the old by the new. Elara is the sacrifice in the creation of Dutugemunu as the symbolic embodiment of state and nation. Dutugemunu's respect for Elara signs his repossession of Buddhist equanimity, as the victory of the Anzacs signs their Christian purity of purpose in the midst of violence and their achievement of the identity of nation.

The mythic Australian-Turkish relation is vital to modern Anzac celebration. In 1985 the seventieth anniversary of the Gallipoli landings was celebrated. In a special edition of the journal *Australia Today: From*

The Well of Contemplation, Sydney War Memorial. The statue is located in the center of the memorial. Three female figures support the sacrificed male. They represent the sacrifice Austalian women must bear in the death of their men. The dome above the statue is set with stars representing those who have fallen in war.

The Well of Contemplation: sacrificed male.

the *Heart of the Nation* considerable space is devoted to the Turks. It includes a feature on the Turkish leader at the time, Kemal Atatürk, and an announcement that the Turks had named the Gallipoli landing area Anzac Cove and that Australia had reciprocated by inaugurating an Atatürk Memorial Garden in Canberra on Anzac Day 1985.[11]

I have concentrated on the centrality of the Anzac tradition within the ideological structure of Western Christian civilization. That Australian nationalism is a variation within this ideological form is obvious but is often played down out of concern to assert the specificities of Australian identity. The inclination toward such concerns is itself ideological, and the neglect of the embeddedness of Anzac within Western Christian consciousness reduces any understanding of the power of Anzac symbolism and the force of the egalitarianism embodied in it. Anzac is a "secular" religion but it forcefully engages historically developed Western religious ontologies, in a way no less than the Sinhalese nationalists engage a Buddhist ontology.

My emphasis in no way detracts from the importance of other influences upon Anzac and Australian nationalism in general. At the time of Anzac there was a burgeoning of nationalist art and literature reflected in the work of such figures as Henry Lawson, "Banjo" Paterson, C. J. Dennis, and artists of the Heidelberg school, who romanticized aspects of Australia—the bush, the New Man, the urban larrikin, country folk—nationalistically. Some of those involved in the stirring of Australia's national consciousness supported the Anzac cause enthusiastically. Paintings from the Heidelberg school hang in the Australian War Memorial. C. E. W. Bean and H. S. Gullett, the two great chroniclers of war, carried these ideas of the bush and the New Man, for example, into their interpretations of the Anzac events. I will discuss some aspects of ideas such as the bush in a slightly different context later, but I maintain that it is appropriate to subordinate discussion of them within broader ideological processes, some further aspects of which I shall now pursue.

Australian troops were notorious trophy collectors, even before the call went out from Bean and others for the soldiers to collect "relics" from the places in which they fought. The word *relic* was used at the time, and it indicates the sacred nature of the acts rather than the mere collection of trivial mementos, or outright theft which it most often was.

Some of the relics are now on proud display in the War Memorial in Canberra. Among the more notable is the Shellal mosaic. During a lull in the fighting an Army chaplain in Palestine put troops to work in the archeological excavation of an early Christian church. The mosaic that they unearthed was duly sent back to Australia.[12] Also on display is an inscription "commemorating Athenian casualities in the Gallipoli area . . . against native Thracians . . . probably in the 440s B.C." A note below the inscription states that it is "applicable to the British, Australian, and New Zealand soldiers killed in the same locality more than 2300 years later." Another display is of a wooden statue of St. Roch, patron saint of the plague-stricken, which was presented to the Australian War Memorial by a member of the 3rd Division Salvage Company, who found it at La Neuville, France, in August 1918. These are placed directly across from the spot where the biographies and exploits of Australia's own heroes, the winners of the Victoria Cross, are presented. Thus the spirit of the source, and of the heroic ideals of the beginning reveal a continuity with the symbolic heroes of the new nation of Australia.

Those who possess relics and treat them as sacred identify with what they are ideologically held to represent *and* embody them within the person or—as in the instance of the War Memorial—enclose their spirit in the ideological order of the nation.   If such is true of relics, it is also true of death.

The Anzacs in the Dardanelles, those in Palestine, and those in France and Belgium through their death in essence "occupied" the lands in which they fought and were buried.   In their death, moreover, they were united with the history and traditions of those nations on whose mud and soil they battled.   A verse in the Anzac Book goes

> Bury the dead
> By whose dying, splendidly,
> In that harsh dawn, volley-litten,
> Was our new war-saga written—
> We who "had no history."

Scholarly literature on nationalism, especially in Europe, characterizes nationalist ideological imagination as asserting a continuity unproblematically with the past, a continuity in meaning and import that never existed.   This is a signal point of the critics of current Sinhalese Buddhist nationalism.   Australian nationalism is to some degree a variation. Australian nationalists explicitly recognize a gap, a radical disjunction in their history.   Anzac gains symbolic significance in this context, for the Anzacs forged a link in the ideological chain that had been broken.   There is further import to this observation. White Australians, then and now, are ideologically ambivalent toward the lands of their birth or ethnic origin.   As convicts, free settlers, refugees, or immigrants they were cast out, driven, separated, not just from the land of their beginning, but from their history.   This was given a spatial emphasis in the geographical distance of Australia.   The sense of separation is ideologically counterbalanced by the sense of belonging to that from which one is separated— a feature of many immigrant societies.   This deep ideological ambivalence is powerful in the self-consciousness of Australians, is everywhere evident in the art and literature of the nation, and is a strong part of its historiography.   Such ideological notions are deeply ingrained in the work of well-known modern Australian historians such as Manning Clark (1968) and, especially, Geoffrey Blainey (see chapter 7), but all too often they seem unaware of the power of these notions as they impose their own interpretations and judgments upon history.   This aside, what is stressed here is that the ideas of separation and belonging are potentially in contradiction.   The separation from origins negates claims to membership in the enduring history and traditions of the origins.   The power of such a contradiction is accentuated by the same ideology which continually stresses belonging through such agencies as language, religion, and education.

It is in the context of this argument that Anzac and the key symbol of death find significance. The Anzacs in dying resolved the contradiction between separation and belonging. Their death and reembodiment with the earth of the Middle East, the Mediterranean, and Europe brought Australia in from the cold and in a relation of equivalence with those from whom Australians felt estranged.

The idea of the equivalence of nations does not sufficiently describe the symbolic meaning inscribed in Anzac. There is a strong sense of equal but superior. This is evident in the chronicles and the ever-increasing numbers of books and articles concerning the qualities of Australian soldiers. They are frequently described as not merely equal to but finer than their peers of other nations, ideologically counterweighting an earlier inferiority and thus signing, metaphorically, the process of the Australian achievement of nationhood. This was basically a move from a colonial position of subordination, outside history, to an autonomous position, reunited with history and now instrumental in the forging of history. I present a final, but extensive quotation, from Gullett's official history of the Palestine campaign to create a sense for the nationalist historical moment of the events. He is setting the scene for the movement of the Light Horse towards Damascus. A Major Macpherson is leading the advance.

> The country as usual teemed with biblical and historical associations. Macpherson's ride carried him along the old Roman road down past the stony uplands about Hattin, where "in crusading times the courage of Christendom was scorched to the heart, so as never to rally in all the east again." [Gullett is citing from George Adam Smith's *Historical Geography of the Holy Land*] . . . "The Crusaders, tempted, it is said, by some treachery, came forth to meet Saladin. A hot July night without water was followed by a burning day, to add to the horrors of which the enemy set fire to the scrub. The smoke swept the fevered Christians into a panic; knights choked in their hot armour; the blinded foot-soldiers, breaking their ranks, were ridden down in mobs by the Moslem cavalry; and although here and there groups of brave men fought sun and fire and sword, far on into the terrible afternoon, the defeat was utter." But now, more than 700 years later, Christian soldiers were to ride again over the parched field of Hattin, a simple, wholesome young manhood, conscious perhaps of no high Christian purpose, but single-thoughted in their voluntary duty to their race and country. They bore no relics of the True Cross to inflame their courage; they rode with no mail to protect their splendid young bodies; occasional blasphemy and scepticism marked their vivid speech. But no sworn and fiery Crusader of old carried a more terrible sword against the foe, and none rode nearer to the Christian precept to do justice, love mercy, and walk humbly before his God than these seemingly careless young light horsemen (Gullett 1938, 735).

The Anzacs were not just conceived of as making history but as creating an Australian history to be seen as such on the comparative, contestlike, world stage of war. The ideological stress on war, at the time of the events surrounding Anzac and since, as a kind of sporting event in which rival qualities and skills are matched and tested cannot be overlooked. The Australian history made and pointed to by the Anzacs as the history-making action of a new nation was a history simultaneously continuous with previous orders and transcending of them. The Anzacs signed an order that was uncontaminated by the corrupting entropy which characterized the European nations at war. They embodied the originary pure spirit which signaled the emergence of civilization—symbolically carried in the ancient Greek heroic ideal common in Anzac iconography—a spirit stilled in Europe's decline.

The dominant symbolic themes of the Anzac tradition, themes of warring struggle, death and sacrifice, gain significance in the foregoing ideological context. The horror and suffering of war is one of the chief messages of Anzac. These aspects per se, like the simple glorification of war, which is an often-realized potential of the Anzac tradition, obscure other symbolic dimensions of Anzac that account more profoundly for the centrality of Anzac in Australian cultural life and Australian nationalism.

As I have said, the warring of the Anzacs in historical description and representation is replete with metaphors of a biblical, cosmogonic kind. The hell and strife of war are the originary chaos. The trenches, tunnels, and mud of the fields of war are primeval, indicating a merging with the earth, a reduction to that life-giving clay out of which the form and spirit of a new nation are to be formed. The death of the Anzacs represented as sacrifice is a consciously overt symbol of rebirth. This sacrifice is presented as one of pure and potent youth, a holy, cosmologically regenerative sacrifice.

Sacrifice, of course, for most cultures is a potent symbol of transformation, condensing in its process both the nature of an older order and the form of the new, transformed order. This is no less true of the nationalist symbolism of Anzac. The huge death tolls, the sheer wastage of life, endlessly recalled in the histories and other commentaries on Anzac are metaphors of the decline of human society. The bureaucratic error and mindless authoritarianism often held responsible for the destruction of the Anzacs are metaphors of the degeneration of the old social order. The defeat at Gallipoli achieves some of its significance in this context, for it is, as the record often relates, a defeat of men determined in circumstances outside their control. Their later victories occur in situations in which they are perceived as fully formed in a new, powerful, and self-determining identity.

The youth of the sacrificed, moreover, and the heroic purity of spirit of those killed at the hands of the English and European sacrificers point to the nature of the new order to be established. This new order is one that takes its form through an ideology of egalitarian individualism, the symbols and metaphors of which flood the accounts of the events of Anzac and the Australian cultural discourse surrounding them. A fuller discussion of the new order heralded by Anzac, in the course of an analysis of Australian egalitarianism, has been reserved for the next chapter.

Nationalism as Religious Form

War and death in war are common themes of modern nationalism. The Australian nationalist cult that surrounds them demonstrates the religious form of modern nationalism. More, Anzac supports a general thesis that the cult of nationalism has become the dominant religion of modern nation-states. Dumont's observations on the West, in contrast to "traditional" Asia, appear to be well supported. The "political," the political nation, the territorially sovereign nation and its people, is not encompassed and subsumed within a traditional, typically hierarchical, religio-cosmic system. It has broken free and appropriated as it has transformed ideological and ontological principles of the former subordination of the political into a sacred scheme and practice. What many scholars recognize as the secularization of the modern industrial world can be interpreted in another way. Rather it is the transformation of the religious as the sacralization of the political.

This process of the sacralization of the political in nationalism, whereby it becomes the sacred encompassing, universalizing form, assumes the attitude of an attack on religion. This is so even as it enfolds its ideas and enlivens the deep ontologies of religion, giving them powerful force in new directions. Here is some of the source of the danger of nationalism. The political nation being made the object of devotion assumes messianic and proselytizing dimensions. I consider these to be features of the recent American bombing of Libya as they are of the present tragic conflict between Iran and Iraq. For Australia, the devotional form of the nation—and the wider, extremely nationalist idea of British Empire which preceded it, nationalism in its most devotional and universalizing manifestation—was an inspiration for the fight. Devotion, perhaps most intense at the moment of conversion, inspired the ferocity of Australian troops, what Bean calls their love of a fight. That Australians might love to fight could be seen as ideologically constituted, in the passionate idea of autonomy, for example, but more relevant here, as an act of prayer before the nation, as the duteous and righteous act in the name of a god.

The sacralization of the political through the secular attitude is represented by Bean, possibly the most important architect of the Anzac tradition. He stated in 1916 "I am not a religious man. I don't know that I bear any allegiance to the Christian Faith" (cited in Inglis 1985; 102). Bean and others, in their nationalist functionalism, wished Anzac ceremonial to be universal in appeal and not afflicted by religious sectarian differences, which even in present-day Australia are politically and socially divisive. In the ideology of Australian nationalism expressed here, the nation is subordinated to religion through internal religious division. Such an idea is congruent with the formation of nationalism within egalitarian thought, a point to which I shall later return.

The participation of the clergy in public Anzac ceremonial, now as at all times in the past, is noticeably muted. The clergy perform as the representatives of the state, and the order of prayers and songs is selected to give as little denominational or sectarian offense as possible. The music at the Anzac memorials is played by military bands or by members of the Salvation Army, which is conceived of as the least denominational of Christian organizations, and therefore the most unifying. In the popular folklore of Anzac, members of the Salvation Army were always present at the point of conflict and prepared to tend the soldiers, regardless of their religion. But I note an additional symbolic connection between Anzac and the Salvation Army. The Salvation Army is an army which is yet not an army. So, too, the Anzacs, for they were a fighting force, a free citizen army of volunteers, which was yet not an army. The celebrated indiscipline of the Anzacs achieves significance in this symbolic context. Both the Salvation Army and the Anzacs are better in what they do— more compassionate and efficient fighters—in their negation of the artificial and conventional organizational forms of established religious and military orders. The Salvation Army and the Anzacs manifest the essence of what is natural in humanity that imposed orders deny. I stress the ideology of these values. Recent historians of the events of the war have striven to determine the empirical facticity of these attributes and have underplayed their constructed ideological nature (Gammage 1975; Ross 1985).

The presence of the Salvation Army at Anzac ceremonies contributes to the secular religiosity of the occasion. The Anzac memorials or cenotaphs are located in public, not religious, space, although they impart an air of the sacred to the secular space they occupy. The architecture of the memorials usually blends classical and Christian themes. Small-town memorials are often of a solitary "digger" in a pose signifying death and also peace and guardianship. The imposing War Memorial in the national capital of Canberra approaches the manner of a Mesopotamian tomb, and this sense continues in the iconography inside the Memorial, which encircles the central Pool of Reflection. This Mesopotamian aspect of the War Memorial underlines the originary, primeval quality of Anzac symbolism and traditions discussed earlier. I hasten to add that this opinion is entirely my own, though the Memorial is described as an example of "Byzantine revival" architecture. A critic of the Memorial, an architect, noted the ambivalent aspects of the building in 1928, at the time when the plans for construction of it had been accepted. "It only

The East Window of the Hall of Memory, Australian War Memorial, Canberra. The figures represent (from left to right) the qualities of Coolness (in action, especially in crisis), Control (of self and others), Audacity, Endurance, and Decision. (Photo courtesy Australian War Memorial)

requires some alteration in the windows and doors to make it a typical eastern mosque" (Sydney *Morning Herald*, 13 April 1928). Completed in 1941, the Memorial has been added to since. New wings give it the appearance of a cross when seen from above. The hybrid aspect of the building is symbolically appropriate to a religious-political form, emergent from deep religious and ontological foundations, yet itself encompassing, universal, and not subordinate to any of the religious forms from which the nationalist political religion sprang.[13]

The sacralization of the secular, which is clearly evident in Australian Anzac nationalism, occurred in a broader Western historical movement, the Enlightenment, and in the development of scientific, economic, and political rationalism. These ideas were produced in, as they produced, social and political and ideological transformations in Europe and America. Rationalism, defining itself as an attack on the sacred and the mystical, discovered in these transformational processes its own sacred and religious nature. Revolutionary France and America are particularly obvious and poignant examples, Australia no less so. Australian religious rationalism is powerfully expressed in the virtually sacral nature of common sense pragmatism, and practicality. This is a powerful message of the Anzac tradition. It is virtually sinful in Australia to defy common sense or practicality.

I pursue the nature of Australian nationalist religion through an inadequate overgeneralization of aspects of Australia's historical formation, but in the context of the Enlightenment and its political and social process in Australia. This is important, for I stress these processes as critical to the constitution of Australian egalitarian individualism, the spirit of Anzac. I do so as part of the general thesis that Australian nationalism takes its form in egalitarianism and as such is nationalism of a particular cultural kind. Its symbols, for example, are quintessentially egalitarian, which unites their meaning with other, specifically Western, nationalisms but cannot be reduced to the essential symbolic form of all modern nationalism. The following discussion is also important for an understanding of the separation of nation and state in the Australian nationalist conception.

Australia as a Model of the Western Nation-State

Australia's historical beginning took root within the rationalist ideological argument of eighteenth- and nineteenth-century England. The convict settlement at Sydney, while a pragmatic solution to England's shortage of prison accommodations, became also a conscious experiment of the colonial state in philosophical rationalism. The degradation of the convicts was often horrendous and savage (Hughes 1987). The absolute subjection of the convicts, their loss of humanity and abjection, is inscribed in the ideological consciousness of many Australians. The antagonism to state power that some Australians express, however, is not necessarily driven in the facts of convict history. The antagonism is formed in an ideological attitude in which the convict past has symbolic import. This ideological attitude took form in the development of egalitarian and individualist consciousness that were born under the historical conditions of a transformation into modern Europe from the seventeenth century on. These changes and the growth of modern forms of the state were represented in the political and social philosophies of men such as Hobbes and Bentham. Bentham has been credited with being the primary influence on the forming of Australian egalitarianism by at least one commentator (Collins 1985). This is somewhat overdrawn, but certainly the prison society of New South Wales did in later days take on some aspects of the rationalist, reformist character symbolized by Bentham's "panopticon" (Foucault 1979). All aspects of convict life came under the moral scrutiny of the eye of the state, and the organization of convict society became an exercise in individual and social reconstruction according to scientific rationalist principles (Hirst 1983). The intense rationalism of Australia's beginnings is a marked feature of the cultural life of the nation's social and political institutions. Such rationalism is enshrined in the Federal Constitution, which clearly defines Australia as a secular state representing no religion or particular religious denomination.

The Anzac rites and traditions refract the powerful individualistic thrust of the philosophical rationalism of the founding of Australia. Australian ideological individualism, however, cannot be reduced in a historicist-idealist sense to its rationalist start—as will be seen in later analysis. What I stress here is that Australian nationalism and Anzac are emergent in character in the conditions of a rationalist age. These conditions also comprised the familiar transformations, for example, outlined by Benedict Anderson (1983), into modern capitalism. Some of these were discussed in relation to Sinhalese nationalism and included, among many others, the spread of literacy, the growth of state and private bureaucracy, the ending of community isolation, class formation, and so on. All these contributed to the particular nationalist imagination of community and are possibly most appropriate to those societies that have a depth of history. The relevance of such processes to Australian nationalism might not at first glance seem appropriate.

The foregoing argument is evolutionist in the sense that the present is a transformation upon prior conditions and therefore continuous with the past and ultimately reducible to it. If we exclude the Aboriginal population, which was homogenized in a process of annihilation, there was no historically and cosmologically legitimated social hierarchy and there was minimal specialization of knowledge. It takes some stretch of the imagination and much careful construction to see Australia's population as once distributed among local communities with distinct traditions in Anderson's sense. But it is precisely these factors which, although they appear to make Australia a separate case, reveal Australia to be an almost perfect example of the ideological form of modern Western nationalism. Australia, moreover, demonstrates the egalitarian form of such nationalism. I regard this as distinct from Sri Lanka nationalism, which, while it gathers force in and through the circumstances in which egalitarianism takes root, subordinates egalitarian thought to hierarchical ideological form. In Australia, egalitarian ideology is dominant. This fact owes much to the formation of Australia within the ideological developments of Western rationalism. Additionally, the strength of the egalitarianism owes much to Australia's birth in the state before it was ever a nation. This also contributes to the powerful opposition between nation and state in the conceptions of many Australian egalitarians and establishes Australian nationalism as an important variant from other Western nationalisms with which it is cognate.

Australia could be understood to have begun in the conditions toward which Europe and Asia were changing. Its political form was influenced by the historical processes taking place in Europe. The colony of New South Wales almost from the start could be described as an advanced prototype of the modern state, constituted in conditions to favor the growth of a cult of nationalism. While Australian society develops amid political, economic, and ideological processes that affected the formation of modern Europe and America, especially, its development is also distinct. Its evolution can be seen as a steady growth outward from concentrated, undifferentiated centers.[14] These centers were unified in a single bureaucratic order and, most important, were in effect united in space and in time. Australia, therefore, from its inception took form under historical conditions fundamental to the ideological character of modern Western state nationalism. As Anderson stresses, nationalist ideology emphasises the unity of a people in space and time. Not only do the people stand in a common and equivalent relation to space (territory) but the population is engaged in the one temporality; that is, the imagined character of the national community accentuates a notion that each national member is interlinked with every other in one time frame. All progress through time in unison.

Australian metaphors of space and time have always carried the sense of unity and equivalence referred to in the foregoing. Space and time, moreover, are coincidental. Ideologically, Australia was and is conceived of as a vast open space over which white Australians spread progressively and uniformly. Notions of the outback and the bush, which are critical to the ideological self-representation of Australians, express both a common relation to the one open space and other notions such as the originary and generative quality of this space. Space in the Australian conception is also time, and it is the timelessness of the space that receives particular emphasis. This orientation in the world was present at the historical outset. It was formed perhaps in the ideas of the Enlightenment and compounded in the strangeness of the flora and fauna and in the "primitiveness" of the Aboriginals.

The Aboriginals were initially represented pictorially in the Rousseauesque image of the Noble Savage (Hughes 1970; 29–35). In recent decades Australian Aboriginals have virtually become symbolic archetypes of the unity of space—land, environment—and time. In this white Australian imagination, the Aboriginal concept of the Dreamtime has received particular focus.

This Aboriginal concept is described by Stanner (1956; 111) as conjuring "up the notion of a sacred heroic time of the indefinitely remote past . . . still part of the present." It is also a concept that stresses the unity of humanity, indeed all forms of life, with the earth. They are in animate and regenerative unity. Stanner is aware of the likely misinterpretation through Western ideas of the concept of the Dreamtime. He resists what he calls the reduction of Aboriginal ontology to Western individualism or rationalism. Munn (1970) examines the notion, for example, of autonomy in Aboriginal Dreamtime thought and shows how Aboriginals largely realize an autonomy, an autonomous power, at death. So realized, this power of their being becomes regeneratively fused with the environment. I cannot do justice to such complex ideas here. All I insist upon is that non-Aboriginal Australian ideas of the Dreamtime are born of the magical thought of a modern Western nationalism. Such ideas have nothing to do with the Aboriginal concept and are mystical in the sense that the Aboriginal's is not.

Nonetheless, it is through such mistaken mystical notions of Aboriginal thought that Aboriginals have assumed significance as symbols of nation. Inglis (1967; 34) cites an instance of an Australia Day ceremony in 1961 wherein Australia was symbolized on the dais by "putting a stuffed kangaroo and emu on the right, a stuffed aborigine on the left, and a coloured portrait of the Queen in the centre." Aboriginals have come to represent a system intimately engaged in their destruction.

Aboriginals have become so close to the center of nationalist thought that they have suffered from it. An Aboriginal who departs from Australian nationalist ideals, often inspiring a particular Western conception of the purity of tribal life, its unity in space and time, and its "natural" authority rooted in the Dreamtime, can contribute to discrimination and administrative hardship exercised by members of the dominant white Australian population. The experience of Aboriginal urban and fringe dwellers is frequent testimony to this (Collman 1979).

Many anthropologists in Australia are not immune to such conceptions. There is a zeal in Australian scholarship that relates to the question just how ancient Aboriginals are. That they are often represented as the most ancient, older than anything in Europe, is important, quite apart from any empirical validity, within Australian nationalism.[15] Aboriginals and their Australian world are made older than history and thus encompass all history. History, the making of history, the rejoining of history, it will be recalled, is a major problem within the ideology of Anzac, which presents one resolution to the problem engendered by nationalist ideology itself.[16]

There is a degree of symbolic overlay between Australian nationalist conceptions, for example, of bushmen and Aboriginals. The more famous of Australia's recent bush or folk heroes—men such as Bill Harney, also an Anzac, Xavier Herbert, Jack Absalom, and Harry Butler—are often represented as in close association with Aboriginals. They have that nationalistically valued identity with the earth which the former also achieve through their intimacy with Aboriginal lore.

The Australian nationalist ideological emphasis on unity is present in the value placed upon the idea of the nation as sharing the one space and time. It is also present in metaphors that stress natural unity, a unity of humankind with nature and of order, both individual and social, as being founded in a unity with nature. The separation or breaking of this unity weakens the nation and may visit the destructiveness of nature, or a natural anger (see chapter 7) upon those who threaten a harmonic unity or are unwittingly part of such disruption. This receives excellent demonstration in the Azaria Chamberlain case, which after many years still looms large in the national imagination. Azaria's mother, Lindy, was charged with her murder but alleges that the baby was killed by a wild native dog, a dingo. The case has divided Australians passionately. The event occurred near Ayers Rock, the natural symbolic edifice of the nation. It is a sacred place of Aboriginals but is now also an important tourist center. A best-selling book, *Evil Angels* (Bryson 1985), defends the mother. The facts are immaterial. What is of interest is an interpretive paradigm of the book. It attaches significance to the increase of tourism in the area. An artificial world—a critical problem in the Anzac tradition and Australian nationalism—is presented as breaking a pristine natural unity. The dingo is the evil avenger of a natural world thrown artificially out of joint. The cover of the book depicts the menacing shadow of a dingo on the red desert earth.

The nationalist metaphors of unity in space and time and a harmonic unity with nature are vital to egalitarianism, especially its Australian form. I have discussed briefly the metaphor of the bush. This is not merely a symbolic fantasy of those largely confined to the towns and cities of Australia's highly urban society (Ward 1966). It is a metaphor consistent with egalitarian ideology, which, as I will explore in later chapters, stresses personal autonomy, a natural individualism, unity in similarity, and consensus. The bush and other metaphors capture these ideas and others which are ontologically central to egalitarianism.[17] I stress this because the egalitarian form of Australian nationalism is dominant in the political and social culture of Australia. Few stand outside it.

Nationalist Ideology: Cynicism and Compassion

The foregoing discussion has located symbolic themes that are vital in Anzac within a broader ideological context. Nationalist ideals present in the Anzac legend and rites are prefigured in ideological forces emergent in the historical constitution of Australian society. Anzac enshrines and condenses into sharper focus ideological themes already present in the Australian world. It does not emerge in an ideological void. The point is important not only for an understanding of Anzac and Australian nationalism; it is crucial to a wider sociological view of ideological processes and their relation to the social order.

Two aspects of the sociological discussion of ideology are raised. The first concerns the power of ideology over the imagination and the degree to which it determines or influences social action. The second is related to the first and refers to what many scholars have discovered to be the distorting and mystifying nature of ideology. As I argued in chapter 2, those who have framed their analyses largely in these terms have stressed the pragmatic function of ideology.

Such approaches have not only been extremely materialist but also reductionist in both an individualist and historicist sense. Quite apart from any abstract philosophical or theoretical objections to these points of view, they obscure significant aspects of the power of ideology in social life and can lead to the posing of false questions. An example of the latter is the one frequently asked of Anzac by commentators on the Australian scene concerning the durability of the Anzac tradition. A question such as "How long will it last and continue to hold sway over an Australian imagination?" is not false in itself and may be interesting to ask. It becomes false, however, when Anzac is reduced to a mere pragmatic function and is conceived in a means-ends framework.

Common in the literature surrounding Anzac is an argument by which the Anzac tradition and ceremonial is presented as not just an ideological construction in the interests of promoting a strong Australian national identity and sense of unity, but a construction designed to ameliorate powerful forces of social division and discontent in Australian society, both at the time of Anzac and since. There is much evidence to support such a contention.

The first Anzac march was held in London in 1916. It was organized in the wake of the Dardanelles disaster and its horrible loss of life (McKernan 1980; 120). Australian and British authorities were concerned over its demoralizing effect. The public recognition of the heroism of the surviving Anzacs was regarded as essential to negate the drop in morale among the men.   For Britain it was politically important to ensure the continued support of its erstwhile colonies in its war effort.   Britons were encouraged to turn out in strength to cheer the marching troops. In Australia there was a flagging enthusiasm for the war, especially as the appalling destruction inflicted on the soldiers in the Middle East and in Europe became increasingly evident.   Australian political and military leaders were conscious of the propaganda value of an acknowledgment by the state of the heroism and sacrifice of the fallen.   The development of an Anzac tradition accorded with the numerous stirring recruitment posters.   Immediately at the end of the war there was a problem of social order.   Returned soldiers rioted in the streets of Melbourne, manifesting dimensions of class-based hostilities.   It has been suggested that a conservative motivation to mollify gathering angry divisions within Australian society exacerbated by the war was behind the early establishment of the Anzac tradition (Sydney *National Times*, 25 April 1986).[18]

These are pragmatic reasons of a cynical kind and should not obscure a more compassionate pragmatism.   Most politicians, including the military command, were probably as shocked as were the soldiers and civilians at the loss and terror of the war.   There was a general feeling and demand for rites of national mourning, not only to commemorate the dead but to assuage the remorse of those families and communities devastated by the ravages of war.   During the First World War some small rural communities lost virtually all their able-bodied men, often in a single battle.   Some places in Australia have such names as Pozieres, Verdun, Ypres, Amiens, and Paschendaele.   These are places in the main where returning Anzacs were granted crown land.   The carnage of the war left many small communities bereft of many of their able-bodied men.   Their death created an emotional sense of belonging to those far-off places where the Anzacs had died.

It should be stressed that an important motivation behind the support for Anzac was a concern to celebrate peace rather than war and to record the shocking degradation and waste of humanity entailed by war.   This is a message inscribed in the traditional Anzac memorial service and is made starkly apparent in the long lists of the dead at the memorials.   It was an idea held by the Anzacs themselves and is fervently reiterated by many of those who march today.   Compassionate reasons such as these seem to be important forces behind the establishment of the Anzac tradition.

No doubt there are numerous other reasons for the development of the Anzac tradition.   Its centrality, however, as the national symbol of Australia cannot be reduced to the dynamism or manipulation of influential persons or interested sections of the Australian population, of people like Bean, of prominent politicians and other individual representatives of dominant or subordinate class fractions. This in not to play down the importance of their agency, for they undoubtedly contributed to the shape of the Anzac tradition, as did anonymous members of the Australian public, the Anzacs themselves and their families. What is striking is the great extent to which ordinary men and women participated in the organization of the Anzac tradition. The design and sculpture of Anzac monuments has often occasioned great public outcry—and they have been modified to accord with popular taste (see chapter 6). If for example, Anzac can be regarded as a powerful mode of political and social domination by interested fractions of Australian society, it is so hegemonically, through the willing participation of many of those who could be regarded as being from the subordinated sections of Australian society.

If the nationalist importance of the Anzac tradition cannot be reduced to political pragmatism, neither can it be reduced to the compassion or suffering of a wider public, or to a combination of these. The horror and destructive violence of the events surrounding Anzac achieved significance through a structure of ideological interpretation already integral to the organization of Australian society. If Anzac was created as the symbolic focus of Australian nationalism it arose as such from established ideological ground. Perhaps the sheer shock of the devastation of Gallipoli made it an obvious symbol around which to develop the ideals of Australian nationalism, as Bean often discloses in his diaries in the course of setting himself his own creative task of developing the Anzac tradition. Bean, however, was already of an ideological bent before the occurrence of the terrible events in the Dardanelles. The shock of Gallipoli achieved its significance as a shock *within* Australian ideological consciousness. It was this consciousness acting back on itself through the events of Gallipoli out of which Anzac was crystallized as a core nationalist symbol. The point must be stressed. Nationalist ideologies such as Anzac take form through motivated individual and group action of great diversity. These motivations do not exist independent of the ideas upon which they may pragmatically operate, either cynically or compassionately. In the position advanced here, ideas exist together with their motivational possibilities, as evidenced in the action of individuals. The argument here, then, is one according to which ideas are not separated from reality, which is the case in much materialist analysis. The social world and its ideal representations are inseparable and compose a mutually constitutive unity. This position takes neither ideas nor the reality they refract as one logically prior to the other. If Anzac has served the political interests of individuals and groups differentially located within the social and political order of Australia—and this is easily demonstrated—these interests have been pursued *within* the ideological frame out of which the Anzac tradition has emerged and achieved prominence. Anzac cannot be reduced to a social and political world that somehow exists independent of it, as this world cannot be reduced to the ideas elaborated within the Anzac tradition without consideration of such ideas in relation to the historical social world of which Anzac ideas are part. Furthermore, the nationalist passions of Anzac, in accordance with the foregoing discussion, are as much part of the persons and reality of those who would manipulate the tradition as of those whose relation to the tradition is disinterested in any manipulative sense. It is the recognition that the passion of a collective suffering and pride, a critical dimension of Anzac, is no less a part of those who may stand to benefit from it, which accounts for the power of Anzac in imagination and in action. Those who may come to use Anzac are as much in its ideological grip as those whom they address.

The agents of the state have attempted to make Anzac a central rite of the state. And so it often appears. But an examination of the logic of its symbolic organization reveal it as not such a pliant instrument of state control as some would suggest. On the contrary, there are powerful elements of its symbolic argument which indicate that it is a nationalist rite of the people, but a people in ambivalent relation to the state, a relation of distrust and potential opposition.

6

But the Band Played "Waltzing Matilda"

National Ceremonial and the Anatomy of Egalitarianism

The following analysis is built around the rites of Anzac Day, held every year on April 25. The rite has received much descriptive attention in scholarly literature and is widely covered in the newspapers and the press. The day is celebrated in much the same fashion throughout Australia. The rite begins with the Dawn Service, usually at 6:00 A.M. but in some places much earlier, to fit with the precise moment of the Gallipoli landings. This is conventionally held before the central memorial or cenotaph. The brief service is organzied around the Christian themes of death, sacrifice, and rebirth. The formal service ends with a bugler first calling the Last Post, then Reveille, in between which a short prayer is uttered, "They shall grow not old as we that are left grow old," followed by a minute of silence. The formal wreath laying is then performed. Wreaths are laid by representatives of the state, the armed services, local, state or national government, and various voluntary organizations. After the official parties have broken up, individuals and family groups within the congregation then place their own wreaths at the cenotaph. Often these wreaths commemorate the recently deceased who participated in the wars of the past.

Preparations are now made for the march. Men gather in their military units, which are ordered in accordance with the wars in which they fought, from the first to the most recent. The veterans of the First World War head the march, and the Vietnam veterans, who have only recently been permitted to march, bring up the rear. Men march in civilian dress. Some representatives of the armed services also participate, as do the Boy Scouts, the Girl Guides, and children from Legacy, a charitable organization instituted to help the families of veterans. Women who served in theaters of war as nurses and in other capacities also march, though their role is smaller than that of the men.[1] The marchers proceed, to the accompaniment of martial music, to the central memorial area, which is often located in an area at the edge of the main government, administrative, and commercial centers.   At Sydney, Melbourne, and Adelaide, for example, they are at the margins of the central business districts of the city.   In Canberra almost the entire organization of the rite is focused on the Australian War Memorial, which is located at the margin of the city.[2]

When the marchers have reached their destination the Mid-Day Service, or service of commemoration, begins.   This is virtually identical to the Dawn Service.   The marchers break up, join their families, and share in refreshments.   In the afternoon, which is a highly significant part of the Anzac ceremony as a whole, the celebrants repair to their clubs and the hotels, where considerable quantities of alcohol are consumed.

This is the bare order of events.   The description is based on my observation of the main central rites.   But similar services and events take place in the municipal areas of the larger cities and towns.   The main Australian voluntary association, the Returned Services League, which is responsible for Anzac and the organization of the events of the day, has smaller services in its various clubs scattered through the suburban areas.   Men and women who attend the central service often return to the clubs immediately after the Dawn Service to have breakfast before the March.   In one club I attended the men cooked breakfast on outside barbecues while their wives and children waited inside the club.

The Anzac Day ceremonies are always gaining new significance in their developing historical context.   Themes pertinent to its political world are routinely gathered into it.   In my student days in Sydney I was part of a student protest at the rite as embodying outdated imperialist ideas and supporting gerontocratic rule.   During the period of the Vietnam War it became a focus for radical protest as it also provided a platform for the voicing of conservative nationalist sentiment.   The feminist movement sees it as a symbol of Australian male domination, which is certainly one of its aspects.   Since 1981 Women Against Rape (WAR) collectives have made controversial appearances at the rites, attempting to lay wreaths and being violently resisted.   Members of Australia's ethnic minorities are beginning to make their appearance at the rite, especially those who fought in Allied units or as partisans.   At the celebration in Cooktown, in northern Queensland, the bugler is a former member of Rommel's Afrika Corps.   This, however, has created some disquiet and even outrage elsewhere in Australia.

But my interest here is not so much in the changing historical significance of the rite, although I will have cause to consider it.   What I am concerned with is an exploration of some of the principal themes of the rite, vital to the internal logic of its structure, which persist through historical time.   The overall structure of the ceremony has remained virtually unaltered despite its changing import within lived social contexts.

This lack of change is an ideological product of the conditions in which the Anzac rite was created. The spirit of Anzac is maintained in the continuity of the ritual form. To a degree resistant to the political and social forces of the moment, an analysis of the rite that reduces it to context or that merely concentrates on such forces may obscure certain persistent themes of the Anzac argument locked into the ritual form. My purpose is to unlock these themes, without ignoring the importance of historical context. The themes that are present I consider to be integral to Australian life, regardless of whether one participates in Anzac Day or not. The ceremonial of Anzac Day is a way into an understanding of the processes of much political and cultural life in Australia and, especially, of pursuing in greater depth the nature of Australian nationalism and its egalitarian individualist form.

I shall begin with a discussion of the rite at the most politically central place in Australia, the national capital of Canberra. It is here that the relation of state and nation in Australian nationalism receives its most formal display, as is only to be expected. My analysis will then change its descriptive base to the state capitals in the Australian federal structure, particularly Sydney, Melbourne, and Adelaide, where my experience of Anzac Day is most extensive. It is on the basis of my observations in these cities—but also in small towns elsewhere in Australia—that I show certain aspects of the oppositional character of Australian egalitarianism and of the dilemma of the state in the context of its nationalism.

Nation, People, and State

The organization of ceremonial space in Canberra, this most planned of Australian cities, is noteworthy. The focus of the ceremonial is the Australian War Memorial. This faces the buildings of the National Houses of Parliament. The temple of the people—and symbol of nation—confronts the edifice of the state. Initial plans for the building of the War Memorial provided that it be erected on the hill, Capitol Hill, where the present Houses of Parliament stand. Bean objected to this importation of an American model but was eventually well satisfied with the decision to locate it at the foot of Mt. Ainslie, where it now stands opposite Parliament at the far end of a broad, red-gravel boulevard, Anzac Parade.[3]

The Canberra Anzac rite involves the returned soldiers in civilian attire, but grouped according to their wartime military units, marching from the Parliament House end of the boulevard to the steps at the foot of the War Memorial. Seated above these steps and looking down at the ranks of advancing men are the dignitaries of state, including the official representatives of the diplomatic staffs of other nation-states living in Canberra. Symbolically, people and state are structurally transposed: the people coming from the direction of the edifice of state and the state facing the temple of the people. People and state are created as interchangeable; one is made identical to the other.

Furthermore, the identity of people and state is made ritually egalitarian. "Hierarchy," inequalities of power and status implicit in the rite as a whole, is overtly and systematically negated. Thus the structures that bound the ritual participants, Parliament House and the War Memorial, can be interpreted as at symbolically equivalent height. The state balances the people. In the ritual process the marchers—the people—can be seen as moving from a position below the edifice of state toward the representatives of state who are seated above them. But these representatives are seated below the War Memorial. The whole rite, of course, is conceived as a homage by state and people to the fallen, which theoretically unifies state and people in relation to the fallen. It is also conceived as an occasion when the state gives homage to the people.

Anzac ceremonial in other Australian centers refracts a similar fundamental people-state opposition and apparent resolution in identity. Observations in Sydney, Melbourne, and Adelaide indicate that the opposition is of a far less balanced form than at Canberra. This is consistent with Canberra's position as the national capital, the symbolic center of the state and nation, and thereby a place where the idea of the state, and the forces potentially in opposition, will find the most intense expression. Away from Canberra and in the other cities Anzac ceremonial reveals itself more powerfully as a celebration of the people. The agents of the state give homage to the people, and establish an identity with the people. But in a way the state is subordinated, overwhelmed almost, by the people.

This is especially evident in the ceremonial in Sydney, but with local variation it can be witnessed everywhere. Following the Dawn Service, which is held at 4:30 A.M. in Sydney, the entire center of the city, concentrating at the cenotaph in Martin Place, becomes an assembly ground of men in their civilian dress, often adorned with campaign medals and others, gathering into their respective service units. The march is led off by a riderless horse, a pair of empty boots in the reverse position. This is followed by riders who represent the celebrated Light Horse of Anzac tradition, succeeded by a car of state carrying the state governor. Symbols of sacrifice, specifically the sacrifice of the *ideal*, are succeeded by the symbol of state, which—indicated by its position in the parade— is in effect in subordinate unity with the ideal, which is nothing less than the quintessential spirit of the people.

There are two symbolic moments in the Sydney Anzac ceremony that can be interpreted as marking a distinction between people and state and their mutual transposability along the lines described for Canberra. They occur at the beginning and at the end of the march. Situated at the point at which the Sydney march begins and in a direct line with the cenotaph is an empty chair, on which is placed an Australian soldier's slouch hat. A salute is given as the marchers pass the chair. The chair and the hat belonged to Australia's "Little Digger," Billy Hughes, the Australian prime minister from October 1915 and for a number of years following.[4] Hughes, in this symbolic situation regarded as a populist hero, a champion of the common man, a "battler," typifies the spirit of the ordinary people.[5] Thus the salute of Hughes's chair can be interpreted as the people recognizing the nature of its collective identity in the idealized person of Hughes. Further, if Hughes refracts the people, he also symbolizes an ideal of a perfect unity of people and state. This is so in that Hughes, as the prime agent of the state, is the state as an extension of and symbolic embodiment of the people. At the end of the march, which is reached below the Sydney War Memorial located on high ground at Hyde Park and in a parallel line with the State Parliament, the state governor receives—and returns—a salute from the marching men. People and state, in their reciprocal recognition and honoring, also realize an equivalence and sign an essential identity.

The discussion of Anzac ceremonial has pointed not only to a people-state opposition, but also to an identity between people and state. Interpretive care should be taken, however, in the examination of the nature of the people-state equivalence and identity as it has been presented in the analysis so far. The symbolic importance of Hughes is that he expresses an ideal. The Anzac rites represent little real identity with the state. It is rather an identity with the nation and in the person of the federal or state governor, who transcends the governing and practical arm of the state apparatus. The governor, in effect, reflects the collective unity of the people in the nation, which is signed in the marching of Anzac. The marching—or progressive movement—of the people sym- bolizes their generation of the nation. Essentially they, people and nation, encompass the ruling arm of the ordering state. A possible contrast can be observed here between this idea and that of Sinhalese Buddhist nationalism, where the central metaphor is of the state embodying and reproducing the nation.

That the people are dominant and that the people constitute and generate the nation-state are key messages of the Anzac Day events. On Anzac Day the people occupy the towns and cities of Australia. They occupy central urban space, which is also the locus of government administration and authority. In Australia central urban space is clearly marked as principally the area of administration and work and is not conceived of as living space. At the end of each working day and on weekends the centers of the cities and towns are deserted. In recent years civic authorities in Sydney, Melbourne, and Adelaide, for example, have attempted to build up the central areas as places of public and family life along a European pattern—and with a little success. But the point remains: the ordinary family and social life of Australians is enjoyed away from the urban centers. This observation gives significance to the occupation of central space by the people on Anzac Day. They take over that area which is the symbolic focus of state authority and power.

The Authority of State and the Power of the People

The power of the people is asserted. On Anzac Day there is a blossoming of officials, or marshals. These are men—and a few women—who organize the marchers at their assembly points, assist with the control of traffic or the ordering of spectators, and so on. The officials are from Returned Services League clubs, are former servicemen, and are elected by the members of the club. It should be stressed that the RSL clubs are not restricted to former servicemen and include as members a larger number of persons who have never seen military service. In the eastern states of Australia—Queensland, New South Wales, Victoria, and the Australian Capital Territory—the RSL clubs are among the largest centers of popular leisure and entertainment. They are the principal places, with the pubs and football clubs, for the expression of the cultural life of the common man. The RSL, of course, are not the only organizations that provide officials. Voluntary organizations such as Legacy, the Scouts, and others also provide such assistance. Even members of the Salvation Army virtually adopt official status and become important sources of information and direction concerning the ceremonial proceedings.

The various officials that spring up on Anzac Day are the representatives of the people, even the people's police. From the people, they are the legitimate controllers of the people. That this is so is revealed in their relation of contrast with the State Police, who are very much in evidence on Anzac Day. Their presence is clearly a response to the need to regulate the movement of the large gatherings on Anzac Day and to the cultural expectation that Anzac Day is typically an occasion when incidents of public disorder are likely to occur. This very expectation is, in effect, recognition that Anzac Day is potentially a time when the order imposed by the authority of the state may be challenged. Indeed the police are customarily restrained on Anzac Day and do not apply the letter of the law. As far as possible they attempt to present the exercise of their authority within the terms of the spirit of Anzac. The people they attack most freely, therefore, are those who appear to contradict the idea of Anzac itself. Thus, students who have protested what they saw as the militarism of Anzac and feminists who have regarded it as a symbol of masculine destructive oppression are savagely attacked by the police, sometimes with the muscular aid of the veterans. When the police are not trying to merge with the spirit of Anzac they often appear to take a backstage role, giving way to the authority of the people's officials. Even so, there are numerous occasions on Anzac Day when the authority of the police will be resisted by the celebrants, perhaps willfully. In contrast, few instances of the resistance to the voluntary officials, if any, will be seen. The key to an understanding of this is contained in the very fact that the police are not voluntary. They perform their work as work defined by the state, independent of the people. The police, moreover, act involuntarily, not as individual, independent, free-spirited persons who give their service as an act of free will. It is the symbolic fact that Anzac officials embody these aspects of individuality, exemplifying the ideological spirit enshrined in Anzac and Australian nationalism, which gives these officials their authority and power. Acting in the perfect spirit of Anzac, they are the legitimate controllers of the people and symbols of the assertion by the people of their dominant power on Anzac Day.

The comparison between the police and the Anzac officials is, of course, between two very different modes of authority and power. The police derive their authority from the state and a right to use force; they also possess the coercive power of arrest. The Anzac officials have no coercive power. They can act only with the willing assent of those to whom they issue directives. Their determination is the determination of the people. A critical point of difference between the police and the Anzac officials is that the latter, having no powers of arrest, are unable to act against the interests of the people. The police as agents of the state can act against the people. The presence of the police at such a heightened time of ideological consciousness as Anzac Day accentuates the thematic tension of Anzac, which is the potential opposition between people and state. The occasional taunting and baiting of the police by the Anzacs and a certain motivation to disorder is both an expression of the rivalry of opposing powers and an assertion of individual autonomy, of the power of the person, acting independent of the state.

Of People, Power, and Drink

Not only is the power of the people dominant during Anzac Day, the celebrants are quite literally drunk with it. The smell of alcohol is distinctly noticeable at the Dawn Service and in the streets as the marchers and spectators gather. The pubs in all the towns and cities are opened early, and for some celebrants a tot of rum is ritually required—for such was issued to the original Anzacs as they prepared to land at the Dardanelles. But the drinking begins in earnest at the clubs and pubs following the march and the concluding midday service.

The drinking at Anzac is not merely an expression of camaraderie, a spiritous facilitator of sociality. This is a common interpretation and does not reach the heart of the matter (Kitley 1979; Sackett 1985). Drinking is of ideological import in Australia as a sign of personal autonomy, as an ingredient in the formation of personal power. Australian cultural discourse flows with the connection between drink and power. Drink fortifies, strengthens, empowers, as did that preparatory tot for the Anzacs years ago. Drink, specifically spirits, has bite, "nip." Its potency is uncontrolled, and it is the ability to control or tame the power of drink that is stressed in the culture of the Australian male. Drinking and apparently being unaffected by the alcoholic content of the drink is admired, all the more so if large quantities are imbibed. Indeed, Australian males consume huge quantities of beer, not simply because beer may be good to taste and quenches thirst. The thirst-quenching properties of beer in Australia could be doubted in view of the large amounts that require downing before the thirst is killed. Australian men are motivated in Australian culture to drink beer and in large quantity. To "hold your booze" is a highly valued masculine virtue, and those who quickly become drunk, or "two-pot screamers," can be the target of ridicule (as I have often been). The "beer belly" is a major physical indication of drinking capacity, of the ability to hold. An Australian man will point with some pride to his billowing gut and sometimes slap it with affection. Recently the beer gut has fallen into some disfavor, partly as a result of the influence of a cult of physical fitness, which takes as its chief indicator a slim appearance. Before this recent cultural change physical fitness and considerable drinking abilities were taken as synonymous—as the beer advertisements made abundantly clear.

The consumption of drink is to appropriate its power, and the more that is drunk, the greater the power gained. Further, the control of this power, indicated by strength of brew—Cunnamulla Needles over proof rum with a beer chaser can inspire admiration—or quantity consumed coupled with little evidence of apparent effect, is tantamount to signing the power and strength of the imbiber. Alternatively, failure to consume reasonable quantities or outright resistance to drinking is to indicate weakness, a tendency to the female rather than the male. Men in New South Wales often regard the "wowser" states—Victoria and South Australia, which until the 1960s had fairly stringent drinking laws—as "weak" and "female."

The association of nondrinking with the female has historical basis in Australia, where until recently women were allowed only restricted entry into the hotels. These restrictions were founded in ideological conceptions of the weakness of women, their supposed inherent physical inability to hold such strong stuff. The power of booze, in effect could therefore control them rather than be controlled by them, and thus "metaphorically" they were "polluted"—a serious matter, given the cultural emphasis on the purity of women and the centrality of female purity to the maintenance of domestic order. A common word for drink is *piss*—typically beer, but occasionally the word is applied more generally. The term indicates the potentially polluting and destructive properties of drink and therefore the power of those who consume it. Through the ridicule of other men or other intentional demeaning action men are sometimes referred to as "having the piss taken out of them." Essentially this means that they have been weakened, reduced, and feminized in the eyes of their male peers.

It must be emphasised that to get drunk, to be pissed, is not necessarily valued. "You're pissed, mate" is an expression used with some disdain, even disgust. The expression typically refers to someone who is out of control, who does not know his limit, and who is apparently incapable of ordinary rational talk. Individuals who need a "bellyfull of grog" to shore up Dutch—artifical or false—courage are demeaned. It is possible for someone to be so drunk that many of the ordinary physical functions, such as walking, are endangered. Such a person may be called hopeless, but as long as his social action is judged rational, his drunkenness is not deprecated. He has, in fact, consumed large quantities but demonstrates continuing control and command over the power of drink. Being "full" is not being "pissed"; it refers to someone who is filled to physical capacity but generally is not drunk and is still capable of orderly behavior. In some quarters of Australia it is considered reasonable to have a "constitutional chuck"—to be intentionally sick—so as to reduce the level of liquid in the stomach in order that more can be consumed.

The drinking on Anzac Day, therefore, is an expression of individual power, of autonomy, of individual control. It is also, within the cultural terms outlined, reinvigorating and regenerative. The heavy consumption of alcohol on Anzac Day, virtually a cultural and national duty, is literally reempowering. This meaning is iconic with the symbolism of Anzac ceremonial.

The organization of ritual events is such as to trace a transformation from death to rebirth. The main drinking begins at the point of rebirth. The Anzac ceremony engages its participants in their own rebirth as well as that of the nation, and this is signed in their drinking. Further, through their drinking the Anzac Day participants can be interpreted as actively contributing, effecting perhaps, the rebirth, not only of themselves but also of the nation. The Anzacs restoring their individual power and personal autonomy in drink also restore the nation, a nation ideologically conceived as founded upon their individualism.

The symbolic aspects of drink discussed here are by no means unique to Australia. There are many features of Australian drinking lore that should be recognizable to North Americans and British but possibly less so to Europeans. Such similarity is related to the dominant individualist ethos of these cultural regions. As in all cultures food and drink are filled with social significance and symbolically refract the ideology of the social world in which they are consumed. In Australia an extraordinary amount of symbolic effort has been played onto "booze" or "piss" that reveals not only aspects of Australian individualism but also certain features that may be distinctive of Australian individualism or accentuated in comparison with the phenomenon as it can be observed elsewhere. Additional critical features of Australian individualism as it achieves heightened significance in Anzac must be seen in the context of egalitarianism. A brief return to the Australian cultural valuation of drink in relation to egalitarianism will extend an understanding of Anzac as a specific symbolic condensation of the egalitarian individualist ideology.

Drink and the Practice of Being Equal

Drinking in Australia, as everywhere, has to do with social relations. Especially in public places such as hotels, one should not, ideally, drink alone. To do so purposefully is either a sign of dementia or is open to interpretation as aggressively antisocial. Drinking alone in an Australian pub can be a decidedly uncomfortable experience. This is because human beings in Australian egalitarian culture are social in nature. It is natural to drink with one's "mates." Australian male drinking is symbolic of "mateship," a critical theme in Anzac tradition and an aspect of Australian culture continually referred to in Australian scholarship and in popular writing.[6] Mateship is germane to egalitarianism, at once expressive of its ethos and a central principle of social coherence. Much of the Australian literature on the topic stresses it as male friendship. It is certainly most frequent between males, but it is not exclusive between them nor is it exclusively about friendship, although friendship develops because of it. Men have women who are "mates," and many women in Australia are now stressing a kind of mateship ethos among themselves. Mateship can be interspecies. In egalitarian cultures particularly there is a virtual cult of pet lovers, a phenomenon that may not, absurd as it may seem, be unrelated to the principle of mateship. A verse written by a light-horseman in Palestine expresses the sentiments of mateship to his horse:

> How the mateship grew in the depths of you,
> When the waste spread its gauntness wide.
> How you parched with me, how you marched with me,
> Through that hell of a thirst denied.
> (Cited in Ross 1985, 76)

Mateship in my view is an egalitarian principle of natural sociality and reciprocity between equals. It is the basis of natural society, the way society forms, independent of artificial mediating institutions such as those implicit in the concept of the state. The force of mateship, of natural sociality intrinsic to human beings, is most powerful between those identical in nature and acts cohesively upon them. Mateship as natural sociality bridges any unnatural or artificial difference. To reduce the idea of mateship to friendship or to comradeship is not to comprehend its meaning fully and to fail to grasp deeply the Australian antagonism to the lone drinker. The lone drinker is not giving vent to natural sociality and is ontologically threatening.

Australians typically drink in groups, in groups of mates. Those people who are regular drinking companions sometimes refer to their groups as schools—as in schools of fish; Australians also refer to themselves as "drinking like fish," and when full as being "filled to the gills." This term indicates the character of Australian egalitarianism, which stresses notions of collectivity, undifferentiated identity, and unison in movement. Australian males are strongly group-oriented but in a way that neither subordinates the individual to the group nor sacrifices the personal autonomy of the individual.

Pub drinking groups are egalitarian par excellence. The institution of the "shout"—less commonly, "round"—is directed against any social differentiation, or distinction, conceived of as derived from the ordinary working world. Quite simply, the shout involves one person buying the drinks for all the others in the group. It defines membership in the drinking group. Once the shout commences it is theoretically not completed until every person in the group has bought all the others a drink and, ideally, at once. Failure to shout can bring disgrace, and if one departs from a group before shouting for some unavoidable yet under-standable reason—because the wife might "go crook on you" for not getting home at the right time—this must be done with profuse apologies. Often people deposit the required amount of money on the bar as they leave. The shout is an excellent example of what Levi-Strauss (1969) has called generalized exchange, which he identified as the pattern of reciprocal giving of gifts in non-Western egalitarian societies. The shout places all the drinkers into equivalent relation, regardless of social or economic position. Indeed, the shout facilitates the formation of drinking groups that cuts across the social differentiation of the outside world. A person can enter a group on a more or less immediate understanding that he will participate in its life on an equal footing. The shout creates equality and contributes to the marked disposition of Australian drinking groups to encompass persons of different social and economic backgrounds and positions of power in society. The shout is actively antagonistic to distinction—as is Australian egalitarianism as a whole—and in the practice of it there is pressure to resist differentiating factors or else to refuse actively to recognize their emergence should they intrude.

Shouting can be financially crippling, the more so the larger the group, and drinkers tend to close ranks by forming a tightly packed circle. Newcomers to the pub may be given a nod of acknowledgment but in a way which indicates that they should join some other group. Mixed orders that involve more expensive spirits rather than the cheaper and more common beer are problematic for those "short in pocket." The inequality in expenditure between different shouts is stoutly unattended to; all shouts in a school are treated as if they were equivalent. This points up a critical feature of the shout and of Australian individual egalitarianism in general. What can be called the moral economy of the shout values the equality of the persons in the group and their individual autonomy. Any complaint about the relative expense of a shout threatens individual autonomy and can be personally demeaning.

Observers of Australian drinking may detect a certain competitive character to the drinking: the considerable quantities of drink consumed are a consequence of competitive drinking. This feature is one manifestation of the high value placed on individual autonomy coupled with the stress on equality. Drinkers must consume in synchrony, together and at the same rate. They must not fall behind. Not to keep up is to endanger recognition of one's autonomy by others and to give evidence of a certain lack of natural equality. Individual autonomy and the equality of individuals are interdependent. Australians do not deny their autonomy in their egalitarianism; they emphasize it, but they do so in a way that also reinforces the sense of the collective.[7]

The discussion of drinking has stressed the antidifferentiating dimensions of Australian egalitarian individualism. This is a vital characteristic of the Anzac Day marches. The Anzacs march in unison but in a manner that gives full expression to their individuality. They march in accordance with the ideological valuation of the Anzac tradition, which in certain respects is antimilitaristic; that is, while Anzac Day assumes militaristic symbolic form, the ideas enshrined in it in some measure contradict militaristic values—at least as these are conventionally accepted independent of Anzac ideology.

The Anzac tradition lays great stress on the individuality of Australian soliders, giving particular attention to their insubordination, their flouting of the disciplinary rules of the military order, and their independence of spirit. These emphases in Anzac discourse will be discussed further in a later section. For the present they reveal the metaphoric aspects of the military symbolism of Anzac.

The armed services as collectivities marching in unison symbolize the egalitarian ideal, but only insofar as this does not subordinate individual autonomy. The marchers, by giving expression to their own individuality in the march—they wave to friends in the crowd who may call out to them by name or momentarily break rank to talk to relatives or friends— in effect point to the nonmilitary nature of their action. This is underlined by the fact that the marchers generally do not, and many insist that they should not, march in accordance with their erstwhile military status—as officers or as privates, for example. Military symbolism in Anzac has little import outside Australian egalitarian individualism, and the apparent stress on military symbolism in Australian nationalism is fashioned to the service of egalitarian ideals that may even be countermilitary in spirit.

Routine Australian drinking gatherings and Anzac marching valorize the individual in groups. But even more, Australian individualism carries the powerful notion that the ideals of society are embodied in the individual. This is not merely the idea that the individual is prior to society or the atom, with which the wider structures of society are eventually built. It is the notion that the ideals of a perfect society are already embodied within the individual, the Australian male individual. In this conception, individuals are not formed in society; society, in its pure and distilled potentiality, is preformed in the individual.

The Australian ideal of the individual male has resonances with Rousseau's conception of the Noble Savage, although he stressed that the savage was noble because he had no society. This is not the view of Anzac egalitarianism, wherein valued society is already in nature and intrinsic within the individual. Australian ideological thought is closer to the anarchist conceptions of Kropotkin and Bakunin, who saw human beings as naturally embodying ideal sociality and given to the self-effacing reciprocity of mutual aid. Reciprocity and sociality are not produced through the force of society or the state but are already essential in the human being. One sense of the egalitarianism in Australian thought concerns the belief that human beings are naturally given to share and to come to the aid of others. This, of course, is premised on the related conception that all unique individuals are essentially alike in nature and that to help another is identical to helping oneself. Thus ideal society as an expression of egalitarian values is an extension of the individual.

Earlier, attention was drawn to the symbolic link between drinking, the closing stages of Anzac celebrations, and the reempowering of the individual and the reassertion of individual autonomy. A further point can now be added: the closing events can be interpreted as symbolic of a reassertion of the nature of an ideal social world premised on or generated out of the individual ideal.

Autonomous Society and the Order of the People

Observers of Anzac have commented on the "disorderly" aspects of the day, not only the heavy drinking but the relaxing of rules of state order. Noteworthy is the open playing of Australia's traditional gambling game of two-up. Once officially banned, the two-up "schools," in popular folklore at least, flourished in secret places. On Anzac Day the authorities conventionally turn a blind eye to the spontaneous forming of two-up schools in the pubs and the clubs.

Sociologists (Kitley 1979; Sackett 1985) have likened the closing events of Anzac Day to the symbolic reversals described for ceremonial or ritual events in other cultures. A variety of functionalist explanations has been advanced. These have ranged from simplistic psychologisms such as that the events enable the letting off of steam and other repressions caused by society to the potentially more promising thesis of Gluckman (1954) that the events constitute "rituals of rebellion"—that is, ritualized forms of social and political protest organized in an ultimately nonthreatening way and harnessed to the maintenance of the sociopolitical order. The latter argument—unfortunately too often parodied in analyses of Anzac and elsewhere—bears a close connection to the interpretations of ritual advanced by anthropologist Victor Turner (1957, 1969). The reference here is to Turner's general observations on the structure of liminal events in ritual and the form of their symbolic emotionalism, which is defined by Turner as *communitas*. Unfortunately, too, these explanations have suffered when applied to Anzac Day. Thus commentators have focused on the togetherness, mateship in the sense of emotional closeness, interpretational possibilities of Turner's ideas, and have thereby trivialized them. Turner's discussion of liminality and communitas, however, is relevant to this analysis. Its salient features, therefore, will be outlined briefly here.

Liminality, for Turner, is a moment outside time and structure or that period "betwixt and between" one condition of the person in society, as ritually constructed, and another. It is a moment in a process of psychological and social transition—and its model is that of the life crisis rites of birth, initiation, marriage, sickness, and death—wherein different modalities of individual and social experience and order are joined. Liminal periods, for Turner, take on the symbolic character of the personal and social ordering they conjoin. Thus their symbolism is sometimes that of confusion, and their reality symbolically marked as dangerous and often filled with the action and imagery of violence—all of which indicates the powerful conjunction of contradictory forces in the personal and social process and the power of occurrent transition and transformation. The essential aspects of all modalities of the person and society are revealed in liminal periods, and the most poignant symbolic forming of these essential aspects is described by Turner as communitas.

Communitas, in Turner's elaborations, can take a variety of forms. Basically, however, it is an assertion of the oneness of humanity that exists below the differentiation and separation caused by social orders. Implicitly the assertion of communitas is simultaneously a critique of the social orders created by human beings, a criticism of their hierarchy and social distance, and an expression of the character of a fundamental indivisibility of humanity from which the personal and social order is to be constructed or reconstructed.

The concepts of liminality and communitas appear almost tailor-made for an understanding of Anzac. Thus, the drinking and gambling of the closing events can be interpreted as consistent with a liminal ritual moment preparatory to the reassertion of the state and social order—the ideological aspects of these being carried within the liminal period and revitalized through the Anzac ceremony as a whole. The drinking and the gambling both engage notions of individual autonomy and egalitarian unity and conform in their particular Australian way to what Turner would identify as communitas. But the fit is almost too pat. This is surprising since Turner based his distinctions on the study of the rituals of a nonindustrial society, the Ndembu of northwestern Zambia. Indeed, the extension of the concepts to the setting of Anzac ceremonial, the nationalist rites of an industrial nation, obscure some fundamental differences in applicability and meaning.

While the concepts of liminality and communitas may describe some of the outstanding features of Anzac, they do not apply to particular moments of the ceremony but to the ceremony as a whole. Over all Anzac is a ceremonial process within the sociopolitical order, an order which in nationalist ideology is claimed as essentially unchanged and enduring. Unlike rites of transition, especially those of tribal societies, it effects no transformation in identity or in the nature of social reality. It does mark the moment of nationalist recognition, a time of national origination. Liminality and communitas, as described by Turner, are themselves symbolic formings of origination. In this respect they are a unity in space and time, in effect the beginning of all space and all time. Nationalism as discussed earlier asserts nothing less than the unity of the nation in space and time, and such an emphasis is to be expected of the central rites of the nation. In the circumstances of modern nationalism, therefore, national ceremonial is likely to adopt as a whole ritual form, rather than a particular section of the ritual, that which dominantly expresses the origin and unity of space and time.

Furthermore, it is obvious that nationalism in modern, large-scale, usually industrial, nontribal societies is all about idealism, whether of the political right or of the left. A distinction between the ideal and the real is central to the ideological consciousness of modern nationalism and those encompassed within the territories of modern nation-states. Such a distinction between ideal and reality probably reached full fruition in the ideological consciousness of those populations affected by related ideological developments connected, for example, with industrialization, scientific rationalism, secularism, and so on. But whatever may have given rise to the distinction is unimportant here. More significant is that the assertion of ideas and the playing out of action labeled for convenience as communitas in the ideological context just described is the objectified declaration of the ideal which at the same time is conscious that it is not congruent with the experiences of daily life. The critique detected by Turner in that action he calls communitas is probably most relevant to those societies in which there is strong ideological distinction between ideal and reality.

Indeed, on the basis of this analysis I suggest that the concept of communitas is probably most applicable to modern, nontribal societies and, furthermore, to those founded in ideological variants of egalitarianism. This may be why Turner's concepts seem to fit—not because of any inherent properties of scientific generalizability but because of their essential ideological constitution.

I suggest further that the communitas of tribal society is of an entirely different order from that of modern industrial society, a possibility suppressed in Turner, and that an analytical tendency by anthropologists or sociologists to infer a similarity of import should be treated with some suspicion. The tracing of parallels between non-Western thought and practice and Western industrial ideas and action is an ideologial growth industry of the West, in particular. It is ideological in the sense that Western ideas and practices, in common with all ideology, attempt to assert their authenticity and dominance through a process of naturalization; that is, they assert that the social and political situation of human beings is founded in nature and rooted in humanity per se. A trend of the naturalization of ideology is to establish a link with the primitive, with that order conceived as the pure prototype of modernity. To a degree Turner's analytical extensions out of the Ndembu, for all their insight, are open to this charge. In those societies, like tribal communities, in which ritual is understood as constituting and determining the personal and social world, there is virtually no distinction between the ideal and the real. Communitas *is* the reality and is the taken-for-granted ground upon which the real is constituted. It requires no assertion and contains no criticism beyond a tacit realization that where there is no communitas there is no society and no humanity.

The concluding events of Anzac are an extension of the idealizations of the individual and social order of the preceding ceremonial events. They are an actualization of the order that has been modeled previously. This is so in that the ideality of the people is asserted and brought into a relation of symbolic dominance. This ideality takes the form of the people without, or independent of, the state. It is the apotheosis of the natural, spontaneous, society without the artificial ordering and restraining mechanisms of formal authority—the bureaucracies of government, the organizations of private enterprise—and frowning morality, represented by the church and reforming citizenry, who are the recurrent butts of popular folk humor.

The worlds of play and leisure, of the pub, of illicit gambling, spill out into the streets. The ordinary formal and informal rules of order of even the routine everyday world of leisure—the pub and the club—are suspended, and momentary, novel modes of order come into being.[8] Thus in some pubs there are music and dancing, and women—and sometimes children—still ordinarily a rare sight in the front, public bars of Australian hotels, despite changes in attitudes and drinking regulations, are more obviously in evidence. Often these women are the wives of the male regulars.

These events of the afternoon manifest the ideal world of the people. This world is founded in perfect individual autonomy, which in itself generates the perfect society of a mutually oriented and socially engaged collectivity of equals, signed in the metaphor of comradeship in war. Through the preceding events of the day the perfect spirit of the dead Anzacs is made continuous with and embodied in the living. In effect, the potency of the dead, released through their sacrifice, inhabits the living, whose reciprocal action, in accordance with the ideals of the dead, maintains the spirit of the ideal nation and society. The drinking and the gambling on Anzac Day are virtually sacred duties. They are the sacralized practices of ordinary men. The living, as the ceremonial of Anzac Day reiterates, are the custodians, indeed the guardians, of the spirit of Anzac—of its individual autonomy and social egalitarianism. Some of the aggressiveness that celebrants do occasionally display on Anzac Day is not a mere consequence of drink, for example, but is motivated by their sense of guardianship. A feature of the closing events of license should be stressed. Their atmosphere is as often maudlin as it may be joyous. This fits with a dominant tone of Anzac Day as a whole. It is a rite of mourning, and there are features of its closing stages that resemble an Irish wake more than anything else. But perhaps the note of sadness is even more poignant, revealing the deeper tragedy of the idealism that is integral to egalitarianism. The ideals that Australians celebrate on Anzac Day are present only at the peripheries, at the margins of the everyday routine and working world. They are presented in ritual as being at the center of Australian nationalist consciousness and at the root of the nation. The sadness of the closing events may, in part, be a recognition by the celebrants that their ideals and their individual autonomy are, in reality, swallowed up in the artifice of imposed orders. When Australians mourn at Anzac they may not only be sorrowing at the death of their comrades in war and since but also at the experienced reality of their own loss of autonomy and their inability to determine their own lives in the ordinary social and political world.

The entire discussion, especially the point of the argument now reached, demonstrates a general feature of nationalisms elaborated within an ideological consciousness of egalitarian individualism. This is, of course, the claim that the nation is founded in the people and upon their individual qualities. It carries the dominant idea that the nation-state is nothing other than the transcendent realization of that which it encompasses territorially. The nation is individual, a person, and the individuality of this nation is fashioned according to the character of that ideal individual present at its beginning.

All those anthropological, sociological, and psychological national character studies of Germans and Japanese and those researches, notably by anthropologists, who generalize about the personalities of peoples living in defined cultures, have been engendered largely in those centers of scholarship that are included in nation-states formed through individualist egalitarian ideologies. The arguments of the students of national character manifest the same kind of nationalist ideological form as the very national orders they sometimes criticize and are potentially active in the reproduction of the types of prejudice against which they may inveigh.

There is an additional aspect to nationalist argument of the egalitarian individualist kind: the nation as the transcendent individual is also the guardian of the ideal and distinctive human qualities at its source. Within this conceptualization the nation in essence appropriates the spirit of the people, and its different state apparatuses are seen to function ideally in the interests of the reproduction of the ideal individual qualities that the nation embodies. The social and political discourse in Australia, as elsewhere in the West, over morality, legal responsibilities, education, ethnicity, and so on, is constructed in accordance with such ideologically constituted nationalist concerns.

Anzac Day in many respects can be interpreted in the light of the foregoing. Thus the events of the day are a peeling back of superstructure of the state to reveal the vitalizing spirit of the people underneath, at the base. The reinstitution of the state after the holiday of Anzac is symbolically the appropriation and embodiment of the people by the state. This is a valid understanding, critical for the legitimation of the state.

Among nation-states formed within the conditions of egalitarian individualism the issue of legitimacy has an enduring problematic specific to it. This is so because the individual autonomy preached as a central part of egalitarianism potentially conflicts with the loss or surrender of this autonomy to others, specifically agents of the state. One resolution, part of the fury of Western political philosophical discourse from the seventeenth century on, is precisely the argument that the state embodies the pure spirit of the people and is the guardian of this spirit. Further, the individual autonomy of the people is protected in the organs of the state, even against the autonomous actions of others who may deprive individuals of their essential autonomy. The state—but not necessarily its individual agents—is legitimate in its very embodiment of egalitarian individualism and in its protection of the related ideals. Well-known political philosophies of the state such as those of Hobbes and Locke extended the terms of the argument: the state, specifically the rational sovereign state, was the institution that guaranteed the rights of the individual and maintained the order of moral society. The state as it was conceived, moreover, assumed the individual function of producing society. In accordance with this idea the people relinquish their autonomy to the state so that, paradoxically, their autonomy and social order can be preserved and perpetuated. The state is charged as the legitimate guardian of the people and the reproducer of society.

The foregoing, a model for and of the nation-state in England, bears important similarities to and differences from Australian nationalist ideology. Sacrifice in war, the most common symbol in modern Western nationalism, in Anzac as elsewhere, is the most powerful metaphor of the surrender of personal autonomy. Death in war is the ultimate sacrifice, not only because it is a loss of life and of human potentiality, but also because it constitutes the effacement of self. This is sacrifice indeed in societies fueled by ideological individualism. Death in war as tirelessly intoned in the nationalist litany is the quintessential gift of the people to the state.

Anzac Day as a whole can be interpreted as taking its symbolic form in the ceremonial structure of gift exchange. Thus the events model the gift of the people of their services and lives to the state and the acknowledgement by the state in return of this gift. The final stages of the Anzac celebration find their significance in this structure. For the state, by relaxing the rules of its order and bureaucratic authority and giving the cities and towns back to the people, returns to the people their autonomy, which was initially their supreme gift.

Egalitarianism and the Idea of Nation

In the sense described, Australian Anzac ceremonial and celebration must be among the more perfect representations of the Western theory of the modern nation-state. There are, however, certain critical features of Anzac Day and of its general ideological composition that indicate important variations within, or departures from, the Western, more specifically English, model of the state. The main variations appear at the related levels of the state as guardian of the people, the state as reproducer of society, and the surrender by the people of their autonomy to the state. The variations at these conceptual levels, it is stressed, are matters of degree, not absolutes. Refracted through Anzac Day they represent a marked degree of ambiguity, not to say tension, in the relations between nation—people—and state as these can be conceptualized. This ambiguity, which of course is by no means absent from other Western state nationalisms, achieves its form in Australia as a historical working out of alternative possibilities of egalitarian individualism. Australians, the people from Down Under, popularly represent themselves as the inverse of many things Northern Hemispherical, especially English and European. Indeed, ideologically their egalitarian individualism goes in the reverse direction.

The argument of Anzac is not that the state is the guardian of the people but that the people are the guardians of the state. More precisely, the state—its instituted bureaucracies and other agents and organs of government—mediates the guardianship of the nation, a unity of space and time, by the people, a collectivity of individuals. Essentially, the nation and the people are identical, the nation being the higher encompassing and organizing form.

The primary symbol of the nation, as in all modern nation-states, is the armed services. Within the Australian Anzac tradition the services, as previously explained, are a symbolic forming of egalitarian individualist ideals. The services, moreover, are presented as the fighting face of the people, created by the people and protecting society—the social relations of which are constituted through egalitarian ideals—which is generated by the free will of the people.

That the services are the people as ideologically conceived is revealed in the antimilitaristic character, even in the midst of the militarism, of the Anzac ceremonial, as described earlier. Looked at this way Anzac Day conforms perfectly with Durkheim's argument about religion as society worshiping itself. His classic study, *The Elementary Forms of the Religious Life* (1965), based on an analysis of traditional Australian Aboriginal society, probably accords more closely with the white Australian ideological practice of Anzac. Durkheim's general sociological argument on religion certainly reflected his own position within an ideological world of scientific rationalism and egalitarian individualism. In the ideology of Anzac the people guard themselves, the nation. This points to a specific resolution of the problem of the loss of autonomy in the situation of modern Western state nationalism. In effect, the people do not surrender their autonomy. Their sacrifice is a gift to themselves in the interests of autonomous control or determination of their own perpetuity as a nation. Their autonomy and individuality are only momentarily lost and are held in trust by the state, not appropriated by it. The state does not, as evidenced in Anzac, achieve a stable identity with, or encompassment of, the people. Uneasy lies the Australian state.

Two earlier points concerning the significance of the Anzac ceremonial now require modification. While Anzac reveals the people as the basis of the nation, it does not expose them necessarily as at the root of state or as embodied in it. Further, the closing events, which can be interpreted in the context of Western theories of the state as a reciprocity of autonomy, are simultaneously more and less than this. Thus the events are ideologically a return of autonomy per se and not a mere symbolic acknowledgment of the value of the gift while permanently appropriating it in safekeeping. An ideological and transformational resolution, whereby the state is presented as constituting nation and people and producing and supporting society is incomplete, these functions remaining with the people.

Anzac Day betrays an antagonism between people and state and a degree of conscious separation between the two. This is reflected in the attitudes of the public when the armed services have become identified with autonomous state decision or have misconceived their symbolic role in Anzac Day and have appeared too nakedly as a representative of the agency and power of the state, not the people. Conventionally, military might in the form of displays of weaponry is subdued if in evidence at all.

When, at the height of the Vietnam War the army attempted to turn Anzac Day in Adelaide into a recruitment drive by heading the parade with tanks, the organizers of the ceremonies and the Returned Services League, an association noted for its right-wing, militaristic views, were acutely embarrassed. The Vietnam War was extremely divisive in Australia, among the veterans as among the general public. It offended the ideals of Anzac, moreover, for not only was it conceived of as an unheroic war at the time, it was service by conscription rather than by the exercise of individual and voluntary will. The Vietnam veterans gave up their autonomy unwillingly and unheroically in the face of the power of the state and thereby revealed the state as not of the people. Vietnam veterans for a long time felt unwelcome at the Anzac march. Their exploits have only recently been added to the Anzac tradition in the national War Memorial. Time has allowed the Vietnam War to be presented in the Memorial as a heroic occasion, thus, as in the case of the Second World War, offsetting the fact that the service was forced, not voluntary.[9] The recent acceptance of the Vietnam veterans in Anzac is also connected with the growing view of the Vietnam War as the cause of the pointless suffering of Australian men, an example not just of state bureaucratic bungling but an instance of the state harming the people. The acceptance of the Vietnam veterans was clinched by the evidence of state suffering unleashed on the men as a result of the wartime use of the defoliant Agent Orange.

The closing events of Anzac Day have the sense of Gluckman's "rituals of rebellion," as some have asserted (Gluckman 1954). But if so, unlike the traditional Swazi rites upon which Gluckman bases his argument, they are not transformed in the encompassing institution of state. There are no ceremonies that formally close Anzac Day. The drinking and gambling of the afternoon, which are recognized as important to the day, just peter out, a hangover merging into the routine of ordinary life. Although the state makes every effort to muscle in on the day the formal state apparatus is in many ways made marginal to the occasion. This is especially so in the state capitals away from Canberra, the national capital. Anzac Day is the celebration of nation and people independent of the state. Anzac Day is unofficially, by the action of the people, Australia's national day. The formal day of the nation as state is Australia Day. It is a day that is treated as little more than an extra holiday by Australians. The agents of the state are attempting through strong appeals to Australian nationalism to make it a more celebrated occasion. So far there has been little success. But the nationalist interest in Anzac Day appears to be on the increase. The number of civilian spectators who appeared in the streets for the 1986 Anzac parade in Brisbane and Sydney, for example, was greater than in earlier years.

Heroes and the Natural Order

The Anzac tradition and the symbolism of Anzac Day articulate an ambivalent view of the state, a view within which is ingrained the state as potentially the enemy of the people and a strong inclination to regard state interests as separate and not necessarily identical with those of the people. This fundamental attitude of Anzac is driven from within an egalitarian individualism which is crystallized in the Anzac hero, the symbolic type of the tradition. This hero is immortalized in monument and in the interpretations of both popular and scholarly historians. It is this hero whose symbolic form is assumed by the marchers on Anzac Day. The people become hero and in their collective embodiment of the Anzac heroic ideal display some of the aspects of an Australian individualism that generates an enduring distrust of the state.

The Anzac hero has many qualities. The more noteworthy, perhaps, are his lack of discipline, verging on insubordination; his ingenuity and common sense; and his self-effacing, often self-annihilating, assistance and loyalty to others. These qualities are ideologically conceived as natural to the hero. In his possession of them the Anzac hero manifests in uncontaminated form what is essential in all human beings. A brief consideration of these qualities will extend earlier analysis on the import of egalitarian individualism in Anzac and, too, the function of this ideology in the nation-state opposition that is characteristic of Australian nationalism.

The celebrated indiscipline of the Australian soldier is actually a metaphor of his autonomy and his resistance to an order imposed artificially from outside the individual. His sometimes riotous escapades, no less part of the Anzac legend, are ideologically valued as the surfacing of an essential autonomy in conditions under which his independence has been unnaturally subordinated. Indiscipline, in addition, is an indication of the vital purity in nature of the individual. Brought under legitimate control it is the force of the characteristic courage of the Anzacs, which leads to their eventual superiority in battle. Thus, the rioting of the Anzacs on Good Friday (see chapter 5) in the brothel quarter of Cairo—action which, incidentally, has its moral defenders—was the manifestation of a pure vitality, a vitality realized in the courage and conquest of suffering at Gallipoli.[10] Ultimately, therefore, what may appear to others as indiscipline is, in reality, not so. It is rather the manifestation of the vitality of autonomy, the essence of individuality. The implicit critique of externally constituted social orders contained in the metaphor of indiscipline is carried further in the idea of the inherent common sense, the fundamental rationality, of the Anzac hero.

Rationality is natural to the individual. It appears both as common sense and as ingenuity, naked cunning. Perhaps, the single most-commented-upon aspect of the Gallipoli campaign is the retreat. As the story goes, the Anzacs left the bluffs of Gallipoli under the eyes of the Turkish troops but unnoticed. Only six lives were lost, a fact that is regarded in tradition as nothing short of miraculous. The "miracle" of this event, immortalized in the National War Memorial, owes all to Australian ingenuity. Tins were attached to the triggers of rifles left in the trenches and drip filled with water so that they fired at random, creating the illusion that the trenches were still manned. The retreat in effect is symbolically presented as a victory for ingenuity and common sense. The defeat at Gallipoli is in reality a victory for the people. Their inherent rationality permits their escape unharmed in the face of the enormous irrationality and failure of common sense of the state that was instrumental in the horrific death of the Anzacs.

Indiscipline, insubordination, and common sense as the heroic qualities of the Anzacs are interrelated. Thus the insubordination is valued as often the legitimate protection of the individual against the irrational and autonomy-destroying potential of superiors or those who act not as natural individuals but as representatives of an imposed order.

The individualist ideology of Anzac is not unambiguously anti-authoritarian. It constitutes instead an argument concerning the conditions of legitimate authority. Authority is legitimate when it is exercised by a person demonstrating natural common sense and who gives evidence of his right to position as a function of other qualities, perhaps enhanced, which are natural to individuals in general and thus shared with those whom he commands.

The commander-in-chief of the Anzacs was General Birdwood. Born English he was yet unlike his countrymen as typified by Australians.[11] He fit the Australian cultural category of the down-to-earth "good bloke." A photograph in prominent display at the War Memorial shows him swimming naked off the shores of the Dardanelles. To swim naked, of course, is to shed all signs of identity in an imposed social order.

The question of authority and the hero raises the related question of egalitarianism as inscribed in Anzac and the Australian hero. Egalitarianism has a variety of senses. As already noted it is understood as the perfect spirit of sociality that is fundamental to the nature of man. It refers to both the quality of person and the quality of social relations. This can be glossed as a form of self-effacing humility whereby individuals do not assert the dominance of self over other in accordance with their social identities in the nonnatural world. The aspect of egalitarianism referred to here appears to be grounded in Judeo-Christian thought, as Dumont and others have argued more generally.

In the Body of the People: Dawn Service at the Australian War Memorial. Australians, many of them civil servants and politicians in Canberra, carry candles into the War Memorial in memory of Australia's war dead. (Photo courtesy Australian War Memorial)

One of the most heroic symbols in the Anzac tradition is the stretcher-bearer, Simpson. The legend is that he was a private who had enlisted under an assumed name; his real name was Kirkpatrick. He had a record of insubordination. Simpson was, however, known to everyone from the general on down. Nicknamed Murphy, Simpson, often against orders and under withering fire, would extricate the wounded and bring them back to safety, carrying them on his donkey, Duffy. Patsy Adam-Smith describes him as "An Englishman with all the qualities of a legendary Australian." Indeed, while in Australia before the war Simpson had "waltzed matilda," tramped through the bush, independent and outside the constructed differentiating society, carrying all his worldy goods—his "bluey"—on his back. He is thus the individual embodiment of the transformation to national identity that is the core of the Anzac message and one that I shall pursue in relation to Australia's immigration policies in the next chapter. Simpson died at Gallipoli in the course of his saving work. Patsy Adam-Smith, in full ideological flight, gives this account of the significance of the event.

> [It] is one of the great tragedies of that war of tragedies, for "Jack" Simpson was a *real* man, and when he died real men wept in the sight of others. He had flouted the rules and "never heard" of the regulations. In camp before he left Australia, in Egypt, and at last on Gallipoli, he was a man to have with you when the whips were cracking. In the back streets of Cairo when there was a stoush on and the call went out "Aussie Here!" he answered and was as nippy with his knuckles as the next man (Adam-Smith 1978, 122).

Simpson is virtually a saint, and a bronze statue to him, labeled simply "Man with a Donkey," is on prominent display in the War Memorial. Like most saints he is in his person almost an inversion, a negation of identity formed in a differentiated and hierarchical social order. Simpson's negative, saintly aspect is a model of egalitarian ideals, of the compassionate and equal treatment of other without concern for self or social identity. The Anzac egalitarian heroic ideal as indeed saint is iconographically evident in the stained glass windows, not unlike those one may expect to find in a church or cathedral, of the Hall of Memory in the National Memorial.

> Each of the fifteen panels in the three windows portrays a figure in the uniform and equipment of the 1914–18 War. Each figure typifies one of what were judged to be marked qualities of Australian service men and women (Australian War Memorial, Canberra 1975).

Egalitarianism and Inequality

The egalitarian idea of Anzac specifies that human beings are equal in nature and that their social relations follow from this natural equality.

This does *not* argue that individual differences do not exist. Indeed, the character of Australian egalitarian individualism, like the individualism elsewhere in the West, is precisely the opposite. Individual differences do exist, but as unique differences in nature. Anzac egalitarianism stresses a commonality in nature. It is not an argument which states that individuals are naturally equal—that is, that there are no natural individual differences separating them. The egalitarian interpretation, one rooted in the tradition of Western philosophy, of the equality of rights, of opportunity, encapsulated in the expressions "Fair go, mate," "Fair crack of the whip," or "Fair suck of the sauce bottle," is based in the related notion of individual autonomy. The social egalitarianism of Australian nationalist–Anzac ideology extends from above. Social difference must be a difference founded in nature. The only legitimate difference is that premised upon and growing out of a demonstrated natural difference. All social differences, in the ethos of Anzac egalitarianism, must ultimately discover a legitimacy in a reduction to the natural. The ideology of social egalitarianism is set, not against social difference per se, but against that which is not reducible to qualities held in nature. Ingrained in this interpretation is the idea of the potential artificiality of society, society as a social product not reducible to man in nature, society as sui generis. In this aspect of egalitarianism there is almost a sense that society, which is sui generis a world of social relations formed independent of nature, is evil and is set against nature.

Australian egalitarianism is directed against the artificial and the imposed, and Australian humor takes this form. It is typically deflating, sarcastic, and reductive. Ordinary good-humored discourse works on the principle of understatement. Common expressions are "You're not wrong Norelle" (You are absolutely correct, if a bit obvious), "Not hot today, Jack" (very chilly), and so on. Occasionally a negative indicates a positive: "Old Bastard" can be an expression of intense affection. The Anzac Book overflows with examples.

The egalitarian attack on social inequality is upon those social identities and relations not founded in differences that are based upon a commonality in nature. In practice the force of egalitarian ideology is present in the concern of persons to demonstrate their social distinction as natural. This is clear in the cultural attitude toward intellectual and physical pursuits.

Sport in Australia is probably more highly valued than intellectual activity, perhaps because it can be linked more readily to demonstrable differences in nature and to the power of pure spirit. But I suspect that in the Australian imagination there is a ranking of sports that has to do with the degree to which the skills they require are based on natural talent rather than that which is artificially produced. The social relations and the individual inequalities formed in the Australian sport world in many ways constitute an ideal social reality. Entry into this reality and acceptance as a legitimate participant enables the presentation of identity formed in a social reality potentially conceived as unnatural to be shown as "actually" based in nature. Sport is the arena for the conversion of the unnatural into the natural.[12] It naturalizes that which is conceived as socially produced and reproduced. For this reason sport is an important symbolic arena for the playing out of contradictions integral to egalitarian ideology. What is natural and artificial in the sport world is the constant stuff of discourse. Heated disputes repeatedly revolve around the entry of social and political forces from a socially created and therefore unnatural world into the realm of sport.

This brief discussion underlines the ideological significance of the sporting metaphor in the Anzac tradition. An outstanding hero of Anzac, Lieutenant Jacka VC, is the symbolic center of a World War I recruitment poster which has scenes of sporting life in the background. The poster reads "Enlist in the Sportsmen's Thousand—show the enemy what Australian sporting men can do."

Education, specifically problematic within Australian egalitarian individualism, is an area in which arguments premised on politically right and left positions are focused. The social distinction based on educational learning and qualification is not necessarily the outgrowth of natural talent—a fact that is obvious to academicians and to the population in general. Considerable effort is poured into educational argument and funding, to demonstrate that unequal educational opportunity, created by sending children to privately funded schools, either is justifiable because it is the exercise of individual autonomy or is in some other way based in nature. Children are already naturally talented, for example,—and thus can, perhaps should, attend unnatural, inegalitarian private schools— for they are the natural extension of their parents, whose power and position is likewise based in nature. Just conceivably the private-school emphasis on sport—character building, school spirit, and so on—is motivated in part by the ideological concern to naturalize their social production of distinction. In this sense private schools can be understood as one of the principal institutions for the reproduction of an egalitarian ethos. It is paradoxical that those centers of egalitarian educational practice, the public or state schools, where natural intellectual talent is ideally to be given its opportunity—and the inhibitions of an artificially created social world of unnatural inequality are to be overcome—can become the symbols of antiegalitarian, autonomy-depriving, state power. What I am suggesting is that the issue of education in Australia, the debate about private or state education, is ideologically framed within a people-state dialectic that engages ideas such as those concerning the conversion of the artificial into the natural.

The valuation of natural talent in intellectual pursuits, as in sport, is common to the experience of many who have grown up in Australia. At school students should not be seen to study if their academic success is to be accepted as legitimate. A natural brilliance must be displayed. This ideological theme is present in the characterization of prominent Australian politicians and in their attitudes toward each other. The present prime minister has a "God-given brain," a statement made by his mother that was used in a popular biography (written before he became leader of the Labor Party and was elected prime minister) which energetically builds Hawke in the Anzac image. He is variously described as "a Wild Colonial Boy," a "middle-aged boyish man," a boozer, and a Digger. Hawke's opinion of his predecessor, Malcolm Fraser, is cited: "he's got a second-rate mind . . . needs to work tremendously hard to get on top of information" (D'Alpuget 1982, 311).

Australian egalitarianism is not antagonistic to inegalitarian distinction per se; it establishes the ideological terms of its existence. This is that distinction, inequalities in power and status, should be demonstrated as extending from individual qualities found in nature.

The egalitarian practice of negating or underplaying achieved identity in a social and political world is constituted in a particular consciousness in which a potential disjunction is perceived between the commonality of man in nature and the artificial, constructed, and imposed world of status and power differentiation in the ordinary working world of political and economic life. The underplaying of identity is also congruent with a second principle of Australian egalitarianism, that of individual autonomy. Indeed, the underplaying of identity and recognized status and power in social relations is a valued cultural method of asserting and gaining legitimacy for such distinction.

To underplay one's identity in the face of others' awareness of distinction is to be become a "good bloke," for it constitutes a manifestation of naturalness. It is a rule for the operation of bureaucratic, managerial, or organizational power that individuals who wield it act at the same time as if their position in the structure is of little moment. A person who engages this rule, which can be understood as protecting the other's natural autonomy, may on occasion be referred to as an "original," "a real original," "a fair dinkum bloke," or "a dinky di [Aussie]."

The negation of differentiating identity, the suspension of the signs of an unequal world not founded in nature, unites figures such as General Birdwood with the men whom he controls by virtue of the very structures from which he distances himself. Through this principle of egalitarian suspension, evident in the form of Australian humor, as it is in the sanctification of Simpson, inequality and hierarchy are created and legitimated in the realization of their common basis in nature.

"Tall poppy" is a conventional Australian expression for that person who not only sets himself above the crowd but systematically presents an identity formed in the structures and processes of an artificial world. Tall poppies are offensive in the Australian egalitarian conception, for they sign a separation from others (the possession of qualities unnaturally produced—schooling (being self-taught is a natural wonder), inherited wealth, and so on. Tall poppies are more frequently those who invert the principle of egalitarian suspension; that is, they assert dominance, leadership, and superiority by virtue of qualities that separate them from others. They refuse the natural sociality of egalitarian suspension and assert the distinctions and differences born of created social realities, those which are not reducible to the natural. Some of the most notorious tall poppies are politicians. They insist on an unnatural world and become the agents of its imposition.

Australian egalitarian individualism is an ideological form which recognizes that the various aspects of human experience are not congruent with its ontological thesis concerning the autonomous commonality of human beings in nature and society as an extension of the natural. This is the basis of its particular idealism and the foundation of the continual egalitarian attempt, in the practices of Australians, to render reality in accordance with the ideal. At the heart of Anzac is the recognition of the possibility that society, rather than an extension of man, is a negation of him. This becomes most apparent in the political institutional form of the state and its bureaucracy. Their power subsumes the individual and can appropriate that generative potency which Anzac ideology argues strongly to be natural in man. This is the procreative power to generate society, which the state assumes to itself. It is problematic in relation to Australian egalitarianism and constitutes an Australian ambiguity toward the forces of state power.

The broad kind of ambivalence described is present in most modern nationalisms, particularly those of the West. It is out of the anger of the populace against forms of state oppression that many modern states took their present form. The danger of state excess in the political ideologies of state formation has led to the variation in the formal political order of certain states, as it has led to a complex framework of constitutional law. The very framing of constitutions has illustrated consciousness of a need to protect the people from the state. State constitutions that supposedly enshrine the ideals of the people are in many nation-states a matter of some national pride, as reflected in continual reference to them. The long-term scholarly interest in the state—and the more recent critical concern with state nationalism—is formed within an ideological consciousness of ambivalence, at the very least, toward the state and the structure of state power.

The Anzac tradition, however, is perhaps among the most highly developed of those nationalisms that give evidence of powerful distrust of the state. Society is in man and in nature, and ideally in the Anzac tradition it is no more than the sum of its parts. While this is undoubtedly an aspect of other egalitarian individualisms they appear to have achieved a resolution whereby society is conceived of ideally as based on but greater than the sum of its parts and that this greatness is enshrined within, and ensured by, the state. The state has been created as a higher, transformed dimension of the natural, and as such it is often represented as having an identity with God and as protecting God's natural law. Unlike the United States, for example, Australia has no individual hero who, like Abraham Lincoln or George Washington, combines in his person nation, state, people, and individual.[13]

Australian nationalism has sacralized the people and their practices. In this distinct variation on Western egalitarian nationalism, the Australian version highlights certain aspects of egalitarian ideological systems. It accentuates individual identity as critical to social and political life and generates a crisis of legitimacy for the state, for its agents, and for its institutions.

Anzac Day celebrates the identity of the Australian individual, his—and, to a lesser extent, her—natural qualities, and the force of natural sociality among those who share the one identity. This social bonding and essential harmony in identity is the potential of the individual and is generated independent of any external agency, manifesting itself in all its purity as comradeship and, above all, mateship in conflicts and in wars that engage national others of different identity. War reveals the sociality born of mutual recognition in identity a sociality that is in the individual and society. Indeed, the natural sociality of the individual generates society and its institutions, notably those of the state. The individual, the collective individual or people, and their bonded cooperative order, the nation, are one. The higher units, people and nation, are premised on the individual. In contrast to Sinhalese Buddhist nationalist principles, Australian nationalist ideology, like all egalitarian ideologies, places the primary value on the individual and makes the individual—and the qualities inscribed within and generated by the individual—creator of the whole. In Sinhalese Buddhism, the whole, ordered in the principle of hierarchy, constitutes the parts and their personal integrity.

The value placed on autonomy, on individual self-determination, and on the determination by an autonomous nation, is a powerful part of egalitarianism generally and is particularly strong in the Anzac tradition. Drinking, fighting, gambling, and insubordination are the metaphors of both an Australian and an Anzac culture of individual autonomy. I note that this autonomy is one created independent of the state and that individuals, by exerting it, actually gave birth to the identity of the Australian state. This is underlined in ideology, wherein the national day of principal ceremonial significance is Anzac Day, not the day the first settlers landed or the day on which Australia formally achieved its independence from England. The state, then, is determined through the autonomy of the people and in effect is subordinate to and included within the people. Quite the reverse is true of the Sri Lankan situation discussed earlier.

In effect, Anzac and Australian egalitarian individualist nationalism argue that the moral order and its revitalizing and reconstitutive powers are with the individual and the nation. The state is not a moral entity unless it is embodied in the people and the nation. The state is not necessarily immoral and evil but it can virtually become so when it moves into encompassing, and incorporative position. In other words, the state becomes threatening and destructive when it denies its determination in individual and in nation. Again the Sri Lankan material throws the point into relief. The state in Sinhalese Buddhist thought becomes powerfully destructive, indeed moves outside itself, when it becomes reduced to its fragmented base, metaphorized by the demonic, and the incorporated parts become determinant. In Australian thought, if the state or other agents and institutions of potentially supraindividual power, such as corporate organizations, industrial firms, and bureaucracies, begin to assert their power in such a way as to deny autonomy and be unreducible to the qualities of individual and nation, they risk identification as morally evil and become the legitimate objects of resistance, often violent.[14] The people can assert their inherent morality even against the state, in which their identity is not formed, as it is for the Sinhalese.

The ideological import of the Australian conception can be witnessed on Anzac Days when some prominent and not so prominent politicians, representing both the political left and the right, make it a point to march in the body of the people.[15] Recognition by those in power, in governing state institutions and in private enterprise, that they can be identified as evil and illegitimate—not Australian—motivates them in their concern to be identified with the people. They recognize this and act accordingly because they conceive of the world in the same egalitarian ideological terms as those from whom they may expect resistance. In Australia at present huge efforts are being made by the state and other agents of propertied and industrial power to assert an Australian national identity. This effort is being made at a moment of political and economic crisis and transformation in Australian and world history. This is not merely a mechanism of cynical ideological control. Those in power are acting within an ideological framework of their own awareness of their potential illegitimacy within Australian nationalism. Anzac is not a duping of the people, telling them that they have a power when they do not. I referred earlier to the sadness of the closing events of the day, saying that this indicates a recognition by Anzac egalitarians of their lack of autonomy in fact. This view was portrayed excellently in the well-known Australian play *The One Day of the Year* (Seymour 1962). The play, popular during the 1960s, caused an outcry and angered some Anzacs, perhaps the anger of truth recognized. It dealt with generational conflict, the growing antiwar attitudes of Australian youth, but focused on the tragedy of the returned soldier-father who had to confront his own failure and lack of power. What I draw attention to, however, is a power the people may indeed have in their egalitarianism, though not that of individual autonomy. Their ideas may be determining in a situation in which the rulers are, as I have argued, internal to the ideology, which they therefore cannot fail to engage. Furthermore, the people are powerful in the negative sense in that their egalitarianism creates, as I have said, a constant crisis of legitimacy for the state and its representatives. Australian egalitarianism ideologically enshrines a resistance to and suspicion of the state, which may motivate the officers of the state to greater efforts to conform to the will of the people. The representatives of the state are going to extraordinary lengths at this very time as Australia approaches the Bicentennial of the landing of the First Fleet to embody the nation in the edifices and ideological order of the state. This can be dangerous, as the chapter to follow will indicate, for there are possibilities in egalitarianism that can cause great suffering when harnessed to the machinery of state, a suffering perhaps even contradictory to some of the ideals of Anzac, yet consistent with its logic.[16]

I am not saying that Australian nationalism enshrined in Anzac is not a force of domination. My argument is directed toward showing how, indeed, it can achieve such a powerful function. Anzac egalitarianism in domination has force, not because it is merely a weapon of cynical use by persons external to it, but because they are deeply part of it. Australian egalitarianism, insofar as it is integral to the constitution of being, of the way people habitually and unquestioningly tend toward the horizons of their experience, can lead to the ready acceptance by the powerful and weak alike of arguments and of a social and political course that may cause them and others considerable suffering, even against some of the ideals they express. There is a logic within egalitarianism that can be manifest, as some commentators on the Australian scene argue, in a fragmented conception of the social order, a view of inequality and the suffering that may be related to it as reducible to individual qualities and not founded in social relations. The intense stress on individual coherence in autonomy can be a factor in breaking the kind of unified class action that is important in Marxist analysis. The sacralization of the individual and its practice and, in Australian political culture, the presentation of the male as "holy" hero, is a significant ideological element in the Australian subordination of women and in discrimination against them. The ceremony of Anzac Day identifies the male as heroically unified with nature and thus a generator of such unity. The male encompasses the female as a greater, more potent natural force. Through his sacrifice he comes to constitute the female identity, her very being, as he did the nation. The vital, powerful regenerate nation in Australia is male. The symbol of Australia is male, not female, as it is in many other countries. England is referred to as the "Mother Country" by Australians whose own country, transformed through the action of men at Gallipoli, becomes symbolically male.

The iconography designed for the Sydney War Memorial and the disputes over it further demonstrate the point. This memorial is perhaps the most cosmically egalitarian of all the memorials in Australia. Most of the important memorials in Australia—those in Melbourne, Canberra, and Adelaide, for example—list the names of the dead. Not so in Sydney. The dead appear individually, however, each as a single star in the firmament fixed into the central dome of the monument. This dome is the canopy over a statue contained in the Well of Contemplation. It depicts a naked youthful soldier lying on a shield and hung like Christ over the Sword of Sacrifice, supported by three women—mother, wife, and sister or daughter. The women, as the brochure, issued at the time of its design, states, signify their "burden of sacrifice," which they share "equally with the men" but which was created ultimately through the sacrifice of the potent youth of the male in the creation of the nation. In my interpretation the dome and sculpture together signify the embodiment of the female in the male, the constitution of the being of the female in the male, and ultimately her reproductive and fertile capacity as having been created through the male. This interpretation is supported by the rejection, after social and religious protest, of two other monumental statues designed for the memorial (White 1981, 136).

The rejected statues signified "Crucifixion" and "After Sacrifice Victory," respectively (see illustration). The former shows the crucified body of a naked woman, her head bowed, and at her feet are the bodies of the dead soldiers. The latter statue shows the naked woman resurrected, hands held regeneratively aloft, but with the dead men still at her feet. Much of the outcry was centered on the moral decrepitude of the naked female form.[17] I consider, however, that there was possibly a deeper motivation. To present the female form in such a way was not only to deny the regenerative force of the male but also to deny the fundamental ontological and ideological position that the female is embodied within the male.

It is entirely conceivable that the considerable opposition of feminists in Australia to their cause, not only from those who march on Anzac Day but more generally, is connected to the particular centrality of the male in Australian egalitarian ideology. This is far from an original point, though I think that an inspection of the logic of Anzac and Australian nationalism creates a stronger analytical understanding of the phenomenon. For women to assert equal rights, an autonomy independent of the body of men, is to act like the state separating from the body of the people. In Australia they can become virtually demonic, "Damned Whores," as expressed in the title of one well-known book by an Australian author,[18] ontologically threatening, not just to individual male beings, but also to the ideal ordering of the social world as a whole.

Australian egalitarian nationalism, then, can defeat its own ideals. It creates identity as particularly problematic, particularly identity which does not conform to that identity which determines the whole. This

The Crucifixion of Civilization, Sydney War Memorial. (Model; never erected)

After Sacrifice Victory, Sydney War Memorial. (Model; never erected)

brings me to the issue of the next chapter, the character of intolerance in Australia as an aspect of the function of egalitarian ideololgy ingrained in practice. I shall concentrate on the relation between Australian nationalism and modes of thinking and acting in relation to ethnic identity. The discussion will be extended by issues related to the conceptions of nation and state addressed through the analysis of Anzac to isolate some further features pertinent to a cultural understanding of social and political processes and the forms of inequality and suffering that may be intimately connected with them.

7

Ethnicity and Intolerance

Egalitarian Nationalism
and Its Political Practice

"What is more surprising in the Australian Dominions, is, that . . . this
great country is flat. To this prodigy may be added the admirable
uniformity of languages, customs, buildings, and other things which are
to be met with in this Country. 'Tis sufficient to know one quarter, to
make certain judgement of all the rest; all of which without doubt
proceeds from the nature of the people, who are all born with an
inclination of willing nothing contrary to one another."

Gabriel de Foigny
A New Discovery of Terra Incognita Australis (1676)

Egalitarian individualism is most apparent in issues that concern race and
ethnicity. It is ingrained in the heat of argument and other action—in
the establishment of national and party political policy and in the
patterning of everyday personal ethnic or racial antagonisms and prejudices—and it can be seen as a motivating force in interethnic violence,
which is becoming increasingly evident among various ethnic fractions
of Australian society.

Recently, an outstanding Australian historian, Geoffrey Blainey, well
known for a succession of influential and popular works in which he
describes the growth of modern Australia, has achieved prominence for
his vocal criticisms of Australian immigration policy. These were widely
reported in the press in 1984, and his ideas continue to have currency in
the media and in academic and lay discourse.[1] Blainey is strongly criticized
by numerous members of the Australian intellectual community, who
consider his argument racist and a harking back to the populist prejudices
that produced Australia's White Australia policy. This was a policy that
restricted immigration into Australia to those peoples conceived of as
originating, ancestrally at least, in Europe. The policy was enshrined in

the Immigration Restriction Act of 1901, one of the first acts of the Federal Parliament of a newly independent Australia. The Immigration Act remained in effect until after World War II. The bias was in favor of English-speaking immigrants, and various categories of intending immigrant were discriminated against. Southern Europeans and other Mediterranean peoples were regarded as undesirable.

The White Australia policy was stimulated in a social and political setting of racist fears that were mainly antagonistic to Asians.[2] Preceding the Immigration Restriction Act were the Chinese immigration restriction acts passed in Victoria (1854) and New South Wales (1861). These acts, while the apotheosis of anti-Chinese feeling, also manifest in the slaughter of Chinese on the goldfields, were part of a general anti-Asian consciousness.[3] It is a consciousness that has perhaps never disappeared from many Australians of European extraction. In the present conditions of increased Asian immigration to Australia—attendant on the official ending of the White Australia policy and a move to the pluralist policies of "multiculturalism" since the early 1970s—there has been a reemergence of anti-Asian sentiment. Herein is some reason for the anger and fear expressed toward Blainey. There is much substance to the charge that Blainey's argument harks back to the White Australia policy and the sentiments that fueled it. Blainey makes this quite explicit in an open reference to a massacre of Chinese at one of the Victorian goldfields during the mid-nineteenth century. He refers to an occasion in 1982, while making a television documentary on Australian history, when he visited a Victorian goldfield that happened to be the scene of an outbreak of murderous violence against Chinese. Blainey muses that in this confrontation with his past there was "a lesson for us to learn. . . . In the gold era, Australians had also experienced what is now called a multicultural society. Their experience convinced them that such a society didn't work; and at that time clearly it didn't work" (Blainey 1984; 22).

The shadowy ethnocentrism and racism that haunt Blainey's argument share much with the tradition of Anzac. Scholars have traced the eagerness with which Australians volunteered for military service during the early years of World War I to a widespread concern to affirm a powerful identity with the causes and issues of England and Europe. It was a concern motivated from within an ideological consciousness that white Australians were isolated within a sea of alien, mainly Asian, peoples and cultures. There was anxiety at the growing industrial and military might of Japan, especially after the recent Japanese defeat of Russia.

The chroniclers of the Anzac tradition were avowed supporters of White Australia. Bean wrote in defensive sympathy, shortly after his return to Australia from England, of the Australian fear of having "his country flooded with Orientals" (Sydney *Morning Herald*, 1 June 1907). Later, in the *Spectator*, Bean argued that "The Australian sees a good deal of the Oriental. He has the Queensland coolies, and the Chinese quarter in every town. . . . He knows what every Briton who meets them knows— that, living together, the Western demoralises the Eastern, and vice versa" (cited in McCarthy 1983; 53). There are clear similarities here to the views expressed by Blainey in *All for Australia* some eighty years later. Like Bean, Blainey argues from the standpoint of a Eurocentric view, seeing Australia isolated in a region of cultural difference and otherness. This is not an opinion new to Blainey; it is deeply part of his historiography of Australia as a whole.[4] His immensely popular, award-winning *Tyranny of Distance* discovers its entire raison d'être in Australia's cultural isolation. This book, published in 1966—and engendered little outrage— carries the powerful message that the relative "peace" and "harmony" of Australia are derived from its British slant and strong controls over immigration (Blainey 1966, 321).

The similarity in the views of Bean and Blainey is to be accounted for by much more than a reference to their racism. Their arguments are motivated within the logic of their nationalism, which guides their particular diligence as historians and which is a logic constituted according to the principles of egalitarian individualist ideology. Blainey's *All for Australia*, far more than a racist tract, as many have argued, includes an essay in the logic of egalitarianism. It is here that Blainey's work shows a deep unity with Anzac and reveals the hidden dangers of democratic egalitarian ideology, especially when this ideology is harnessed in the service of the construction of nationalist identity. Racism, to be disparaged wherever it may emerge, reveals a specific logic, direction, and motivation through the ideology that encompasses it, and to combat it successfully demands attention to the ideology that engages and constructs it and gives it some of its particular force.

Nationalist Individualism as Text

Australian egalitarian nationalism equates individual, people, and nation. In line with such an idea Blainey identifies the nation as a person. This is clear from the outset, where he ties the issue of immigration to notions of national independence and national direction: "Real independence consists in knowing oneself rather than in trying too hard to seek the praises or favours of neighbouring nations" (p. 20). The nation as individual is also autonomous; its autonomy is prior to its engagement in relations with others. This logic, which determines ideal—in egalitarian terms—international relations, is also the logic that governs intranational relations. Thus as the nation is an autonomous person equivalent to other nations, so the nation is an internal amalgamation of autonomous individuals, which are interrelated according to a principle of consensual equivalence, in such a way as not to threaten individual autonomy. In accordance with egalitarian ideology, this is achieved by individuals freely exercising their opinions or will. It is an ideological position that is closely related to the people-state opposition and to the fact that the people are the guardians, the determinators, of state direction and order, as already discussed in relation to Anzac myth and ceremonial. It is from within such an ideological egalitarian individualist position that Blainey now presents an attack on immigration policy. Using the language of reduction appropriate to the ideology, he states that:

> In the last resort it is not the politicians, it is not Canberra, which determines whether an immigration program will succeed. It is public opinion which decides. . . .
>
> The flaw in the old White Australia Policy was its arrogance, its insensitivity, its lack of proportion. The flaw in this new immigration policy is its arrogance, its insensitivity to a large section of Australian opinion (Blainey 1984; 25).

Blainey's critique is also a prediction—of the failure in the policy— the prediction in a vital sense being the legitimation or rationale of the criticism. Essentially, the argument is that chaos and disorder will invade the calm and harmony of the present order as it has been historically formed. In effect, Blainey is arguing that racial clashes will occur *because* of the violation of virtually sacred Australian egalitarian principles. The autonomy of the people-nation has been denied by the state, and the state, thus acting determinately and independent of the people, causes the people to fall into violent, destructive strife. This, it will be recalled, is one of the core arguments of the Anzac tradition. The horrors of Gallipoli and of the war in Europe are in part a consequence of the denial of individual autonomy and equality, and the annihilation of individuals is iconic with the appropriation of their autonomy by state forms. As a coda to the establishing theme of his argument Blainey reiterates the principle of the people against the state and the idea that the people are not in trust to the state.

> Democracy is not like a long-term loan of property to be entrusted by the people to the government and its small group of advisers. And yet in recent years a small group of people has successfully snatched immigration policy from the public arena, and has even placed a taboo on the discussion of vital aspects of immigration (Blainey 1984; 35).

The stage is now set for Blainey to extend his egalitarian logic, which is explicitly ahierarchical. Just as individuals are not inferior or superior in accordance with their positions in society, so nations as social systems or, better, as collectivities which achieve their unity in accordance with certain principles—be these democratic or nondemocratic in Blainey's sense of the word *democracy*—cannot be ranked according to a scale of superiority or inferiority. Here Blainey seems to depart from the argument of Anzac. The Anzac chroniclers were far from loath to engage in the practice of ranking national types from top to bottom. Apparently having learned the lessons of history, Blainey distances himself from the prejudices of imperialism and European nationalism. Exuding liberal tolerance, he states:

> Within Europe were nations who saw their own people as even more special than other Europeans, for the nationalist fervour of the era increased the emphasis on national qualities and traits. In the twentieth century Hitler carried the mistaken idea to a terrible extreme. Many of Jewish descent, understandably, are frightened by any emphasis on race (Blainey 1984; 38).

On closer inspection of the text, however, Blainey has made minimal modification, if any, to the Anzac line, formed as it was at the height of the imperial era. The ranking of nations pursued by the troops and chroniclers was in accordance with two factors: the qualities of the persons representing the nations in conflict and the egocentric valuation of these qualities, the systematic comparison of the national self with the national other.

In the nationalist thought of Anzac, nation and individual are mutually reducible. The person embodies the nation and has inscribed within his or her being the social order of the nation as ideally typified. In accordance with this idea the qualities of the nation are made nakedly apparent in those conditions under which routine or everyday social orders are suspended—thus the critical importance of war (and, increasingly, sport), wherein the qualities of individuals as bearers of the nation are laid bare.

War for the Anzacs was, like sport, an "equal opportunity" arena. Here the qualities of nation embodied in the individual could be tested and evaluated—national self evaluated in relation to national other and vice versa. The evaluation by the Anzacs, and the consequent assertion of national superiority or national inferiority, was fundamentally in accordance with a logic of similarity or difference from the national typical self. I stress this because although victory and defeat—winning and losing—are important elements of the egalitarian individualist logic of the Anzacs, they are of secondary rather than primary consideration in the national ranking process. A further point should be added which extends an understanding of the importance of war in Australian nationalism. While the ideal of nation may be embodied in the national person, not all facets of the characteristic social activities of that person may be given to or inherent in the individual as bearer of the nation. It is possible that the qualities of the individual as manifest in certain kinds of action are properties of the situation conceived as independent of the individual and produced by certain artificial or imposed aspects of the social and political world which are sui generis and not reducible to the person. War tests for national quality. It can reveal the artifice and falsity of national presentation as it can expose, negatively or positively, the "true" person beneath the routine social mask. Here is a vital aspect of egalitarian individualist argument. Surface form and even that characterized as the form of the nation may not be congruent with the real qualities of person and nation as these are ideologically conceived. Assumed difference, moreover, may obscure a fundamental similarity.

Examples of the foregoing abound in the Anzac tradition. Thus, to the horror of the Australian authorities and other observers, the Australian troops in Egypt appeared to be drunken, destructive, brothel-frequenting, thieving louts. Where such action could not be valorized as the ideal of free-wheeling individualism it was largely explained away as the fault of enforced idleness, which prevented the emergence of the truly virtuous form of individualism. The selfless heroism of these same troops revealed itself in the actual conflict.

The Anzac tradition also underscores the point that fundamental similarity can overcome supposed difference. This is one aspect of the oft-repeated respect of the Australian troops at Gallipoli and in the desert for "Jacko" Turk. It was a respect based in the recognition of an element of idealized self-identity in the war-revealed qualities of the other. The Turks demonstrated courage and valor, and as was true of the Australians it appeared to be their basic quality, a quality exploited by the state that determined their suicidal slaughter.

In the Australian egalitarian individualism of Anzac the extent to which the fundamental qualities of the individual-nation are similar is the main principle of ranking. These qualities, ideologically, are not necessarily evident in surface or presented features. Thus the Turk is different on the surface but basically similar. The same argument is present in the traditions of World War II. Italians, as far as the Australian troops were concerned, demonstrated individual cowardice in battle, an unwillingness to fight. Consequently, and in accordance with the ideology, Italians as a nation were ranked low. Such an idea was undoubtedly fueled by anti-Italian prejudice in Australia, which predated the war and in turn exacerbated postwar tensions attendant on increased Italian migration to Australia following the end of hostilities. But the point remains. Italians who on the surface were similar declared themselves to be fundamentally different.

Nationalist thinking in the Anzac tradition is by no means free of notions of inherited national characteristics or of British imperialist prejudice. I stress this, however, to indicate that the nationalism of Anzac cannot be reduced or dismissed entirely by reference to imperial thought of the time. Indeed, the particular emphasis on basic qualities and the fact that these may not meld with surface appearance is an ideological element at variance with some imperial prejudice and to a degree may be conceived of as antagonistic to imperialistic rankings. It is consistent with an egalitarian, individualist nationalism, fashioned in the circumstances of newfound independence, where in a new identity must be asserted in accordance with principles that resist those which defined a previous national subordination.

Blainey's view of national difference or similarity has affinity with the nationalism of the Anzacs. While Blainey eschews a ranking of nations his argument for limiting Asian immigration and suggestions for immigration policy generally engages principles similar to those used in the Anzac tradition in its ranking of nations. Thus English and other Europeans, for example, should be given preference over Asians because the former are similar to the dominant resident population in Australia whereas the latter are different. In relation to the conceived self-identity of Australians, English are evaluated as better because they are similar. Paradoxically, Blainey may be more *racist*, as the word is understood in current usage, than the argument of the Anzac tradition, for which racist is virtually unproblematic. Thus, Blainey characterizes potential immigrants as appropriate or inappropriate for Australia on the grounds of his assumption that they embody as personal qualities the form of the social system by which their nation is characterized. He argues unproblematically from the nation to the person. The Anzac tradition, as I have explained, is more reserved on this point. Dissimilarity is to be proved rather than assumed.

Blainey is opposed to notions of innate or inherited national or racial characteristics. The rejection of such assumptions alone, as Blainey supposes, does not transform what many understand to be a racist thesis into a nonracist one. Indeed, ideas of innate racial characteristics are unessential if it is also maintained that individuals embody—as a function of socialization and language for example—the primary qualities of the social and political world into which they have been born; that is, if it is held that they are virtually identical microcosms of macrocosmic cultural reality. The idea of biologically inherited racial or national characteristics is even less necessary when it is assumed, as Blainey does, that individuals can transport to the country of their immigration, as a function of their embodiment, the central characteristics of that social and political world into which they were socialized.

The views presented by Blainey are a variation within egalitarian individualist thought. Blainey and Anzac could be seen as representing polar extremes, but within the one ideological scheme. Thus, while Anzac asserts that ideal society is an extension of the individual, Blainey asserts that the individual is an extension of society. One view is an inversion of the other. Their theses are transposable, however, and can be reduced to a similar argument, because both are conceived within egalitarian ideology. Thus, in both the individual-nation is basic. While Blainey and Anzac can be seen as starting their arguments from opposite poles, at certain points in their theses the individual is conceived of as reproducing the social order.

For Blainey and for the Anzac tradition difference produces conflict and disharmony.   Mateship, or the community of mates, which in Anzac thought is the natural society, is founded in natural individual similarity. The unity in action and consensus of mates and their ultimate harmony emerges from their similarity.   This similarity is rooted in their individual being.   Blainey, pursuing this logic of mateship, argues that society is given to internal disruption—even naturally given to internal strife—if it is composed of individuals who embody social difference.

It is now possible to see a deeper significance in Blainey's reference to the past Australian history of anti-Chinese violence. He refers explicitly to the murder of Chinese at the gold diggings of Lambing Flat in New South Wales, in 1861.   This occurred, as did similar events in Victoria, before the enactment of government legislation to restrict Chinese immigration.   What I think is the strong inference in Blainey's argument— to be compared with the idea of war in Anzac as revealing natural man— is that the nonregulated, natural society of the gold diggings demonstrated, in effect, a natural law.   This is that Chinese, as the symbolic Asians of Australian history, were radically different from the others and that the difference they embodied was the general cause of the strife.   They could not enter into social relations with others; they remained separate, nonintegrated, and thus a disruptive ingredient.   As if to drive the point home Blainey states that it took considerably fewer people of Mediterranean extraction—surprising, in Blainey's logic, I assume, because they were more similar socially to the majority of residents—to engender murder and mayhem in the gold town of Kalgoorlie in 1934 (Blainey 1984; 72).

The Arithmetic of Nationalism

The multiplication of difference, which Blainey sees as the structure of Australian immigration policy, is, for Blainey, antagonistic to the ideal of national ideological unity, an ideal he shares with the Anzac chroniclers. Such multiplication is tantamount to the internationalism of Australia in the sense of creating a multitude of nations within Australia.   It is virtually assumed by Blainey that Australia will enter into a state of war within itself, if it is not already at war. Blainey's selection of evidence and occasional use of military metaphor are clearly designed to create this impression.   Blainey introduces a letter written to him as coming from "Cabramatta, a *front-line suburb* (my italics) of Sydney" (Blainey 1984; 124).   The following is from the letter itself:

> Of course people from the same countries tend to congregate together. Perfectly natural, and many of the other things Asians do are understandable.

Evidently such practice is natural because the letter writer admits to the same practice.   With the assertion of national identity, however, the letter writer indicates alarm at the possibility of losing identity as a consequence of the increase of Asians in the local territory.

> We are Australians and what is so shameful about that? Are our ways of life so terrible, are we to be branded as unworthy because we choose to like to keep our ways? How can anyone not be upset at the falling standards, the deterioration of our way of life and a feeling of being a stranger in one's own town.
>
> With each passing week the town of Cabramatta is becoming more and more like an Asian town (Blainey 1984; 125).

The construction of the immigration process by Blainey and his Sydney correspondent as producing a situation of virtual national territorial dispossession by members of another nation and a situation almost of nations at war is thoroughly congruent with egalitarian individualism. Immigration as endangering the nation of those already in occupation is in accordance with the idea that individuals embody nation.

Thus the arithmetic of nationalism in contexts structured within egalitarianism. A nation is the sum of its individual parts, each of which replicates the whole. It follows that nations, therefore, increase in size as a function of the multiplication of their replicate parts. Nations must multiply likeness, not difference, otherwise national identity is weakened. Size in the numerical sense of multiplied particle identity is a key to the conception of national ownership. The control of defined national territory is directly tied to the number of like parts—unit embodiments of national identity—in occupancy. National power and national social coherence —aspects of power in egalitarian conception—are properties of numerical size. The control, domination, and weakening of the national other is in egalitarian ideology particularly conceived in relation to numerical regulation. Thus the concern in regimes dominated by egalitarian ideology to reduce the numerical size, for example, through the extermination or forced deportation and emigration, of national ethnic populations identified and categorized in accordance with the egalitarian logic of difference and similarity. Americans and Australians in the Vietnam war conceived of "body counts" as a sign of the weakening of the enemy. A basis of the very early fear of Asia, of the "yellow peril," in Australia was the numerical size of Asia as indicative of power and potential domination.

Blainey refracts egalitarian ideology—though certainly no less than does the Australian Department of Immigration, which he criticizes—in his discussion of the statistics of immigration. The slightest change in the proportion of national or ethnic minorities entering Australia constitutes a weakening of Australian national coherence.

A reduction in unitary national identity, in the national power of numerical dominant groups, achieved by the multiplication of difference, also produces a sense of personal dispossession and a feeling of loss in personal power. This is so because of the identity of the individual or nation in egalitarian nationalism. The person conceives self as also the nation. A reduction in like selves or an increase in different others as a property of ideological conception generates a sense of strangeness, perhaps of powerlessness. In the ideology of egalitarian individualism the very words *majority* and *minority* conjure up the meaning of domination and subordination and of power and weakness. Blainey's correspondent, who is described as "writing a little roughly" on two pages "torn" from a pad, is angry because of being "swamped" and converted into a powerless minority.

Inegalitarian Equality

Blainey extends what he sees as an important democratic principle underlying his letter writer's anguish, that of distributive justice. This has two aspects which Blainey discusses in particular, free speech and equal access to the wealth of the nation. Both are premised on the egalitarian principles of individual autonomy—and by extension the autonomy of the collective individual categorized according to likeness in identity—and upon the idea of the essential equality of individuals. These principles are negated, and the ideals of a democratic society are undermined, should they for any reason be abused. Few in Australia would disagree. Blainey gives examples of the contradiction of the high principles that he enunciates.

There is a muzzling of the democratic right, it would seem, of long-term English-speaking residents of Australia to voice their resentment of national or ethnic others. Blainey expresses some of their opinions. He gives the instance of the worry of one woman who lives in a block of flats also occupied by Vietnamese families. After mentioning her complaints about cooking smells, the comparative affluence of other ethnic communities, and the names of those "nationalities who in her view produce the worst garbage" he outlines the woman's worry about the present and future situation of her eight-year-old son:

> An Australian, with an Australian mum, he is the odd boy out; and every day, she says, her son is bullied: "One morning when he was hurt I just lost control and grabbed an Asian child and slapped him across the face. All the Lebanese mobbed me, calling me obscene names and spitting." She privately predicts race riots: "There will be bloodshed in this country" (Blainey 1984, 133).

The significance of the foregoing should be seen within the logical structure of Blainey's argument as I have outlined it so far. There is, for example, a continuity between Blainey's assessment of the import of the prejudice and violence expressed toward Chinese on the goldfields and the sentiments he cites here. The woman expresses the tension of difference and the conflict which is natural to difference. But, further, through publishing the woman's opinion, Blainey not only vents her democratic right to free expression, he also suggests that the autonomous and equal right of "old Australians" to free expression is routinely denied by inequities in the social system that are counter to democratic spirit.

A serious inequity to which Blainey points is that of class. He cites the following statement of Charles A. Price, a person influential in the formation of Australian immigration policy—opposed to the White Australia policy yet an assimilationist and like Blainey opposed to the multiplication of difference:

> Academics, professionals and politicians, especially those living in
> affluent suburbs, are often very insensitive to the feelings of native
> Australians whose neighbourhoods are being transformed by the influx
> of peoples with quite different customs and ways of life (Blainey 1984,
> 126, cited from Canberra *Times*, 17 May 1984).

This is echoed by Blainey in his voice as champion and mouthpiece of the underdog. Thus he represents the old Australian urban working class as the most affected by the immigration of difference: in the situation of a competitive labor market in a depressed economy, in the effect on the quality of schooling for children, and in routine social relations:

> The neighbourhood is probably more important to the daily life of the
> storeman and packer than to the prosperous lawyer. . . . The disruption
> of that neighbourhood [for the unskilled man] by newcomers must
> strongly affect his daily life and sense of security (Blainey 1984, 129).

Blainey argues that the socially powerful, and hence vocal, are better able to control the effects of immigration on their social and economic lives. Few would disagree with him that the structure of social and political inequality as it exists in Australia has discriminatory and prejudicial consequences. Favored by their social circumstances the well-to-do have no need to express open racist sentiments (Blainey 1984, 126–128).

But there is a hidden agenda in Blainey's discussion. He is stating in effect that all Australians are essentially the same in their suspicion of difference, a tension which is by definition natural in humanity. In true populist egalitarian style, Blainey exposes the "liberalism" of dominating groups as artificial and false. Their liberalism is not vital in the individual per se. It is rather a property of an inegalitarian social and political order dominated by such individuals, an order that obscures their real nature as individuals. Those who argue for liberal multicultural policies, who defend the immigration of Asians, are, from the standpoint of their elevated positions, blind to a reality with which others less fortunate than they must live. An important implication of Blainey's argument is that the truly authentic people are the "old Australians of the working class," as he presents them. It is they who reveal the authentic consciousness which for Blainey is the natural dislike of, and separation from, the cultural, ethnic, or national other.

Such a position may appeal to populist class sentiment but it is founded on a premise which would be rejected by most serious analysts of class relations, not to say by many of those "old Australians" whose views Blainey purports to represent. The problem at hand, however, is to account for Blainey's view. He is not alone in his opinion, as his presentation of supporting evidence indicates.

Blainey's view is constituted in a historically formed cultural common sense, widespread in Australia, of which Blainey is the proven scholarly adept. Blainey is a folk historian—rather than a historian of the folk—who is trapped in the very interpretational categories he presents.[5] Like so many Australian historians, notably those of the Melbourne school, Blainey represents these categories and assumptions, unquestioned and unexamined, as the underlying analytical basis for an understanding of the events he selects and describes. My point is not that Blainey has the facts wrong. It is much stronger. Ignoring the interpretational procedures whereby he apprehends reality, and also the procedures of understanding of those whose opinions he advocates, Blainey can at best only present appearances and at worst confirm the veracity of modes of interpretation forever beyond his grasp. Imprisoned in his view, moreover, Blainey's statements resonate with broader meaning which not only rouses the cultural passions but reveals the inegalitarian potential of egalitarian logic in the Australian setting.

When Blainey joins nation to class he contributes to a fragmented understanding of a social order upon which he reflects. Those who may otherwise be conceived of as being in a common class relation within the overall political and economic structure are now conceptually opposed. In effect the Australian working class is divided from the Lebanese working class, the Vietnamese working class, and so on. Insofar as such a conception may be more widely held, national or ethnic identity negates a potential unity which may be present in the structure of class relations, as I have already argued for Sri Lanka.

The subordination of class to ethnicity or nation and the fragmentation of the significance of class relations in ideological conception is integral to the logic of egalitarianism, especially in nationalism. In egalitarianism, the individual and identity are in unstable relation. Indeed, this must be so in an ideology such as that of Australian egalitarianism wherein the value is placed on the unique natural individual that is prior to or independent of the socially constructed individual in identity. Identity is the principle whereby different or unique individuals are brought into social association. It is a principle of categorization in accordance with which people are related and rerelated on the basis of identity. Identity shifts according to situation, but the individual is a constant, essentially unchanged in inner constitution. Indeed, a worry among some Australian egalitarians in their shifting identities is that their individual natures may be changed in their assumption of new identities, such as promotion to the position of boss at work. There is a tension toward the substantialization of identity in egalitarianism, identity becoming integral to being, part of one's very substance. One can substantialize class identity, and the analysis of class relations in some social science analyses within egalitarian societies, rightly or wrongly, proceeds in this way. Certainly this is a view in everyday life. Thus an individual may continue to claim an identity as a member of the working class even though that individual is a company director controlling the lives of thousands of industrial employees. The identity which is most valued is that which is the most inclusive. This, which is determined ideologically in conjunction with social and political processes, establishes the level at which identity stabilizes or beyond which it ceases to be significant or valued in cultural conception. This is where identity stabilizes, and when it stabilizes it substantializes, fusing with the individual at root. In egalitarian nationalism identity stabilizes most inclusively at the level of the nation or ethnic group which is defined as a manifestation of the essence of the individual at base. This, of course, overcomes the fundamental dilemma of egalitarian individualism, which asserts the primacy of the individual. The identity valued as the most inclusive and most relevant across diverse situations, further achieved in the sacralization and reification of individual essence as culture, is realized as also substantially the individual, so the tension between individual and identity in egalitarianism is resolved. Furthermore, the thesis of egalitarianism that the individual is prior to and determinate of society, that the whole is conditioned in the parts, is also satisfied. Thus the egalitarianism which values nation and ethnicity as the most inclusive catgegory of identity association must reduce and subordinate the importance of other identities and relations. Indeed, if my analysis is correct, egalitarian nationalists should be antagonistic to the possibility that other forms of association, like class, may be critical, even determinate. Class is merely identity but nation is spirit.

The scheme I have outlined for egalitarianism must be distinguished from the conceptual scheme of hierarchy, for example, as it is apparent in Sinhalese Buddhist myth or exorcism described earlier. To write of the individual as separable from identity is impossible. The person is constituted in the whole and manifests in his or her inner being a moment of the process of the whole. The manifestation of the person as demonic is a property of the fragmentation of the whole. It is not an identity to be sloughed off at will, but a dimension of the person, integral to the person as to the whole, to be transformed by acting on the whole. Cosmically determinate principles operating through the power of hierarchy interrelate all aspects of the person as a continuous process. The person in all aspects of a hierarchically constituted being is potentially relevant through all situations of social experience. In this conception, furthermore, the situation is not determinate, but the whole and the person in the whole is theoretically constitutive of the situation. To put it another way, if the whole is demonic or manifests a fragmented reduction to nonhierarchically incorporated parts, contexts of social action become demonic, as does the person.

Ethnicity and Unbalanced Opposition

The analysis of ethnicity in modern industrial societies occasionally appears to conform to the egalitarian conceptual scheme as I have outlined it. The approaches of Gluckman and Mitchell, discussed in connection with Sri Lanka, are certainly consistent within an egalitarian frame. They and others, such as Barth (1969), Wallman (1979), and Abner Cohen (1974), drew consciously on Evans-Pritchard's classic study (1956) of segmentary lineage process and politics among the politically acephalous cattle-herding Nuer of the Sudan. Evans-Pritchard employed the concept of "situational selection," by which he argued that the relevance of identity and its meaning were determined in social situations. The relevance of identity in social interaction was dependent on the presence or absence of other significant identities in social situations. Identity was relational, significant only with regard to other identities, which were recognized as different but which associated individuals at a similar level of inclusiveness within the social order. Applied to Australia, for example, the identity *Greek* is relevant only in contrast to *Italian* or *Australian*. It is not relevant to be defined as Greek in relation to *dockworker, Sydneysider,* or *Crow-eater* (South Australian).

I have said that the approaches to identity of Evans-Pritchard, Gluckman, and Mitchell are consistent with egalitarianism. Indeed, it is important that Gluckman and Mitchell explicitly state that while they use the principles of the Nuer model, the formation of ethnic categories and their significance in the towns of Central Africa is a cultural manifestation of processes determined in a modern industrial society. It is possible that the principles of the Nuer model, at least as they are used in modern ethnic studies, may not be universal, as is often the methdological suggestion, but specific to a modern world. Since the Nuer model has been reproduced in Western anthropological thought, it has every claim to be interpreted as a methodological forming of historically developed, largely Western-centered egalitarianism.

The notion of "balanced opposition," also made famous in the Nuer studies, in which it is argued that social categories of equivalent degrees of inclusiveness come into existence through a principle of opposition, is everywhere thematically apparent in Blainey's rhetoric. Australians, Vietnamese, Lebanese, Italians, and so on are presented as "equivalent" and as "naturally" opposed. As equals they have the equal right to mutual abuse. Defending the right of old Australians to free themselves of socially imposed inhibitions, Blainey observes that "If social comment is fair and accurate, it should be made with equal ease about Vietnamese and Australians," (Blainey 1984, 42).

Here the ideologically inegalitarian potential of egalitarianism is exposed. Ideas of equivalence and balanced opposition can negate or obscure aspects of the world, of the political society that produces them. Engaging Blainey's usage, "Australian" and "Vietnamese" are patently *not* equivalent units, although their phenomenal constitution is in accordance with egalitarian principles.

The association of nationalism and egalitarianism in the Blainey argument and more widely in Australia activates the inegalitarian possibilities of both and transforms egalitarian thought into an ideology of domination. Asians and other identified ethnic minorities are not only made symbolic of a national weakening, a loss of power, but are also created as symbols of class oppression and the negation of the Australian ideal.

Ethnicity and Class Populism

The egalitarian individualist logic of Australian nationalism, demonstrated in the Anzac tradition, is one that asserts the national identity of self and other according to a system of values which valorizes equality. The egalitarian Australian national self is explicitly valued as the superior, and deviations from it, especially in the direction of perceived inequality or hierarchy, are devalued. Blainey asserts that Asian hierarchical societies are intrinsically no better or worse than those societies or nations typed as closer or more similar to Australian democratic society. But given the logic of Australian nationalism Blainey is implicitly setting a higher value on Australian identity as epitomizing the democratic ideal. His repeated hortatory statements about the need to retain democratic principles make very little sense otherwise. Blainey's presentation of other "Australian" opinion, while couched in the language of equality, equal rights and fair go, are ideologically concerned with the maintenance or restoration of "old Australian" domination.

The structure of egalitarian practice, as exemplified in Blainey and excited by nationalism, demonstrates further inegalitarian potential when tied to populist notions of class. The popular conception of class, as I have already intimated, takes its form through nationalist egalitarian individualist ideas. When it is invoked it makes nonsense of ideas of balanced opposition and essential equality. In the nationalism of Australian identity, the self-referential characterization or stereotype of the national other tends to generate a complex conception of the national self and a relatively simple conception of the national other. Thus in Blainey's discussion, for example, Vietnamese are Vietnamese are Vietnamese. It is virtually only old Australians who have social classes. Australian nationalist egalitarianism engages its ideological force to the work of external typing and to a discourse on the processes of internal social differentiation.

Populist ideas of class such as Blainey's follow the argument of the Anzac tradition as does much Australian class nationalism in Australia generally. The Anzac tradition incorporates the logical sequence: English : Australian :: hierarchy (inequality) : equality :: society (constructed and imposed) : society (natural, mateship) :: individual (artificial) : individual (authentic). This, the logic of Australian identity and of the way Australian nationalism continues to order an external world, is also fundamental to much popular cultural discourse concerning the internal social order of Australia. Replace the terms *English* and *Australian* with, for example, "ruling class" and "working class" (as they are used in everyday language and in some scholarly writing) in the argument of the Anzac tradition and the logical sequence I have outlined remains unchanged.

In Australia, the words *English* and *Australian* are metaphors of class distinction. They mark, or typify, individual action as representative of a particular class style. The terms are also cultural statements of the different modalities of the social and political order as a whole. On the one hand is its tendency toward social inequality, which is the property of society sui generis, and on the other hand is the movement to natural orders, an order based in similarity, an order of natural equals undivided by the superficialities of social convention and of other forms of imposed order.

The Australian comedian Barry Humphries has created the famous role of Edna Everage, who derives her humor from her play on the tension between inequality and equality in Australian nationalist ideology. It is significant that her most devoted audiences are in England and in Australia. She works in the space between two nationalist self-recognitions. I suspect that for the English she satisfies the stereotype of the essential vulgarity of Australians. For Australians she represents the absurdity of English pretense. Within Australia, moreover, Edna Everage—as in England—is the symbolic type of the upwardly mobile Australian, losing her or his naturalness in the conventions of social superficialities but continually revealing her "common" base through a variety of social gaffes and absurdities. Edna loves English royalty. One Australian television station used her as a commentator on the wedding of Prince Andrew. Edna Everage's very transvestism is an obvious symbolic commentary on the superficiality of hierarchy and the ultimate absurdity, destructiveness, and posturing of imposed orders. She is an "unnatural" woman encompassing the "natural" man underneath, who actually surfaces in other Humphries characters, Bazza Mackenzie and Les Patterson.

Bazza was the first character developed, and his escapades, organized around his wild-eyed natural innocence but natural vulgarity, graced the pages of the English magazine *Private Eye*,—an antiestablishment journal run largely by the self-critical members of the establishment. While Bazza's aunt was Edna, Les Patterson now appears to be her true inner identity. Les Patterson is presented as Australia's cultural attaché, and he plays up to an Australian love of "natural" vulgarity, most of it in the form of overt obscenity. He is not quite natural man, though—and thence much of his absurdity—for he sports a knighthood and thus displays an unnatural appreciation of hierarchy—the fundamental Australian ideological dilemma.

Edna Everage—now Dame Edna, for she, like Sir Les, has been honored—has an undeniable surface hilarity, but she also discloses the way a mode of egalitarian thought deeply ingrained in Australian nationalism permeates a popular understanding of social processes. There is a powerful tradition of class struggle and a strong devaluation of many forms of inequality in Australia. But these often take cultural form through the ideology of Australian identity, through the conceptions of a Dame Edna and a Blainey. What is dangerous is that the joining of ethnic issues to the passions of class through the mediation of nationalist egalitarianism creates the national or ethnic other as potentially an object of class distrust and hatred.

National and ethnic identity as critical elements of an interpretive framework for understanding class inequality and suffering lay at the root of the White Australia policy and of the argument of assimilationism. The egalitarian logic of this bears discussion. It demonstrates additional inegalitarian aspects of egalitarian practice in a nationalist setting.

I have referred to *English* and *Australian* as metaphors of opposed possibilities of the internal social order of Australia as it is popularly conceived. Indeed, Australia, or the nationalist egalitarian ideal, discovers its form in relation to its conceptualized opposite, that of inegalitarian, hierarchical, England. Historically and ideologically, many Australians understand their social world as having a strong identity with England but simultaneously as being its inverse. Australia, through its progress to independence, succeeded in effecting a transformation of the English scheme of things. While inequality, the ideals of aristocratic birth, the privileges of socially produced position, and so on are the unifying principles of England, equality metaphorized by the underclasses of England, constitutes the organizing principle of Australia. Ideologically, England and Australia are bound, together composing a unity of the strongest similarity *and* difference.

This conception of Australian nationalist thought extends an understanding of the reason many Australians express identity with England even as they assert a distinct Australian identity. The latter reproduces the former. It is the reason many young Australians must visit England as their ultimate destination when they first journey beyond Australian shores. The sense of a historical identity with England is produced ideologically, as it is emotionally, in the very constitution of an Australian identity. Some of the basis of Blainey's argument in favor of an increase in English immigrants—or persons of nationalities similar in type—rests in the foregoing ideology. Thus Blainey's support of certain aspects of assimilationist immigration policy and, more generally, the development of assimilationist ideas in Australia as elsewhere can be seen as a product of egalitarian individualism per se.

On Making Australians

Assimilationist ideas work on the principle of transformational conversion, of changing a national other into the national self. As a logical outcome of ideology, this transformational act is likely to operate most successfully when it is performed on persons who are already conceived of as sharing aspects of the national self. English or British are therefore preferred. To transform them is also to repeat, incidentally, the original act of national creation.

Making people into Australians, the object of assimilationist ideas, is to reassert ideas that are integral to the domination of categories of persons who are seen as the natural embodiments of the original nation. This is why ethnic minorities and supporters of multiculturalism in Australia opposed assimilation. The stress on Australian identity brought into play other features of egalitarian nationalist ideology. It invoked notions of national superiority and an inegalitarian ranking of nations, which is the thrust of the multiculturalist complaint. Furthermore, the emphasis upon becoming Australian is contradicted by a critical aspect of the ideology underlying Australian egalitarian conceptions of national identity.

There is in the ideology of Australian identity a strong sense that society, the nation, is integral to the person before socialization, and there is a further sense that society—and by extension the state—does not create the person. In such an ideological context, persons naturalized by the state cannot become "completed" Australians and may be accorded secondary status, often in accordance with the ranking of their former national identity. People in Australia refer to themselves and are referred to by others as, for example, Greek Australians, Lebanese Australians, and so on. In Australia there is considerable concern as to whether individuals are first-generation, second-generation, and so on, Australians. There is a question on the latest national census which asks specifically for this information. It seems that with the exception of English—or persons similarly acceptable to the paradigm of national self—who already constitute the preliminary stage of transformation in nationalist ideology and historiography, persons cannot easily embody the essence of a new nation.

Egalitarianism as an ideology that promotes inequality as an aspect of the logic of its practice is further revealed by Blainey. Employing egalitarian ideals Blainey details the inegalitarian offenses of the immigrant policy of the state, then uses his egalitarianism to support inegalitarian practice. Thus, the family reunion policy unequally favors Asians, for, he states, arguing categorically, they have larger families than other groups of immigrants. On the basis of this "fact'—and I assume through the multiplication-of-difference principle—Asian immigration should be reduced.

In the manner of balanced argument that is central to egalitarian dispute and is often epitomized as the instancing of reason by egalitarians, Blainey presents evidence of the hidden favoring of New Zealanders. He charges the minister for immigration of "defying his own emphatic statements of impartiality."

> Here was one nationality, its people overwhelmingly of the European
> race and white in colour and New Zealand nationality and British
> origin and the Protestant religion, receiving a very special preference.
> A policy that specifically denies preference on grounds of race, colour,
> descent, nationality and religion was, by giving up to 10 per cent of its
> migrant places to New Zealand, defying each of these proclaimed
> criteria (Blainey 1984, 83).

A major thrust of Blainey's point is that contrary to public statement the Australian government maintains elements of a White Australia policy, but in secret. My own view, based on experience, is that this charge is probably correct. The alleged secrecy of government policy is a serious crime in egalitarian individualist thought, for it denies to the individual the right to exert free will. Most, as actors interpreting reality through the assumptions of egalitarian thinking, would agree. But it must be realized that the crime of secrecy, an act of state against the interests of the people, is appealed to in connection with the wider argument of Blainey's text as a whole. He is not amazed that aspects of the White Australia policy persist. Instead he takes it as evidence for the force of his egalitarian assertion that similarity, not difference, is the sine qua non of social and national coherence. The Australian government, in spite of itself, gives rise to the law of similarity. In other words, the government is unnaturally, through the artifice of secrecy, covering up what is natural in human nature.

The paradoxical extension of this position is that the failure to recognize the natural law of similarity is to produce inequality. For Blainey achievement of the egalitarian ideal is not to impose an artificial similarity over an essential difference. To do so is to lead to the generation of social and political inequality rather than to develop equality. Blainey exposes a key limiting condition of egalitarianism as he conceives of it, that it rests on the potentially inegalitarian rule of the multiplication of sameness.

Perhaps the most tragic aspect of Blainey's idealism is its pragmatism, whereby he must recognize the impossibility of perfect equality, thus legitimating the practice he recommends. In a way he makes his idea of equality perfectly absurd in the support of his pragmatism.

> If Australia were to treat all peoples of the world as equally eligible to be immigrants, it would, in fairness, have to advertise in all lands, offer subsidies to potential migrants from the poorest lands, place immigration officers in dozens of new lands (Blainey 1984, 119).

Moral Pragmatism

Economism best describes the form of Blainey's pragmatism. Reason is justified by cost and even reduced to cost. He reasons that it is costly to transform difference into similarity. "Khmer minors" are a greater burden on the taxpayers than young men from Britain (Blainey 1984, 114). It is costly to teach Asians English. Where the rates of unemployment among Asians in Australia are not high, Asians compete unfairly with old Australians for jobs (Blainey 1984, 74). Blainey's pragmatic economism is not merely practical common sense, it is the elaboration of economic concerns as also moral concerns. The economy as morality, money as the measure of moral value—even morality itself—and not simply the unit for commodity exchange, is deeply part of egalitarian ideology.

The moralization of the economy in the emergence of egalitarian ideology in Europe has been examined by Dumont (1977), as I have remarked elsewhere in this volume. Such moralization is coincident with the development of individualism and modern nationalism. In my view Dumont's great insight is that the economism and the moral value placed on economic pragmatism are not reducible to capitalism, to processes of *embourgeoisement*, or to the ethos of competitive individualism, as some may argue. Rather, these aspects, together with the conceptual tools of those, like Marx and his successors, who are vociferously critical of such phenomena, were born in the great social and political transformations which gave birth to egalitarian thought and in which vortex Australia was to some extent caught. Regardless, however, whether Dumont's argument can be accepted at this point, the everyday practice of egalitarianism in Australia reveals the practice as a moral economy.

I do not have to demonstrate this by reference to daily government statements which treat of the economy as some kind of moral condition, as an object toward which a moral attitude, often reformatory, must be taken. This is common enough throughout the Western world.

The outstanding foci of egalitarian ideals in Australia are the drinking shout and gambling, two-up especially. In the former, money acts morally through the medium of drink to effect the equality of mates who otherwise may be positioned unequally in the routine social order. In the latter, money both manifests its intrinsic egalitarian character and indexes the idea that wealth, as the basis of social position, falls to the individual as a quality of the individual qua individual. Embedded in the idea of luck is not so much a mystical property as the notion that the fall of fortune runs against that system which may otherwise, unnaturally, produce social inequality. I stress that in Australian egalitarian thought gambling refracts the essential morality of money, which is also connected with its movable quality expressed in gambling. The idea of gambling accentuates the capacity of money to separate itself from its embeddedness in a wider social and political system: to be attracted through the determining autonomous force of individuals. This force, or luck, a passing natural quality constituted within and emanating from the individual, acts independent of the system. It places money and person in forceful intimate relation, and the system is subverted and individual circumstances are raised. When the force of luck deserts, through no fault of the individual, the system once again determines. Luck is the metaphor of the power of individual autonomy. In a way it can be likened to nature in Australian egalitarian individualism, for it is the force within the person which generates position and relations in the world and against those orders and powers that are imposed. Money is virtually moral in Australia when it gathers to the power of the individual, when it is an index of that which is naturally given. Money becomes potentially immoral, in the ideological context of Australian egalitarianism, when it is fixed in the social order and becomes socially reproduced, when it is inherited and multiplied through the social forces of inequality. Proudhon's famous anarchist dictum, "Property is theft," a dictum fashioned in the circumstances of the development of egalitarianism, is an idea not inconsistent with populist thinking in Australia.

The foregoing is sharpened in comparison with some attitudes toward money in Sri Lanka. Consistent with Dumont's broad argument concerning the valuation of immovable property over movable goods in "traditional hierarchical" societies, in Sri Lanka the demon sorcerers—destroyers of the moral order of the cosmos and of the person—are merchants. They are the traffickers in movable property, and they transform order into disorder through the medium of money. Money attacks hierarchy and the social order. Whereas the egalitarian values this propensity morally, the hierarch devalues it as evil. And so, as I have recounted for returning labor migrants from the Middle Eastern oil states to Sri Lanka, dangerous money is ritually rehierarchialized and reembedded within the Buddhist moral order of the Sinhalese social and political system as it is ideologically conceived.

Therefore, when Blainey makes an appeal to economic pragmatism he is not merely being economistic in the sense of ignoring other political and social considerations. He is organizing his thought along the lines of the very ideological guts of a cultural order from within which he writes. Economism of the kind manifested by Blainey is central to egalitarianism and is a principle of the cohesion of the order of society as a whole. The power of Blainey's argument, its potential persuasiveness as common sense, is derived from its ideological foundations and, more important, from the possibility that it constitutes the interpretational ground, not just of Blainey and his supporters, but of those who would sharply criticize Blainey and who understand themselves to be outside the orbit of his ideological assumptions.

Where the "Facts" Lie

Criticism of Blainey has been extensive. Most of it turns on his alleged racism, the dangers of raising the ghosts of long dead ideas, his sociological theoretical inadequacies and, worst of all for some, his misinterpretation of historical evidence. These criticisms are without question necessary in a political society such as that of Australia, where the public statements of such respected scholars as Blainey have considerable force and where academic experts have real influence on government decisions. In this connection it is well that a significant body of experts dissociates itself from potentially inflammatory comments that may legitimate prejudice and provoke human suffering. There is a strong sense in much of the discussion, however, that if the facts are fully presented, more reasoned counterinterpretations are given, and the political and social background of Australia's past and present are filled out, Blainey's absurdity will be revealed, his legitimacy will be destroyed, and the embarrassment—largely to an intellectual community—he has caused will disappear. But such a view can be self-mystifying. The power of Blainey's argument is contained in its inner logic, not so much in the facts themselves or in his particular interpretation of them. It is this inner logic that constitutes the facticity of Blainey's position, which not only influences the structure of his interpretation and guides his selection of information and the significance he accords it, but also gives Blainey and others occasion to discount and even passionately to resist alternative evidence and interpretation. In an important sense, the so-called Blainey debate on race is like a play without an author. Blainey is merely the impresario and director, whereas the plot is far greater than anything he could have created. He is the play's creation, which nonetheless took particular form in his direction. This is true to the extent that Blainey's argument is part of an embracing framework of cultural ideas and principles whereby many in Australia, from all walks of life, interpret all manner of experience conventionally and come to realize themselves and others in the world.

The knowledge that Blainey presents a cultural argument reduces its persuasive force. It has no validity independent of the premises upon which it is based, premises that are themselves cultural. But if such is true for Blainey it is no less true for those who engage Blainey in debate or, in Australia, otherwise address human issues of related or different kind. Thus with regard to ethnicity, the assimilationist position, of which Blainey's is the outstanding recent example, and the multiculturalist position—that of the bulk of Blainey's critics—are not necessarily opposed to the extent they appear to be on the surface.

Egalitarian Difference

The two positions can be conceived of as logical transpositions of each other. The primary distinction is that while the assimilationist values sameness, the multiculturalist values difference. The distinction is considerable in connection with immigration policy, for ideally the former conceives of national unity as founded in sameness, whereas the latter conceives of unity as not affected by the multiplication of difference. The multiculturalist argument is well supported on humanitarian grounds alone, for it directly combats the potential discrimination, prejudice, human anguish, and suffering which often seem to flow in doctrines that value essential similarity. The multiculturalist valuation of difference, however, also asserts the logic of similarity;[7] that is, the idea of similarity is the principle for the establishment of different communities and is conceived of as the basis for their cohesion. Assimilationism and multiculturalism are different valuations within an egalitarian ideological scheme, and they share all the other key terms of the scheme. Thus in the two points of view, the individual is the basic atom of the whole, for whom ethnic identity constitutes both the essential, primordial, quality of the person and the critical dimensions of the whole—the ethnic community and the nation—as these are characterized. The qualities of the ethnically or nationally identified person or whole are then conceived of as being generated or regenerated through interaction with like persons or wholes. For assimilationist and multiculturalist alike, incidentally, the psychological integrity of person and sociality itself may be threatened if the individual does not engage in environments populated by like others. The old Australians, whose interpretations of experience Blainey cites, apparently understand a weakening and loss of personal integrity through the multiplication of cultural difference. Those in favor of multiculturalism identify the functional utility of ethnic communities for new immigrants because they help in adjustment. This is not merely adjustment to a strange administrative and political situation. Often implicit in the argument is the idea that persons cast adrift from communities of ethnic sameness are likely to experience psychological disorientation or fragmentation of the self. I must make it immediately clear that I am not arguing for or against the empirical validity of such positions. All I am stating here is that regardless of their empirical validity, assimilationist and multiculturalist argument are close ideologically and can be shown to be grounded in the one egalitarian individualist logic.

A number of points follow from the foregoing. Ideologically it is but a short step from being an assimilationist to being a multiculturalist. No significant transformation in the way individuals think of or exist in their world is required. It has been noted that some of the staunchest supporters of assimilationism, indeed persons influential in the architecture and organization of the White Australia Policy, are now fervent multiculturalists (Lepervanche 1984, 171–72, 178–79; Wilton and Bosworth 1984, Chap. 2). There is no need to assume opportunism—as Blainey implies in his rhetorical recognition of earlier allegiances of present opponents— in their change of attitude. Such a change is not a radical leap in faith; it is ideologically consistent, and indeed, it may be motivated in this consistency. It is a humanitarian advance over the more prejudicial possibilities of the one logic.

A trap, however, awaits multiculturalists when they participate in the same ideological ground as their opponents. At the very least they run the risk of reproducing assimilationist argument and weakening their position. Some of those who have attacked Blainey have in effect supported his underlying position. Thus we are told that many Asians are not different but the same—they are "democratic" and not "hierarchical" (Ricklefs 1985, 39; Hassan and Tan 1986, 30); that many do not require skill retraining, are competent in English, are predominantly Christian (Hassan and Tan 1986, 4, 26, 37; Ricklefs 1985, 41; Parkin 1985, 26); and so on. Many who have criticized Blainey have not abandoned the egalitarian individualist view that social cohesion and unity are based in the similarity of individual parts—a similarity forged on the overdetermining principle of ethnic or national identity. Such identity continues to have significant explanatory currency in the interpretation of individual and collective fortune and suffering. The dangers of this kind of argument have already been explored for Sri Lanka.

Marie de Lepervanche puts the case strongly for Australia in the context of a Marxist analysis. She addresses the situation of growing interethnic tension in Australia. "The culture of the immigrants and their ethnicity per se are not the determinants of hostility; the structural position they occupy and the structural relations they participate in are determining in class systems" (Lepervanche 1984, 214). Extending on this point Lepervanche argues that the ideological primacy given to ethnic identity in assimilationist and multiculturalist points of view mislocates the primary sources of inequality, suffering, and violence. These sources are founded in the social and political order of Australia as a whole and in the wider articulation of the country into an embracing world political economy. Assimilationism and multiculturalism, in the determinant import they give to ethnicity or nationality, obscure class forces and function ideologically in the interests of class and other forms of social domination.

I am in considerable agreement with this argument. But I have concentrated my discussion upon another force which is at once more enveloping and more fundamental. It extends an understanding of the reason issues of ethnic identity and race relations are of dominant concern in modern nation-states and why much of the content of the issues discussed seems to be a replay of older argument and earlier historical experience. My position is in many ways an old one. It is the phenomenon of nationalism itself, which has direct bearing on the centrality and form of a discourse and practice in relation to questions of race and ethnicity. But more, the power of nationalism to evoke ethnic sentiment and a spirit of racism is contained in the egalitarian roots of much modern society, in the very egalitarian constitution of the modern nation-state itself.

The Dangers of Nationalist Egalitarianism

Egalitarian individualism is virtually the ontology of the modern state of Australia. It constitutes nothing less than the being of the state, the logical scheme, emergent in historical processes that are centered largely in Europe and America, within which the state of Australia came into existence. In the historical and political process of the formation of the independent nation the meaning of the ontology assumed a particular ideological form that constitutes the identity of both the nation-state and the persons who realized it as integral to themselves. What some may recognize as Australian culture took form through the ideological process that arose from the historical engagement of an egalitarian ontology. In this course, egalitarianism assumed a specific meaning and became embedded in the institutions of everyday life; it was entrenched at the root of institutional formation and was reproduced and often transformed in institutional practices. It is through processes such as these that egalitarian thought in Australia constitutes the dominant, most powerful and encompassing ideological form. I stress this because nationalist sentiments and ideas variously defined as racist find their potentially distressing and destructive force in the meaning of egalitarianism as it has emerged historically in Australia.

Critics of the Australian scene have pointed to the racism, the dangers of individualism, the pitfalls of an egalitarian ethos, and so on (McQueen 1970; Conway 1985; Burgmann 1984). The criticism often manifests a kind of compartmentalizing fragmentation. Nationalism and racism are separated from their integument within a more inclusive ideological whole. It is assumed that the potency of nationalism and racism resides in the manifest phenomena themselves and that through the simple acts of definition and recognition their dangers can be defused. The position I have presented here is not of this kind. The potentially destructive and socially fragmenting powers of nationalism and racism are inscribed deep within the very ontological and ideological formation of the modern Western nation-state. It is the ideological form of egalitarianism in Australia which not only has the potential of exciting a damaging nationalism and racism but also can impart to such practices much of their impetus.

Furthermore, I have focused on what I call the inner logic of Australian egalitarianism. In other words, I have concentrated on attempting to lay bare the interpretational structure, the principles according to which many in Australia apprehend their reality and assert the significance of experience within it. These principles are rarely available to the conscious grasp of cultural participants or of those who would analyze their action. I certainly could not claim to have escaped my own ideological constitution in this analysis. But no analysis can be external to ideology, and all I can ultimately claim is that I have made some attempt to penetrate to a degree the realm of tacit assumptions, of the taken-for-granted, which lie at the root of common sense in the culture of everyday life in Australia. Here is the significance of my analysis of Blainey. He presents far more than racism or poor scholarship, as many of his critics have charged. He argues with the dangerous authority of an unexamined common sense, which in its uncritical application to serious human matters of the present, or to the reconstruction of a past made relevant to the present, can generate untold damage. The exploration of Blainey's common sense and the establishment of its continuity with the nationalist tradition of Anzac reveal the ideological roots of his delusion and that of others who would argue along with him. Blainey's tragedy is that he refuses to question the prison of his own logic, which is deeply part of that historical world into which he was born. He fails, in other words, to pursue the truly liberating possibility of the great ideals of freedom and human dignity that are a vital part of egalitarian thought. He destroys them in a logic of interpretation and practice forged in the conditions of political nationalism harnessed too often to the manufacture and reproduction of inequality and injustice.

8

Nationalism, Tradition, and Political Culture

Nationalism makes culture into an object and a thing of worship. Culture is made the servant of power. Students of nationalism have often commented that the character of nationalism is religious and that the political is made religious in its process. This is effected through the sacralization of the culture of the nation, the two being inseparable in modern nationalism. The culture that is sacralized is highly distilled, spiritualized, and as the essence of the nation defines the conditions of its unity.

The culture of nationalism is a quite specific thing, highly constructed, often carefully planned and worked out (Hobsbawm and Ranger 1983). Australian Anzac nationalism is an example, as is that of Israel (Handelman and Shamgar-Handelman 1986) and the Soviet Union (Binns 1979). The Sri Lanka flag, with the lion of Sinhala in central space, holding the sword of state, was carefully schemed. There was some protest from the Tamil and Muslim minorities, who were represented by colors at the borders. There is dispute over the Australian flag. The official one carries a small Union Jack in the top left-hand corner, symbolizing continuity with Britain. Arguments proceed as to what a new design might be. A few Australians recommend the flag flown at Eureka Stockade, the symbolic revolt of the people against the agents of state.

Hobsbawm (1983) describes the construction of national symbols and ceremonials as an "invention of tradition." This tradition is contrasted with "custom," or the culture of everyday life, which is fluid, changing, and open to continual interpretation. The tradition of nationalism is fixed and static, and the activity focused upon it is often compulsory: people must stand and be silent when the national anthem is played. Furthermore, invented tradition is ill defined and, unlike custom and the everyday practice of culture, has no necessary continuity with the past. Nazism, as Hobsbawm says, was invented and also evolved on established ground. I am not convinced by any of these contrasts. Tradition has little relation to custom or to the past, in Hobsbawm's usage. Australian inventors of tradition are consciously creating a new moment of origin, which points to a future, not to a past. Similarly, when Sinhalese point to the events of the *Mahavamsa* they are referring to history, not in any historian's sense necessarily, but indeed to a moment of origin, which is consciously in the present and extends to the future. Obviously nationalist traditions have to do with origins, but in a highly symbolic sense, a moment which is not *in* time but *is* time, the totality of all time or the beginning of time. The opposition between tradition and custom, furthermore, is false, for in his account of tradition Hobsbawm is describing processes of reification common in religious action. These are processes whereby modes of understanding reality are systematically removed from their embeddedness in the flow of daily life, fashioned into symbolic things, and placed in a stable, dominant, and determinate relation to action. In this way action is formed to the idea and reconstituted in the idea. This is the religious form of nationalism, vital to its power, and integral to an understanding of its inventions. Hobsbawm and other contributors to his view fail to gather the full significance of the fashioning of tradition in this sense. It leads some to reduce the power of such fashioned and potentially determinate symbolic traditions to the social and political circumstances of a situation which are somehow made to exist apart from tradition. The traditions constructed in the religion of nationalism can function to change the world in which they operate. The ways of attaching significance to everyday life, what some anthropologists would describe as culture, can be constricted to the ideas that the traditions embody. The culture of nationalism can become the culture of the nation in the sense that the population begins to interpret experience in accordance with the argument essayed by the traditions.

The word *invention* explicitly carries the notion that some traditions are created and others are not. Ultimately, I cannot conceive of a tradition or mode of cultural action that is not invented. But there are two important implications which must be addressed. The first is the idea that if a tradition is invented or constructed it is less real and less potent than those that are not. This sometimes justifies the shift of the analytical gaze away from the floss of tradition to something that underlies and is separate from it, thereby causing one to miss critical dimensions of the real force and power of tradition. I discussed such an approach with reference to Malinowskian interpretations of the political force of myth in Sri Lanka. The concept of interest is given full material and determining weight and is conceived of as existing outside some form of cultural construction. It constructs rather than being itself constituted within a social process and having specific cultural import. The point was extended to the Anzac material, wherein interests outside the tradition of Anzac are often seen by scholars to be at work. I am not discounting the great importance of class interests but interpretations which state that those motivated in class were external to the ideological apparatus they brought into existence. The fact that the powerful as well as the weak may be internal to the culture of ideology is critical to an understanding of the political force of constructed tradition.

My second point is more important. No tradition is constructed or invented and discontinuous with history. This is so even for the celebrated example of the Scottish highland kilt that was created by a Lancashire Quaker in the early eighteenth century (Trevor-Roper 1983, 21–22). Nothing apart from nothing comes out of a void. Things may take on new form or achieve original meaning, but many of the things that human beings fashion contain aspects of the world from which they spring and to which they refer. The Anzacs referred to themselves as making history and as inventing a tradition. Australians, often those in power, but also artists, poets, writers, sports people, and so on, were and are in their nationalism concerned with making tradition. It is a cultural conception in Australia that Australians have or had no culture and needed to make one. Such attitudes, of course, are part of the culture of many nationalisms, especially those which have broken away from earlier forms of domination and conceive of themselves as starting history anew. But the traditions which are made or the ones recalled to political dominance, such as the legends of the *Mahavamsa* in Sinhalese nationalism, may be ingrained with aspects of those realities that are taken for granted by those who are active in creating the traditions or making them newly relevant. The Anzac tradition is ingrained with an egalitarian and Christian ontology that is deeply part of the historical world out of which it was formed. Likewise, the *Mahavamsa* stories have embedded within them the logical scheme of a hierarchical ontology. The act of construction is one that is not producing an empty tradition. It is an act of essentialism, thoroughly appropriate to a religion of nationalism, which seeks to distill and purify a world of experience into its basic qualities as these are culturally conceived. Accordingly, the selection of traditions and the organization of nationalist ceremonial are not arbitrary—of the "any stirring myth will do" variety—and neither are they mere dressing, pomp and circumstance, chosen because they are presentationally impressive. They are chosen because of what they distill ontologically; that is, they make sense and condense a logic of ideas which may also be integral to the people who make the selection although hidden from their reflective consciousness. Thus the Vijaya and Dutugemunu legends are not just good yarns or natural nationalist stuff because they tell of the Sinhalese origin and the glory of Sinhalese Buddhist power. One reason they are important in modern nationalism is that they are stories which powerfully and coherently present fundamental Buddhist logics of cosmic hierarchy that are integral to daily practices and to the constitution of person.

The ideology of nationalism has passionate force, and it was my focus on the ontology of ideology that I consider to have extended an understanding of this force. My analysis does not reduce nationalist passion to a psychologism, either of the kind by which the traditions or culture of nationalism are seen as being intrinsically emotive or of the kind that reduces to an individual psychology, that sees violence and other passions as integral to individuals, as natural in humanity. The emotions and passions unleashed in nationalism are both of the person and of the world. The emotionality of nationalism flows from the way persons are directed to their experience, to the political and social and economic circumstances of their experience in ontology. Such ontology is integral to the total context of persons, constituting their being and, through the force of ideology, part of the way varieties of situations in experience are constructed in significance. What is internal to the person also extends around the person, and it is by exploring the world around the person, the logic of routine ideas and practices, that some understanding of the parameters of the passions and the conditions of their sometimes explosive realization can be reached. The emotions and the passions are in the world, in the total situation of human action, and in the particular form of the unity that human beings have with the situations of their action and experience. This is the kind of approach I have essayed in this book.

When I refer to the ontology of tradition in nationalism and the ontology of those who select the traditions or come to adore them in the religion of nationalism, I do not imply that the ontologies are the same in their meaning. Meaning is always a property of historical and social and political contexts. It takes particular shape in the logic of ontology but is not reducible to ontology. The meaning of ontology must always be in the world, abstracted from the world of existence; it is the potential logical shape of the world. It has such force only when it is joined to the world of action. The ontological meaning of the events of Dutugemunu was different in the twelfth century from its meaning in the twentieth century. Likewise, the egalitarianism of Anzac at the time of its construction was an ontology which drew its meaning, possibly for people such as Bean, for example, within the context of British Kiplingesque Boy's Own imperialism. This meaning is not the same today, the egalitarianism of Anzac shaping within its logic other discourse born of modern politics, like the argument of Blainey.

If ontologies change their meaning through time, they are also varied in their meaning across space. Different interpretations within reality and indeed competing ideologies can be contained within a single ontological scheme. The feature of nationalism as a dominant ideology is that it can bring a particular ontology and its reasoning into central place. In this situation an ideology of nationalism, through the ontology inscribed in the traditions presented for worship, can unify diverse contexts of meaning in time and in space.

Thus, when the legends of the *Mahavamsa* are made symbolic of the modern Sri Lankan state, their logic is brought into dominant relation to the ontologies of everyday Sinhalese realities. It links with those, I suggest, with which it shares a common logic but not necessarily a meaning. In this conjunction, wrought by political action, the events of mythic history, of Vijaya and Dutugemunu, are united with persons in the depth and ground of their being in current realities. Mythic history is made immediate and the present is extended into the past, a past made existentially real. Similarly, separate contexts of meaning in space brought into conjunction within the one ontology by nationalist ideological action, begin to exchange and to resonate with similar meaning. Thus, the ideological assertion that the modern state and the cosmic state of everyday ritual experience are essentially the same converts one context of meaning into the terms of the other. Meaning across space becomes unified in the logic of ontology. The importance of this expansion in time and space is precisely because it is achieved in the logic of ontology. It is an expansion which reaches into the person. Not only can it be a factor in effecting a sense of ideological unity with others but it can yield to nationalist ideology the power to effect a general orientation or reorientation of a population to the horizons of their experience.

Tambiah (1976, 516), whose understanding of the modern politics of Buddhist states is unsurpassed, stresses the totalizing dimensions of Southeast Asian religio-political systems. My analysis extends within his view. I also note his emphasis on political agency in the conjunctive and totalizing process. In Sri Lanka, *Mahavamsa* history has not always had the same dominant import in nationalist politics as it has today. Tambiah comments that the UNP, well before Jayawardene took control during the 1970s, "tried to keep politics and Buddhism apart or at least within bounds" (1976, 518). I think that the perspective I have developed in relation to ontology increases an understanding of ideological totalization, the way in which the tentacles of ideological argument can spread into diverse situations, capturing human beings in their grip.

Totalization is the tendency in all nationalism and of Australia no less than Sri Lanka. But the form taken by such totalization is often different, both in consciousness and in experience and orientation within such consciousness. Such difference in consciousness is intimately connected with ontology in ideology.

The orientation to history, whether mythic or factual, is very different within the ontology of Sinhalese hierarchical ideology from what it is within Australian egalitarianism. For Sinhalese the past is always in the present and the person is inseparable from history. The person and history form a cosmic unity. People in Sri Lanka are not oriented to the past, because the rubble of history is all around them or because events of history are moments of reference within the ritual occasions in which they participate. These aspects are of undoubted importance, but quite apart from such considerations, a specific orientation to the past, the past as in them and conditioning their continuity in time, is integral to the ontology embedded in hierarchical ideology.

Australian egalitarians are given to placing history outside themselves. The Australian individual is constituted as prior to history, and Australians may be said to struggle toward history, to join with it, and to make it. Sinhalese can fear history, for its possibilities are continuously in them. Australians are disturbed to be without it.   Distance from history is a tyranny, so they journey to Europe to infuse the meaning of its ruins or, in a recent, more Australia-centered nationalism, appropriate the remains of Australian Aboriginals to themselves.   It is an expectation and a fear in some quarters (a hope in others) that Anzac Day will disappear as the old soldiers die and the lessons of history are thus forgotten.   But the egalitarian fear of a separation from history and of isolation by time and distance may be a factor in the very reproduction of Anzac Day as a national event.   Other ways of joining its past to the present, of maintaining a continuity of time and meaning, are always being found in the organization of the day.

Sinhalese stress the nation in history as integral to their psychic unity.   Their history forms the person who has no existence outside it and who realizes an emotional unity with others through history.   Australian Anzac egalitarianism recognizes a psychic unity external to history. History is the product of the psyche and is the example of the psychology of the group.   History functions to bind people together—is the cement for the psychic mix—but is passive and does not generate action, as it does among Sinhalese.   Australians make history, and its recorded and remembered events are the sediment of their autonomous individual will.

Conceptions of ethnic unity and national identity take different form in Sinhalese hierarchy from that which they take in Australian egalitarianism and may be manifest in action.   The hierarchical ideology of Sinhalese nationalism stresses the internal unity of Sinhalese in themselves.   This internal unity, a hierarchical unity, structures their relations to non-Sinhalese.   Thus the principles of the hierarchical interrelation and incorporation of difference which join Sinhalese also condition their relation to Tamils.   Ideally the latter are linked to Sinhalese but in a subordinated relation of incorporation.   They are not part of the Sinhalese nation but are part of the higher encompassing unity of the Sinhalese Buddhist state.   I stress that in Sinhalese nationalism, ideologically and ontologically, the personal and national integrity of Sinhalese is holistically conditioned.   It is in the encompassment of the Sinhalese Buddhist state wherein Sinhalese as a nation are in a hierarchical relation of domination to others that the unity of Sinhalese qua Sinhalese is determined.   Any fragmentation of this unity, a separation of the part from the whole, is antagonistic to hierarchy and produces a loss of personal and national integrity for Sinhalese.   A failure in hierarchy generates opposition, conflict, and suffering among Sinhalese and between Sinhalese and non-Sinhalese.

Australian nationalists conceive of things rather differently. Their identity is not in itself, as it may be described for Sinhalese. Sinhalese consciousness is one of enduring historical unity organized according to principles of internal coherence which is sustained by their encompassment within the state. Australian identity is for itself. It is established in relations of competition, conflict, contrast, and opposition. The metaphor of war in Anzac has import in this context. Australians are defined in the conflict. Dutugemunu's war with Elara does not define Sinhalese and has nothing to do with the establishment of Sinhalese identity. But it has everything to do with the restoration, in modern interpretation, of Sinhalese hegemony and of Sinhalese internal national and personal coherence. The Australian nation is a collectivized individual identity that, in a sense, can only sustain such identity, and unity in identity, by contrast.

These kinds of ideological conceptions of ethnicity, nation, and identity have import and force in the political and social circumstances of their integument. They can establish their vicious cycle. An Australian stress on an Australian national identity, for example, can establish the conditions of its own contradiction. It defines itself in relation to what is not Australian and discovers opposition and conflict founded in the presence of collective national identities that are different. But nationalist egalitarians value unity, unity in essential if unique similarity. So difference is suppressed, manifest in the symbolic violence of the past governmental policy of assimilationism; or difference is excluded, present until recently in the state violence of the White Australia policy. Such ideologically motivated social and political processes may be redirected, and certainly liberalized, but not altered in principle in the recent policies of multiculturalism, as I have suggested. Indeed, surface differences may be tolerated, but in the conditions of nationalism, perceived deeper, ontological difference, may generate racial hostilities. The only radical difference tolerated in such circumstances may be that of Aboriginals—not any Aboriginals, but those regarded as truly traditional, in White Australia nationalist thought the ultimate egalitarian, in perfect union with nature.

In Sri Lanka, the assertion of Sinhalese nationalism sets in train a process of reversing perceived fragmentation of numerous kinds, personal, social and political, through a logic of incorporation. This is not one in which differences are suppressed or excluded. Rather it is a process wherein those who are different are brought into hierarchical subordination within the order of the Sinhalese Buddhist state. This conditions the violence of the state, the violence of Buddhist monks, and the violence of ordinary citizens in relation to those they identify as ethnically different.

In a situation where such a hierarchical nationalism is firmly in place, one heightened in consciousness by an appeal to the traditions of the *Mahavamsa* and to rites which signify similar principles, any move toward separation from the state on the basis of difference will always threaten to bring into action the incorporative violence of the state. Ordinary Sinhalese citizens may encourage the state in such action, for the power of the person is in the authority of the state—as the sorcery rites show—and it is by summoning the power of the Buddhist state that the suffering of person and nation can be overcome. In the totalizing force of Sinhalese Buddhist nationalism any move to separation or exclusion from the encompassment of the state is likely to be resisted. Nothing can exist outside the state, with the possible exception of demons and monks. Another exception may be the Vaddas, the aboriginal inhabitants of the island in popular Sinhalese belief. They are outside hierarchy, often conceived of as wild and demonic. In myth they are the descendants of the children of Vijaya and Kuveni, the "evil" of origination, against which the hierarchy of the Sinhalese Buddhist state is defined.

The foregoing processes, of course, gather their force in specific ideas of the state, the relation of nation to state, of power, and so on. I demonstrated with reference to the Sinhalese legends of the *Mahavamsa* and to the Australian story of Anzac and its ceremonial that such ideas are part of the distinct totalizing ideological form of the respective nationalisms discussed. A general significance of this point is that not all nationalism is the same, which is sometimes too readily assumed. I emphasized, moreover, the importance of taking the traditions and rites of nationalism seriously, for they provide a window into the ideological structure of nationalism.

The distinction between the two nationalisms was thrown into relief in my comparison whereby each was made to reflect critically on the other. Sinhalese nationalism reveals many of the Australian nationalist understandings of their realities to be culturally arbitrary and vice versa. The analysis in my view increased an understanding of the force of ideological factors in the direction of human action. Methodologically, I was enabled to explore the logic of ideas in their context, in myth, in ritual event, and in the practices of everyday life. But in an important sense, when the two nationalisms were juxtaposed, each became quite explicitly part of the analysis of the other—indeed, an aspect of the ethnography of the other. The nationalism of Australia, for example, became the means by which the analytical significance of ideas and events that affect Sinhalese could be revealed. This was so, however, in a setting in which the ideological ground upon which significant difference was realized was also present. To put it another way, an analytical consciousness of the Sinhalese material influenced the way I searched the Australian material and vice versa.

A claim that is often made in anthropological circles is that the study of another extends an understanding of one's own society. The claim is not without difficulty, for anthropologists cannot escape interpreting other realities through ideologies of their own action. This, I add, is not necessarily to be disparaged. Paradoxically, it is the consciousness of difference that is perhaps integral to the character of anthropological insight, to the humanizing and scientific contribution of anthropology. A problem arises, however, when the anthropologist without being aware of it systematically organizes the ideas and actions of different others to the ideological assumptions of the anthropologist. There is no extension of understanding, and the taken-for-granted world of the anthropologist is confirmed, not challenged, which some anthropologists assert is the virtue of their approach to culture. Methodologically, it is no better than those who apply, as Geertz (1973) has argued, universalist theories such as psychoanalysis and economic theories of rational choice, without being aware of their cultural nature. In so doing, the generalist theoretician may misconceive radical difference as an instance of a universal. This is the reverse possibility of that of the anthropologist who presents as difference nothing but an image of his or her own reality. I cannot claim that I have avoided such difficulties. They are intrinsic to any discipline whose subject of inquiry is ultimately itself, the nature of humankind.

My version of the method of anthropological comparison is one by which in the dialogue of the juxtaposition I attempted to sustain the authenticity and integrity of the worlds described without reducing the one to the terms of the other. The analysis, I think, suggested parallels between the argument of nationalist tradition and practice and ways in which some social scientists conventionally interpret reality. The essentialist character of the culture of nationalism undoubtedly aided such observation. The exploration of egalitarian ideas and practice distilled in Anzac nationalism and sharpened in contrast to Sinhalese nationalism displayed arguments concerning psychic unity and group mind and the individualism underlying the conception of the social that are as suggestive of Durkheim as they may be of Hobbes and Bentham. The determination of processes relating to ethnicity and to ethnic identity were shown to be very distinct phenomena in Sri Lanka and in Australia despite other similarities. Sinhalese do form into wider inclusive associations on the basis of identity, for instance, as they do in Australia and elsewhere. This, reflected in caste and in ethnic communalism, was developed in the transformations attendant on colonialism and the formation of class relations under the conditions of capitalism. But Sinhalese conceptions of the internal unity of ethnic categories is vastly different from such conceptions in Australia.

The establishment of ideological and cultural distinctions in my comparison was the basis for opening discussion on issues of general relevance to humanity at this historical moment and of particular import for the political societies examined—thus my interest in nationalism and its connection to intolerance and violence and to the production of human suffering. I was concerned with the relation of constructed tradition in this process. I focused on the conceptions of reality contained in these traditions—of power, of state, of nation, and of person and individual— and, I stress, not upon these phenomena as they may be empirically described or defined independent of such conceptions. Nonetheless, these conceptions are integral to the experience of reality and, I hold, to those who deny their relevance to an understanding of reality and who exclude their relevance in their own interpretations. While I have concentrated on the logic of ideas and their practice, nothing that I have said diminishes the importance, indeed the paramount importance, of world economic and political forces in the production of the kinds of human anguish I have addressed.

Much of the present crisis in Sri Lanka and the generation of intolerance in Australia have to do with their integration within wider processes that reproduce themselves in particular form in the social and political dynamics of the nations discussed. I do consider, however, that such forces gather their power and their significance through the ideology of tradition, which gives to general processes a particular fatal twist. These ideologies in their historical movement are not merely surface phenomena but, through the ontologies they engage and the original significance they yield to them, act at depth, act in the very being of those who participate in them. Here is where much of the hegemonic strength of tradition and ideology lies; its power to release great passions for human liberation and also for domination and destruction.

Notes

1. Dumont reverses the evolutionist position of much Western social and political philosophy. In Marxism and anarchism, for example, egalitarian ideologies and social forms have been seen as historically prior in the evolution of modern society. In the evolution of society the fundamental humanity of humankind was lost in the development of instituted social inequalities. Dumont is concerned to reveal the ideological aspects of this position, which is also deeply ingrained in other varieties of Western social thought, not to mention anthropology. I regard Dumont to be as ideological as those he criticizes and I consider arid the continuation of the search for "basics" along his lines or along the lines of those with whom he disagrees. In this way Dumont remains bound to the issues and debates of eighteenth-century Europe.

2. Dumont's discussion of hierarchy and egalitarianism owes much, of course, to the arguments of Toqueville (1968) and Tönnies (1955) especially. What some may interpret as his valuation of hierarchy over egalitarianism is also an aspect of the romantic "world we have lost" syndrome, which marks much Western social science. It is, indeed, a worship of traditionalism which is a dimension of modern nationalism.

3. The approach to Indian society offered by Dumont has been widely disputed by a host of other critics. He has answered many of these, not always convincingly, in the most recent edition of Homo Hierarchicus (1980). I agree with his dismissal of interactionist and economistic points of view such as those of Berreman (1962, 1963) and Bailey (1960). They refuse to see the ideological constitution and limitations of their own views. Dumont undervalues the potential relevance of class analysis, Marxist or other, in the interpretation of the dynamics of Hindu India. His commitment to a demonstration of their historical ideological constitution leads him to this position (Dumont 1977). I think he throws the baby out with the bathwater. A realization that class forces may take shape in different ideological form is not necessarily reducing all class processes to the same thing. Thompson (1978) has made a clear case for class in the West as being a particular cultural form, and he explicitly attacks a Marxism

that is ultimately an economic reductionism. I show that class in hierarchical ideology has a distinct direction and force not reducible to the terms of much Western class analysis (Kapferer 1983). But this argument requires more space than I have here. I shall note one important point, however, that Dumont is making. It is a point made against Weber as much as it is made against Marx. He does not see hierarchical systems as static forms, as some of Dumont's critics appear to assume them to be. Dumont suggests that institutional orders along the lines developed in the West, but not reducible to them, are a possibility of hierarchical systems and were developing before the Western colonial intervention. Hierarchy does not require destruction in its transformation in order to produce the kind of "material" world characterized by modern capitalist society. I stress that this is my reading of Dumont's argument. While I think it is present in his work, it clearly needs expansion to be at all satisfactory. Beteille (1986), who is Weberian in orientation, is an important critic of Dumont. He stresses the importance of democratic egalitarian ideals and practice in India, a fact that cannot be doubted. But Dumont does not dispute this. What Dumont does state is that such ideas are subordinated in hierarchy. He also implies that it is the presence of egalitarianism in its Indian form that contributes to the ethnic and religious communal rioting. I think, however—as I have indicated in the body of my argument—that Dumont is often too exclusionist in his discussion. Things are either egalitarian or hierarchical, parts or wholes, and so on. Very different ideological schemes or ontological systems can coexist, even in India, as is suggested by B. S. Cohen in his fascinating study of British colonial ritual (1983). It may be that the analysis of the coexistence, the structure of the relation and interpenetration of such ideological systems, would extend understanding. There are numerous other criticisms and developments of Dumont but they tend to be within the terms of his argument (Marriott 1976, Barnett 1975, Das 1982, Beck 1972). He rejects them. Broadly, however, in the context of my argument the points made are of a deeply specialist kind. My understanding of Sinhalese Buddhist ideology fits broadly with Dumont's notions, in which I find many insights, despite my own misgivings and the criticisms of others.

4. Tambiah's discussion of the Thai Buddhist and Sinhalese Buddhist conceptions of the galactic polity is essential reading for those interested in extending their understanding of the relation between hierarchy and the political in the Buddhist state as distinct from Hindu social orders. Tambiah (1976, 40) notes the dualistic structure of the Buddhist system in contrast to the triadic Hindu hierarchical order.

> Unlike the brahmanical cutting of the cake into the hierarchized domains of dharma, artha, kama, the Buddhist slicing is in terms of two levels—the dharma, as cosmic law and as truth (the seeker of which is the renouncing bhikku), encompassing the dharma of the righteous ruler, which attempts to give order to this world. The former brackets the latter.

5. My use of *ontology* and its relation to ideology will be discussed more fully in chapter 3. For the present, I use *ontology* in reference to those constitutive principles of being that locate and orient human beings within their existential realities. Meaning in ontology does not precede the reality of experience but is inseparable from it and is simultaneous with it. The way in which human

beings reach out toward the horizons of their existence is motivated in an ontology whose meaning and force are achieved in context, a context whose significance and force are realized in the depths of personal being or existence. I note a similarity between my use of ontology and other ideas available in anthropology, but there is also a difference. There is a connection between ontology and what a structuralist means by "deep structure," or what an anthropologist such as Turner (1974) means by "root paradigm," or what Ardener implies by "semantic space." But all the terminology of these various approaches also indicates fundamental, basic, generative meaning in their structures, paradigms, and spaces. I insist, however, that the nature of the constitutive and positioning force of ontology is not germane to ontology. Rather, the constitutive or positioning force of ontology emerges through its engagement in specific historical action whereby certain possibilities of the "logic" of ontology achieve significance and derive their potency.

6. Parkin (1985) suggests that dualistic theological systems such as those of Christianity have strong notions of evil, whereas holistic systems such as Hindu and Buddhist orders have weak notions of evil. Southwold, asserting the same argument, is even more trenchant. He begins an article on the topic with the statement "There is no concept of evil in Buddhism: so I concluded on the basis of my fieldwork among Sinhalese Buddhists in 1974–5" (Southwold 1985, 128). This could not be further from the fact. The Sinhalese Buddhists in the area of his research have a perfectly good word—*vasa*; the Great Being of evil is sometimes referred to as Vasavarti Maraya. Sinhalese Buddhists understand this being and another closely associated with him, Suniyam, as terrifyingly destructive and fragmenting. They are the very converse of the Buddha and his absolute negation and the perfect representation of absolute ignorance and nonreason. I note that the area in which Southwold did his fieldwork is close to one of the most important shrines of sorcery and evil for Sinhalese on the island. As I have said, Hindus and Buddhists simply have a different understanding of evil from that of Christians. It is even more dreadful, perhaps, for evil is the very essence of a cosmic destruction that threatens all existence. The suffering of the person is a suffering in the ordering of existence itself, which encompasses the person. This is very different from Judeo-Christian understanding, which, as Ricoeur (1967) clearly argued, locates evil within the person. As Obeyesekere (1980), extending his argument out of Ricoeur's, suggestively states, Christians experience evil, suffering, sin, and personal stain as guilt. Obeyesekere characterizes Sinhalese Buddhists as shame-oriented, in contrast to Christians, and this fits with a notion of suffering and evil as encompassing, extending around the person rather than rooted in the person as an individual, independent of an encompassing whole.

Chapter 2

1. The horrors of the 1983 rioting received extensive coverage in the international news media. Tambiah (1986) provides a passionate account and a thorough analysis of the historical and social background to the conflict. Thornton and Niththyananthan (1985) provide a useful view from the Tamil side of the events, including a detailed account by one of the Tamil refugees. A description

of the events leading to the riots and of the rioting itself by an official of the Sri Lanka Ministry of Foreign Affairs gives the story from the Sinhalese position (Dissanayaka 1983). While sympathetic to the Sinhalese situation, it is critical and provides graphic descriptions of the rioting in Colombo and its patterning throughout the island. There have been other riots by the Sinhalese ethnic majority against other significant ethnic minorities. The Muslim population was subjected to Sinhalese violence in 1915, and there have been small anti-Muslim disturbances in the towns since. The Muslims are predominantly Tamil-speaking and constitute a significant element of urban and small-town business communities. In the 1981 census of the population they numbered 7.4% of the whole island population of 14,850,000. The Tamil population, inclusive of estate Tamils—a separate category in the census—and Sri Lankan Tamils compose 18.2 percent of the total population. While there have been numerous small incidents of anti-Tamil violence by Sinhalese, major riots against the Tamils occurred in 1956, 1958, 1977, and 1981.

2. Other government sources, not publicly admitted, place the number of Tamil dead around 1,000. Tamil estimates are that 2,000 were killed. Tambiah cites other evidence to indicate that between 80,000 and 100,000 were in refugee camps. He refers to the government evidence that 18,000 households were affected by the rioting (Tambiah 1986, 22).

3. The connection is perfectly clear in Evans-Pritchard's (1937) classic study of sorcery and witchcraft among the Azande. Douglas (1956?) associates sorcery with the structure of authority in societies she characterizes as being of the highly ordered grid type.

4. Obeyesekere cites Peiris's study of the precolonial Kandyan kingdom in support of this general contention. Thus persons found guilty of sorcery could be executed and their property given to those whom they had ensorcelled (Peiris 1956, 144). Obeyesekere's implication is that the removal of such traditional institutional controls with the advent of colonial rule is one possible factor in the apparent increase of the phenomenon. Regardless of the adequacy of such an explanation, Peiris's evidence points to sorcery as a concern of state. As will be seen in subsequent chapters, evil sorcery in myth and in modern practice is conceived of as an act against the Sinhalese Buddhist state. Most who visit the sorcery shrines, or have antisorcery rites performed, are seeking alleviation from attack by sorcerers. In their practice they bring the full power of the Buddhist state to bear upon their problem.

5. Catholic Sinhalese, especially those who lived on the coast in the area immediately to the north of Colombo, also participated in the anti-Tamil rioting. My impression is that their status as a religious minority, coupled with class factors, is critical to an understanding of their action. Stirrat (1984) sets the issue into some historical perspective and discusses the relations between Tamil Catholics and Sinhalese Catholics in the present ethnic situation.

6. Sedawatte Dhammaruchi (1979), who wrote the foreword to "Eelam—the Truth," is the elder brother of J. R. Jayawardene, the president of Sri Lanka.

7. As B. F. Farmer (1963) writes, Sri Lanka is one of the few places where the nineteenth-century European construction of the Aryan race continues to have serious currency.

8. Newton Gunasinghe discusses the many perceptions of the ethnic conflict in Sri Lanka in relation to the complexity of the current social situation. He argues that the most extreme "nation beseiged" syndrome, which recommends firm action against the Tamils, is found principally among "middle level mercantile elements engaged in trade competition, sections of the Buddhist monkhood, fractions within the traditional intelligentsia who generally derive from a rural propertied background and cohorts of urban professionals who are generally self-employed." (Gunasinghe 1985, 15). These fractions, who also tend to be supported by the press, commonly give voice to the fact that the Sinhalese are of Aryan background, that Sri Lanka was always a unitary state, that the Government is in direct line of continuation with Vijaya, and so on. Gunasinghe also points to more "liberal" perceptions, including the position that Sinhalese and Tamils have always lived together and should enjoy equality and the position that supports a devolution of power, which would give Tamils greater autonomy. It is impossible here to do full justice to the subtlety of Gunasinghe's argument and the importance of his accurate assessment of the fact that different perceptions of the ethnic conflict cut across various class fractions. The central point for my argument, however, is that the ruling perception, the one favored by government and other dominant class fractions, is one of Sinhala chauvinism and confrontation with Tamil interests by the Sinhalese.

9. Cyril Mathew was sacked from the cabinet in the latter part of 1984. One reason was probably that he is an extremist and was challenging the authority of the president. The general attitudes toward the conflict, however, which he expressed freely continue as regular fare in the press and public speeches by other parliamentarians.

10. Since the late 1940s there has been a consistent program of colonization by Sinhalese of areas once dominated by Tamils. This has been conducted under the auspices of irrigation programs, for example, in the Eastern Province. The ethnic composition has been significantly altered. There are Sinhalese settlement programs being pursued in the Tamil-dominated Northern Province. These settlements have been the focus of guerilla attacks by Tamil separatist groups. The change in demographic pattern is accompanied by a concern of the government to distribute the icons of Sinhalese Buddhist dominance. This is the significance of the restoration of ruined dagabas. It is also the significance underlying the erection of replicas of important ancient monuments in various parts of the island.

11. It is noteworthy that the Kandyan Rebellion of 1848 against British rule occurred in the month of Asala.

12. Malinowski (1926, 21) states that "myth is not merely a story told but a reality lived." He adds, however, that myth "is not an intellectual explanation or an artistic imagery, but a pragmatic charter of primitive faith and moral wisdom."

Chapter 3

1. There are other important accounts of Sinhalese history, such as the *Rajavaliya*, which are commonly referred to. The *Rajavaliya* differs from the

Mahavamsa and the *Dipavamsa* in that it does not appear to have been composed by monks. It was also composed considerably later, during the seventeenth century or earlier. The *Rajavaliya* has far less authority for Sinhalese than the more ancient *Dipavamsa* and *Mahavamsa.*

2. The creation of the parallel reality or island of Giri by Buddha for the demons is of interest in relation to the folk tradition. There is a category of female demons, known as *giri*, in the exorcist traditions of south Sri Lanka. They are demons who chiefly afflict children, but reference to them is made in the large deity ceremonies of the *gammadua* and *devol madua*. The male counterparts of the *giri* demons are the *gara* demons, ambivalent creatures who remove impurity through their prodigious capacity to eat.

3. When Sihabahu returns to the capital of Vanga the king is already dead. The dead king's ministers invite him to assume the kingship. He does so but passes it on to his mother's husband (*Mahavamsa* 6:31–35). There is no mention of such an episode in the *Dipavamsa*. For those interested in the analytical possibilities of the *Mahavamsa* account, I note the connection between the slaying of Sihabahu's father and the death of his grandfather, the king of Vanga. The act of killing the lion could be interpreted as a sacrificial act which bears some relation to the death of the Vanga king—also a sacrifice—and the creation of the autonomous state of Sihabahu and the rebirth of the Vanga state through the establishment of a new line. Sihabahu's mother has also been reborn, and the death of her father is a kind of structural equivalent to the killing of the lion.

4. Much has been written on twinship in anthropology. Sinhalese mythology is a fertile field for extending present analytical understandings. In the Sihabahu-Sihasivali situation I note the significance of twin-sibling incest. The marriage of twins signifies the perfect resolution of differentiation and unit. I think it is symbolically equivalent to the unity of incipient differentiation of the child in the womb. In this sense the marriage of twins is a condensed symbol of powerful origination. I note the possible parallel between the nature of the Sihabahu-Sihasivali twinship and Saivite duality. Shiva is androgynous (O'Flaherty 1973), combining the male and the female in a single unity. The marriage of the twins Sihabahu and Sihasivali gains significance, I think, in this cosmological context. The unity in difference of incestuous twins contrasts with the conflict of similarity between twins of the same sex. The function of same-sex twinship in the Sinhalese mythic traditions is usually to elaborate on the destructive possibilities of contradictions that are present in embodiment. The king's two bodies—the one representing, continuity and fertility, the other powerful violence—find symbolic condensation in the character of his twin sons. In the Vijaya myth, and repeated in the Dutugemunu legend, the violent destructive force of the king (Vijaya, Dutugemunu) encompasses the aspect of fertility and continuity (Sumitta, Tissa).

5. That there are 16 pairs of twins is significant. In ancient tradition the age of sixteen is the age of adulthood, of the beginning of reason, the age of marriage. In many of the demon myths it is at the age of sixteen that the young demons start realizing their demonic capacities. A multiple of 16 is 32. There are 32 marks of the Buddha that signify his encompassment. The cosmic number contains 28 (the 28 kings) plus 4 (the Four Guardian Gods) all of whom are included in 32. I think it reasonable to assume that the fact that Sihabahu

had 16 pairs of twins or 32 sons signifies a direction of movement toward the establishment of Buddhism in Lanka. Vijaya as the first of the 32 indicates his cosmic role in paving the way for Buddhism in Sri Lanka.

6. The women and the children of Vijaya's men go elsewhere. The women in their boat go to the island of Mahiladipaka (Island of Women) and their children go to the island of Naggadipa (Island of Children) (*Mahavamsa* 6:45–46).

7. Sinhalese exorcists distinguish between two classes of rite, those for demons (*yak tovil*) and those for deities (*deva tovil*). The Suniyama does not fit neatly into either class. Perhaps it is closer to the deity rites, for it, like some of the more important rites of this category, does involve a transformation of the demon Suniyam into his divine and protective form. The demon exorcisms proper are concerned with the fragmentation of demons who cannot become encompassing and protective. They differ in the sequential organization of their ritual events from deity rites and may be said to run in reverse direction to them. I am told by exorcists that the Suniyama has a long history. The rite as performed today tends to be similar across different local traditions. But I am reliably informed that in the past different Suniyama rites, distinguishable in their performance structure, were enacted, depending on the status in hierarchy of the patient. The Suniyama was performed for kings and their vassal lords and, I am informed, was reserved for them alone. If a Suniyama was performed that was inappropriate to the status of the patient and the household, then disaster could follow. There is a story circulating in the Southern Province concerning just such an instance and the ensuing misfortune of the family, still famous in the area, is traced to the inappropriate performance. I suspect that the Suniyama, in the past, was performed on the body of the king or lord to purify them of their destructive power and also to reorder the political and social world they embodied.

8. There are other significances that may attach to the half-shaving of the heads of Vijaya—and his men. It could indicate their liminal status (V. W. Turner 1969)—their moment "betwixt and between" one political order and another. The half-shaven heads may also signify their inclination toward Buddhism. Although they are not Buddhists, they are nonetheless carrying out the Buddha's work, for they are in the process of establishing a society which will eventually become Buddhist.

9. The thread in Sinhalese mythic and cosmological thought is a vital symbol of birth and of creation. I take it as symbolically equivalent to the umbilicus. Exorcism is basically a ceremony of reconstitution and rebirth, and the thread, held or tied around the waist, wrist, or neck, signifies both union— union with that which constitutes being, sometimes a demon—and birth. There are numerous other ritual occasions when the thread is significant: a thread is placed on the railing that leads up to the summit of Sumanakuta (Adam's Peak) during a climber's first ascent and a thread is held by monks during the consecration of a new temple or by a houseowner at the opening of a newly built house.

10. I note the possible significance of Kuveni's imprisoning of Vijaya's men in a chasm. When this event is considered in relation to the event of the cave in the Sihabahu myth, it becomes conceivable that the chasm is a metaphor, like the cave, for a womb. Vijaya, by releasing hs men, acts similarly to the way

Sihabahu acted in removing the rock blocking the entrance to the lion's cave. In other words, Vijaya, like Sihabahu, is the agent of rebirth.

11. In the Mahasona exorcism, for example, the exorcist using the noose of god Mangara, a demon searcher and killer, ensnares Mahasona, thereby ending his evil influence (Kapferer 1983). The symbolism of the noose and the symbolism of the thread are identical. Both tie and unite and become a dimension of determination and control. The thread symbolizes order and control, along with its many other symbolic possibilities.

12. The act of cooking food, preparing the nurturing meal of rebirth, in the Vijaya myth shows marked similarity to the *kiri amma* rite as I have observed it in the areas of Galle and Matara in the south of Sri Lanka. In these rites the men pound the rice and prepare the milk rice cakes (*kiri bat*). Usually a number of kin-related households participate. It is a ritual performed for the 7 *kiri amma* (milk mothers), whose function is taken on by lactating mothers from the neighborhood. The rite is also for Pattini. The ritual as a whole is a rite of purification.

13. I stress the parallel between this episode in the myth and the event of the *avamangalla* (death time) in an exorcism. The demons in exorcism are at their most powerful at the time of the avamangalla and in the great gathering-time dance (*maha samayama*) which follows immediately. A word used for marriage celebration is *mangalla,* and for exorcism it is possible to translate *avamangalla* as "antimarriage." This carries the meaning of the event in exorcism for the moment of the greatest gathering of the demonic and, as in the Vijaya legend, is the moment also of the destruction of the demon; it is a moment, furthermore, which is a breaking of the bond—often conceptualized by exorcists and patients as a "marriage"—between patient and demon. This logic of exorcism could be extended to an interpretation of the Vijaya myth, for Vijaya's killing of the demons also marks an end to his demonic self and the beginning of his own transformation into an ordering and righteous ruler.

14. The desire for a honeycomb has many possible connotations in Sinhalese Buddhist cosmological thought. Honey was the first food taken by the Buddha and is a pure food suitable for the gods. Occasionally, however, the sangha is likened to a honeycomb. A honeycomb itself is divided into cells which are likened to wombs (*gaba*). My speculation is that a beehive has the metaphoric potential of a dagaba. As yet I have no statements from Buddhist monks in support of this speculation, but I note that the honeycomb or beehive stands in interesting contrast to an anthill. The anthill is the symbol of Suniyam, who stands opposed to Buddha. In Hindu symbolic thought, the anthill is a metaphor of sacred Mt. Meru, of the Hindu cosmic mountain. These speculations require further research, if there is anything at all to my surmises on symbolism. Viharadevi's longings are loaded with symbolic import of a dense cosmological kind. I speculate that the three pregnancy longings are metaphoric of the Buddhist Triple Gem: the sangha, the honeycomb or beehive, the purity of the dhamma, the sword or water—symbolizing the authority and purity of the teaching—and the Buddha, the lotus.

15. That the garlands should be unfaded is significant. As fresh blooms they are indicative of unfragmented, whole, life. They contrast with the faded, dead, fragmented, blooms which are typically given in offerings to the demonic.

The lotus is symbolic of Maha Brahma, the originator of life, and of the Buddha, who encompasses Maha Brahma. There is a marvelous contrast in the garlanding of Viharadevi with that of the mother of Oddi Raja or Suniyam. The latter's mother dreams that she is garlanded with snakes, with the poisonous negation of life. Sinhalese notice a similarity between the stalk of a lotus and the body of a snake. The body of a snake is also, in cultural convention, linked to vines and other creepers.

16. The feats of Nandhimitta as a young boy are of considerable mythic and analytical interest. I quote the following significant excerpt from the chronicle:

> In the years of his childhood, since he loved to creep far, they were
> used to bind the boy fast with a rope slung about his body, to a great
> mill-stone. And since, creeping about on the ground, he dragged the
> stone after him and in crossing over the threshold the rope broke
> asunder, they called him Nandhimitta (*Mahavamsa* 23:6–8)

Nandhi means "yarn" or "thread." Bound or tied by rope, Nandhmitta is limited or tied in a way that is indicative of similar action in present-day healing rites. The thread-tying of exorcism, for example, limits the power of the demon and protects the patient. Nandhi's tying bears comparison with Dutugemunu's famous recognition of his own restraint. Dutugemunu is told by his father not to attack the Tamils. That night Viharadevi visits him and, caressing Dutugemunu, asks, " 'Why dost thou not lie easily upon thy bed with limbs stretched out, my son:' 'Over there beyond the Ganga are the Damilas, here on this side is the Gotha-ocean, how can I lie with outstretched limbs?' he answered" (*Mahavamsa* 22:85–86). Dutugemunu's limitation is equivalent, symbolically, to the limitation of Nandhimitta. It might be noted that the account of Nandhimitta's restraint follows almost immediately Dutugemunu's famous retort. Nandhimitta, by breaking the ropes, signs the ending of his limitation, a limitation by the ending of which Dutugemunu similarly ends his restriction. It may be noted in addition that Nandhimitta breaks the rope with a grinding stone, which—at the stretch of my imagination—could be a symbol of rebirth, which, given the mythic context, may be further indicative of the future freeing and rebirth of the state which Nandhimitta will later help to achieve. The breaking of the rope, moreover, could be a symbolic breaking of the umbilicus, a connection with the past, and a portent of a new future.

17. In the folk and popular traditions Suranimala is a drunkard. *Sura* means an intoxicating drink. Pronounced as "sura," as I have heard it, it is a term that refers to the gods. Both meanings are possible in the context of the myth, for Suranimala is filled with the intoxicating power of the gods. He has the capacity to run at great speed, as the *Mahavamsa* relates. Suranimala is dressed in Punnavaddhana (garments). (*Mahavamsa* 23:33, 37). A *punnava* is the pot into which impurities are cast—impure menstrual cloths, for example. At shrines where punishing gods are present—at shrines to Devol and Suniyam, for example—a pot (*des punnava*) is used to contain or confine impurity and therefore purifies supplicants. The suffix-*nimala* carries the sense of purity. In my interpretation, then, Suranimala condenses the powerful ambivalent meanings of the demonic and the divine.

18. I think it possible to interpret the ten champions as the ten forms (*avatara*) of Vishnu. Nandhimitta has the color blue in the folk tradition, as

does Mahasona and as does Phussadeva, the last of the ten champions. At Sankapala, in the southeasten corner of Sabaragamuva province, is an important Vishnu shrine. The people around Sankapala say that the shrine is located in the territory of Phussadeva. In my view Nandhimitta and Phussadeva stand in a potentially significant relation of contrast. I think that Nandhimitta represents the Hindu, Vaisnavite, form of Vishnu—Nandhimitta is a Tamil by birth—while Phussadeva is the Sinhalese Buddhist Vishnu. In a sense, the ten champions can be regarded together as moments of transition from Hindu to Buddhist, an idea that fits with the logic of the events surrounding Dutugemunu.

19. The medieval *Thupavamsa* makes the demonic character of Dutugemunu clearer than the account of the events in the *Mahavamsa*, which the *Thupavamsa* follows closely. The *Thupavamsa* states that "Abhaya was enraged with his father the King and fled to Malaya country. From that time onwards, on account of his being wicked to his father, he came to be known as Dhuttagamani, 'Gamani the Wicked' " (*Thupavamsa*, 77). Marguerite Robinson (1968) gives details of local myths surrounding Dutugemunu while in flight outside his father's kingdom. There are some interesting parallels in her account with the Vijaya myth. Dutugemunu establishes a relation with a low-caste woman, whom he forsakes in regaining his kingdom. The events recounted in the "folk" account collected by Robinson indicate powerful themes of personal rebirth again similar to the Vijaya story. Robinson's analysis, incidentally, mixes a Malinowskian analytical approach with a structuralist Levi-Straussian interpretation. I consider that the argument, while important, displays the serious flaws of both analytical methods. The structuralist logic she discovers in the Dutugemunu myth is not the logic of the myth. Robinson's analysis thereby overlooks numerous possibilities of the kind to which my own, perhaps, points.

20. Dutugemunu's mare is, I think, symbolic of the female power, *shakti*, which he rightfully possesses through his mother and to which Tissa has made false claim by holding Viharadevi. Incidentally, Suniyam's mount is a mare. Other similar destructive demonic deities located on the coast also have mares as their vehicles.

21. It is the son of Sumitta, Panduvasdeva, who succeeds Vijaya.

22. Valeri (1985, 67–70) develops a similar argument. He criticizes Girard's Frazerian conception that sacrifice is a scapegoat mechanism by which human beings can release a violence that is psychologically innate. Valeri attacks the reduced place which Girardi's argument must give to the symbolic, representational, and "gift" aspects of sacrifice. It is of some interest that in the versions of the Buddhist Mahasammatta myth of the origin of the state that I have collected in local Sinhalese traditions there appears to be no argument that violence is innate in human beings. Violence is a consequence of the proliferation and differentiation of humanity rather than of humanity itself. For humanity to realize its peacefulness it must in proliferation and differentiation be hierarchically ordered. This ordering can be violent in itself, a dilemma with which much Buddhist teaching and scholarship are concerned.

23. The building up of the destructive power of the king is encoded in the test of strength between the king's champion, Nandhimitta, and the elephant of state, Kandula, outside the city of Vijitanagara (*Mahavamsa* 25:22–23).

24. These events gain further significance in the recognition of Phussadeva as a form of Vishnu. In the ritual exchanges, I think, Phussadeva is signifying the divine status of Dutugemunu and possibly his achievement of Bodhisattva status. Dutugemunu now embodies, in effect, the highest principles of the Buddha, and Phussadeva, as Vishnu, acknowledges his subordination to Dutugemunu as a Boddhisattva.

25. The career of Kalu Kumara is, in fact, a wonderful symbolic inversion of the Vijaya story. Vijaya moves from India to Lanka and is transformed from a demon into a righteous ruler. Kalu Kumara moves from Lanka to India and is torn apart, fragmented, by women in a city of women. Essentially, Vijaya moves from fragmentation to unity, toward the Buddhist principles that govern the apex of the cosmic hierarchy. Kalu Kumara, however, moves in the direction of Suniyam, toward fragmented oblivion. In some of the myths of Kalu Kumara and of his lower form, Kalu Yaka, carried in exorcist traditions, Kalu Kumara (Kalu Yaka) is explicitly associated with Vijaya. Thus Kalu Yaka is the son of the union of Kuveni and Vijaya (Wirz 1954, 39). Exorcists state that at the root (*mulu*) of the sacred Bo tree at Anuradhapura is the dwelling place of Kalu Yaka devatava. This fits with the logic of the myths both in the great chronicles and in the more popular traditions. Given the link between Vijaya and Kalu Yaka— and that it is in Vijaya's transformation out of the demonic that the way is prepared for Buddhism—it is appropriate that the demonic aspect of Vijaya should be at the root, at the source, of the great symbolic tree of Sinhalese Buddhism, which in its growth and encompassment is a transformation of that from which it grew.

26. Wirz (1954, 70–73) presents two versions of the original act of sorcery. Both were collected in the area of Dodanduwa, just to the north of Galle, on the south coast. The most common is the first version, and the copies I have obtained from various exorcists match that given by Wirz. Wirz's version should be consulted by those who are interested in the details of the myth.

27. I have given a summary of one of the more common accounts of the main form of Oddissa, Maha Raja Oddissa. One version of this myth in my possession is very close to aspects of the Dutugemunu legend. Thus, the queen of the king of Vadiga went to bathe in a pond close to the place where a hermit was observing his austerities. The hermit, overcome by a lust for the queen, transformed himself into a baby cobra and hid himself among the petals of a manel lily. The queen plucked the flower and as she inhaled the aroma, the hermit-cobra entered her womb through her nostril. Later in the same version of the myth, when the king learned of the great danger of the queen's son he banished the son to Maya rata or Kotmale, a jungle place referred to as the abode of demons. In the version of the Dutugemunu story in the medieval chronicle, the *Thupavamsa*, Kotmale is the place to which Dutugemunu fled at the moment he opposed the authority of his father.

28. Many scholars have remarked that the Sinhalese Buddhist myths and legends are related to and obviously drawn from South Indian Hindu counterparts. This is certainly evident in the Vijaya myth and many of the demon myths. But I should emphasize that even so a Sinhalese Buddhist message is being put across; that is, the Sinhalese versions of the myths often embody significant alterations in the structure and content of the events in the myths.

These transformations point to contrasts between Buddhist principles and those that are perceived as Hindu principles. In the Buddhist point of view Hindu myths and practices are consigned to the low regions of hierarchical space. Thus myths are transformed in content and in their organization of events to fit with historical political developments—but, I think, in accordance with similar underlying logics of structure. The argument I have outlined for myth holds for ritual practice as well. There are aspects of exorcism that strongly resemble the symbolic events of Hindu *puja*. Exorcism is performed outside the Buddhist temple. This is because demons are understood to deal with ideas and principles which defy unifying Buddhist logic. Thus in Buddhist exorcism ritual, aspects that are central in Hindu worship are moved to the periphery of ritual action— outside the temple. Exorcism itself is considered to be at the base of a hierarchy of Sinhalese Buddhist ritual practice.

29. In this form he is typically referred to as Gambara deviyo.

30. The derivation of the name *Suniyam* is relevant to an understanding of the powerful relation he commands with Buddha. Sanskrit *sunya* translates as "void." I translate it as "oblivion," for it draws attention to the contrast with the Buddha's achievement of nothingness (*nirvana*) through knowledge. Suniyam's oblivion is the consequence of ignorance. In popular traditions Suniyam in his demonic and destructive aspect is explicitly opposed to the Buddha. Thus in exorcisms a bali image of Suniyam, molded from the clay of anthills, is sometimes made. The image is yellow, the Buddha's color. In connection with the Buddha this color has the sense of suffering, death, impotence, infertility, and so on, which the Buddha transcends through his knowledge and teaching. Yellow as the Buddha's color, then, is the converse of that which it may signify otherwise. Suniyam in his demonic coloring of the bali images signifies all that the Buddha overcomes. The face of Suniyam on bali images is that of a pig. According to popular tradition Gautama died from eating pork. At some shrines in Sri Lanka, Suniyam's staff of authority (*danda*) is placed at the foot of the Buddha's Bo tree.

31. My description is based on performances of this ceremony by members of the exorcist (*berava*) caste. Members of this community are professional exorcists, becoming so after a long period of training that begins in childhood. Members of this community are important repositories of Sinhalese Buddhist mythic and ritual traditions, and their significance in this regard still awaits the full recognition they deserve. I described some aspects of the social condition of this community in Kapferer (1983). Another description of the Suniyama rite is given in Wirz (1954). I am preparing for publication a longer monograph on sorcery, and a complete description of the important Suniyama rite will be included.

32. The intimate connection between the order of the Buddhist state and disorder, between violence and the demonic, has been argued by other scholars. Greenwald observes that "violence and piety coexist in the chronicles and that violence precedes the formation of the state." The latter point is the one upon which she seizes. "The point is simply this: in order to have an 'ideal' Buddhist state . . . it is first necessary to secure the very existence of the state" (Greenwald 1978, 25). I contrast Greenwald's argument with my own. My analysis treats violence as part of the process of hierarchical encompassment, a moment

within hierarchization and consistent with Buddhist argument concerning impermanence and cycles of growth and decline. I avoid the kind of interpretational pragmatism—one that steps outside the logic of the structure—indicated by the following conclusion of Greenwald: "In the transition from warrior to master-builder, the chronicled portrait of Dutthagamani not merely recalls the Asokan model, but succeeds in providing the audience with access to a more human and believable Dutthagamani, and so paves the way for his celebration in national reverence which has persisted to the present day" (Greenwald 1978, 31). The efficacy of the Dutugemunu myth, its current appeal, is reduced to a kind of trick in the art of storytelling. My view is that the myth resonates with ontological possibility and it is the realization of this possibility in everyday practice and political ideologizing that renders the myth appealing. My argument, I think, also accounts for the repeated demonic theme in the chronicles that is too often interpreted psychologistically and without appropriate reference to the logic of the structure. Bardwell Smith, for example, comments on the significance of the demons in the chronicles and Buddha's confrontation with them. "Hypostasized into imaginary figures the yakkhas may represent tradition's own realistic fear of man's proclivity toward disorder and evil. In any case, sensitivity toward the demonic remains a permanent ingredient of Sinhalese consciousness" (Smith 1978, 55).

33. The *Rajavaliya* appears to be the work of a number of hands. Gunasekera (1954, iii) states that "in some places the compiler writes as a Buddhist, whilst elsewhere he uses phraseology natural to a Christian." He also states that no copy of the manuscript could be found at the "best-stocked Temple Libraries." His edition is the product of the examination of manuscripts held in the private collections of people living in the larger towns along the coast and in Kandy. I think it possible that there may have been a heavy early ethnic nationalist influence on the construction of the *Rajavaliya*.

34. As this exchange demonstrates, there is some dispute as to the ethnic identity of Velusumana. Velusumana in the *Mahavamsa* is the champion who possesses remarkable skills of horsemanship. The prefix *velu-* refers to the main emblem of the Tamil deity, Murugan, who has the spear (*vel*) as his weapon. Murugan is also worshipped as Kataragama by the Sinhalese.

Chapter 4

1. Sahlins (1981) in his analysis of the advent of Captain Cook in Hawaii, and his subsequent killing and consumption by the Hawaiians, states that by such action the Hawaiians became British. This was expressed in the rapid Hawaiian adoption of the names of prominent English persons and their insistence on flying the Union Jack, even though England declined the Hawaiian request to be included in the Empire. I do not think that President Jayawardene was expressing similar sentiments by his placing of Elizabeth II in the line of rulers of Sri Lanka. England certainly made Sri Lanka British, but I do not consider the reverse to have been true, despite the great influence of English culture on the Sri Lankan elite. President Jayawardene's comment was probably in deference to the presence of England's Prime Minister, Margaret Thatcher, who was in Sri Lanka at the time and who was giving support to antiseparatist

sentiments. If anything the reference to Elizabeth II could have been subtly anticolonial. Sri Lanka's establishment of a president was presented as a democratic advance, giving to Sinhalese a voice denied them under colonial rule.

2. In an article on the growing militant extremism of the Buddhist monkhood (Madras *Frontline*, 15–28 June 1985) especially since the 14 May 1985 slaughter of Sinhalese civilians at Anuradhapura, it is argued that the monks have increased their political power as a result of the ethnic conflict. The article states that the *sangha* is largely drawn from the impoverished peasantry and that they may reflect mass opinion. The writer also asserts that their power in the rapidly changing and technologizing setting of modern Sri Lanka was on the decline. But their significance in the current temperature of ideological discourse has reversed a decline in their importance. I think that the writer of the article is largely correct. I do consider, however, that he underrates the considerable influence of monks, especially in working-class areas. Their influence precedes current hostilities and ideologizing. Many of the monks, of both right and left political persuasion, have identified strongly with the interests of local communities. I know of several instances in which a local temple monk in a working-class neighborhood directed some of the riot action and of one incident in which the monk told a violently rampaging gang to attack wealthy Tamils and not the Tamil poor of the neighborhood. Local temple monks have quite a lot to do with the daily suffering of the people in their areas and gain some power and influence accordingly.

3. In recent years there has been a marked increase of interest, especially among the middle classes, in folk culture. I see this as part of an elaboration of ethnic nationalism. In 1970, when I began work on exorcism, many members of the middle class expressed antagonistic opinions, considering it somewhat declassé and reflecting poorly upon Sri Lanka in the modern world. Now I find that the same middle class is fascinated by this declining aspect of its culture. Some of the current resurgence of interest in folk culture may be the result of certain infrastructural changes in class relations. With the opening of the economy after 1977 has come the emergence of new class fractions rising from previously poor peasant and working-class or lower-middle-class fractions in the society as a whole. These were often deeply involved in practices often labeled folk culture. I think it possible that the new cultural nationalism has some relation to shifts within the class structure. It may account, too, for the apparent revival of deity ceremonies to Pattini, particularly in urban areas, in recent years. Obeyesekere (1984a), who did his research on the Pattini cult during the 1950s, observed then that it was on the decline. I think he was correct for the time but that he would have to revise his opinion today.

4. I have borrowed the idea of imagined reality from Anderson's idea of imagined community (Anderson 1983), which he developed in criticism of Gellner (1983). Gellner argues that the modern nation-state presents itself as a community when, of course, it can only be an imagined community. This is so, Gellner states, because a community is one founded on face-to-face relations, and this is clearly not true of the nation-state. Anderson says that Gellner fails to realize that probably all communities, even small village communities, are imagined in Gellner's sense, for rarely do all members of a supposed community actually participate in face-to-face interaction. For Anderson, it is not that the

nation-state is an imagined community which is significant. It is rather the *style* of the imagination which is the factor of central importance. This style typically includes a notion of solidary unity, a common and simultaneous time frame—all members of the nation-state are moving through historical time together—a common, historically rooted symbolism, and so on. Anderson's argument is similar to the earlier approach to ethnicity of Mitchell, but I also think it a valuable advance in the study of modern nationalist movements, especially ethnic nationalism.

5. The formation of a popular culture can be regarded as an aspect of what Weber recognized as the process of rationalization, which is the historical development of a self-consciousness that takes many specific cultural and political forms and is often produced in the transformations into nation-states. In the Sri Lankan situation the formation of a popular culture parallels other processes of rationalization such as Buddhist reformism.

6. My point of view on ethnicity as presented here draws on the approach initially developed by Mitchell (1956) and extended by Epstein (1958) for colonial Zambia, an entirely different situation from that of Sri Lanka. In my opinion the work of Mitchell on ethnicity—which he called, perhaps unfortunately, tribalism—constituted an important advance the full implications of which seem to have been missed by many anthropologists who have assumed a vital interest in the issue. Mitchell's point was that in the modern urban industrial setting ethnic categories were culturally creative innovations entirely relevant to, and formed within, modern capitalist conditions. He also argued that the ethnic idea, which stressed the cultural homogeneity of an internally undifferentiated category of persons, gained force as constitutive of social relations through the structure of the urban setting. Discussion of his argument became bogged down in sociologistic argument concerning the nature, for example, of categorical relations and "unstructured" situations; Mitchell claimed that the ethnic idea formed social relations in "unstructured" situations outside a preestablished organizational frame, such as those in industrial plants (Kapferer 1969). Perhaps the significance of Mitchell's contribution has been lost because of the tendency of some anthropologists to specialize and professionalize an issue. Ethnicity, or ethnic nationalism, has thus become an area of concern independent of its production in a wider social and political process, so it is occasionally taken as a distinct social phenomenon, unrelated to class and other social processes in which it is clearly embedded. Ethnicity is reduced to the status of a sociological variable to be fed into an analysis together with an array of other factors, appropriate to a sociology of statistics rather than to a sociology of cultural and social structural processes.

7. As I stated at the outset, there is considerable evidence that much of the anti-Tamil rioting was organized—that is, gangs controlled by middle-range entrepreneurs as well as by politicians engaged in the destruction. I have reliable information to the effect that prominent local politicians in Colombo actually arranged for the transportation of gangs by bus to specified areas in the city where they were to attack Tamils. Unfortunately, it was not only gangs who engaged in the destruction; many Sinhalese also willingly joined the mayhem and others simply stood by and watched while Tamils died.

8. Max Gluckman, in his brilliant essay on the structure of apartheid in

South Africa (1958), developed the concept of dominant cleavage. In that situation he wrote of the fundamental division of black from white which overrode other social relationships that interlinked or cut across individuals and groups on either side of the divide. With his love for paradox, he showed how such crosscutting ties could contribute to the maintenance of apartheid. Gluckman's argument is relevant to the modern Sri Lankan situation. In day-to-day relations Tamils in working-class shanty neighborhoods and among the well-to-do members of the urban middle class participate in routine affairs and share a normal sociality. I am struck when I visit a shanty area by the camaraderie that appears to unite families of different ethnic categories. It seems to belie the terror expressed by Tamils in the same areas when they tell of their experiences during the riots and how they had to flee for their lives. Certainly the existence of crosscutting ties may have ameliorated the situation for Tamils of all classes at the time. But these crosscutting ties obscure the fact that a dominant, ideologically generated cleavage exists between Sinhalese and Tamils. The power of this cleavage is that it can suddenly shatter the calm and that the ideas and relations based in it can override all other factors. It is the politically and ideologically wrought dominant cleavage between Tamils and Sinhalese that has come ultimately to define much of Sri Lankan social life. The result is that it can turn both Sinhalese and Tamils against their own class interests. This is not to say that the riots were not to a large extent class driven, a point I have been constantly stressing. A large number of Tamil businesses and industries were destroyed, but I stress that it was businesses and industries and that these were often burned and looted by members of the Sinhalese working class. The point is simple: the effect of the ideological construction of a dominant cleavage organized along ethnic lines in Sri Lanka has been such as to lead subordinate fractions of the class structure to understand their class suffering in ethnic terms.

9. In some shrines the deity-priest (*kapurala*) breaks the coconut, but this is not common.

10. I should stress that far from all the shrines are located in impoverished areas. A few are located on the outskirts of relatively wealthy Sinhalese areas. The location of these, however, often correspond with the "marginal" characteristics of Suniyam and of other demons or deities as well. Thus some are located at points of entry into Sri Lanka or at the margins of areas dominantly Sinhalese Buddhist in population. The main shrine in Colombo for the destructive Hindu goddess, Bhadrakali, is located in the grounds of a Hindu kovil. This temple is on the coast in a largely Hindu and Christian area. Sinhalese Buddhists are the main clients. Symbolically they go to the margins of their religio-political order to gain the assistance of the dreadful powers of self-reconstitution.

11. Taussig (1980, 15–18) makes an important criticism of the assertion of Foster (1960–61; 1965) that the fear of "envy" as the main motivation for sorcery in Latin America is derived from within an egalitarian social ethics in contexts of high competition and "limited good." Taussig argues that the devil beliefs and practices he examines are formed in the transformations into capitalism and may even express a nascent form of resistance to such processes. Foster, to Taussig, is arguing from within a capitalist ethos and fails to comprehend the possibility that sorcery ideas represent an attack on the commodity basis of

capitalism and the forms of its oppressive structures of power. I agree with Taussig's criticism of Foster. My own material, as does the ethnography of Taussig, points to sorcery as being closely connected with hierarchical, rather than egalitarian, ideologies. I depart from Taussig's argument, however. Sorcery undergoes transformations in meaning in modern political and economic settings. It encodes many of the agonies of these transformations. But it is not a critique of capitalism or even a nascent resistance to it. Sorcery, at least in Sri Lanka, is deeply conservative and is intimately connected with the forces of domination and oppression, as it was in the past. Sorcery in Sri Lanka, incidentally, is not a modern practice. My evidence suggests that it stretches deep into Sri Lanka's ancient past.

12. Patron-client relations are a widely reported phenomenon but have often assumed the status of a universally valid sociological concept which can work more or less unproblematically across different cultures. My discussion of the Sinhalese material is preliminary, but I suggest that in the Sinhalese context patron-client relations are not merely a structure of interpersonal ties between the weak and the strong. They are potentially much more than this and follow general hierarchical principles. In a deep sense, the client finds personal integrity through an embodiment in the patron. The power of patron-client ties, I suggest, is in some senses related to this conception. My argument may also extend an understanding as to the reason patron-client relations can overcome differences of class interest conceived through Western egalitarian eyes.

Chapter 5

1. *Anzac* has various uses and connotations in Australia. It refers to the soldiers who fought at Gallipoli, to the ideals manifested there, and occasionally to persons, as in the reference to male surfers of especially good physique as "bronzed Anzacs."

2. In 1916 it was moved in the Senate that the official name of the new national capital be changed from Canberra to Anzac. I cite from Senator Lynch's statements in the Senate at the time and include some extended references of comparison with Washington, D.C., U.S.A. These comments are of interest for an understanding of the degree to which Australians tried to distinguish their identity from that of other nations of a similar egalitarian ideological stress.

> We have a much stronger reason to name our Federal capital "ANZAC" than the Americans had to call their capital "Washington." The Americans had a long struggle for independence. . . . A mighty effort was made by three and a half million people, and it was fitting that when at last they secured their independence and the new American nation was born, Americans should turn to the one man who had made it possible for them to achieve national success and greatness. They immortalized him by naming their capital after him.

> When I speak of "ANZAC," however, and refer to it as the appropriate name for the federal Capital, I would urge that it has wider significance than "Washington," because it represents, not the struggle for freedom by the people of one country only, but the effort put

forward by our sons at the Dardanelles for the freedom of all the
nations at present associated with the allies' cause. . . .

The word [ANZAC] . . . has much wider significance than
"Washington," because it stands for the efforts made by Australians
and New Zealanders on behalf of the liberation of those civilized
nations fighting for the cause of the Allies . . . whereas "Washington"
indicates only the name of a man who led the people of his country in
a successful fight for freedom. . . . The word ANZAC applies not to a
military leader . . . but to the first draft made on the manhood of
Australia and New Zealand in the fight, on a foreign battle-field, for
the freedom of civilization (Hansard, *Parliamentary Debates* 1916,
79:7977–78).

3. Bean embodies many of the elements of Anzac, the legend he was vital in
creating. This is certainly the spirit in which he is presented by his most recent
biographer, Dudley McCarthy, who describes Bean as having been born (at Bat-
hurst, New South Wales, in 1879) "into a people of brutal beginnings. The
cornerstones of these beginnings were rum, the gallows, lash, and the gun. They
were set in a land that seemed scarcely less forbidding: vast, an empty and
unknown continent" (McCarthy 1983, 9). Bean went to school in England,
completing his studies there at Oxford University. When he returned to Australia he was instrumental in creating a romantic, idealized image. McCarthy
cites him thus: "The romance of Australia is not all founded on its past. There
is a deal of romance today in the life of your adventurer outback. There is some
strange pathetic melancholy about the bush and the life there which has got into
the blood of the Australians up-country" (McCarthy 1983, 54). Bean wrote
extensively for the Sydney *Morning Herald*, and after some lobbying by himself
and some fierce competition from a few other journalists he was appointed, in
late 1914, the official war correspondent.

4. Bean describes his own recording and his motivation, in 1920, in the
following way:

In his search for rigid accuracy the writer was guided by one deliberate
and settled principle. The more he saw and knew of the men and
officers of the Australian Imperial Forces the more fully did the writer
become convinced that the only memorial which could be worthy of
them was the bare and uncoloured story of their part in the war (Bean
1981, lxiv).

A fuller understanding of Bean's "obsessive" commitment to detail and the
mythic idea behind it must be gained from reading not only his prefaces to his
six-volume history of the First World War but also the details of his accounts.
These were compiled from his own prodigious notes while he was in front-line
positions, were he was wounded, from on-the-spot interviews with the men and
the officers, and from follow-up investigations among all sides in the war in the
years following its end.

5. According to Ross (1985) the word *digger* assumed its real significance
during the First World War. It had a long history of civilian use before that
time, however. The word was used between Australians as a common form of
address—in the same way as *mate*—until comparatively recently, and it can still

be heard. Ross refers to a work by A. G. Butler, the historian of the Medical
Corps in the First World War, entitled *The Digger: A Study in Democracy* (1945).
Butler attempts to trace it back to English origins, to its use among Cromwell's
troops, among the Chartists and among farmers and miners in Australia. Butler
associates *digger* strongly with egalitarianism.

> Like the Grave, the Diggings have already levelled . . . past distinctions,
> and are fast placing the wealth and property of the country in the
> hands of men of nerve and sinew—men of industry and perseverance—
> men of honesty and integrity; who are perfectly willing to accord to
> others all they claim for themselves—"a fair field and no favour" (cited
> in Ross 1985, 23).

6. Great significance is placed, in the literature of the time and since, on the
fact that the Australian and New Zealand forces were composed of volunteer
civilians, that the soldiers and their officers were not from military traditions.
The symbolic significance of this stress is important for later discussion wherein
I shall argue that Australian egalitarianism separates powerfully the imposed
orders of state forms from those "naturally" composed in civilian society, a
society which ideally does not require the state for it to achieve a mutually
cooperative order.

7. Australians at the time felt that they were fighting an illegitimate war
against people in circumstances similar to their own. They were subordinated
to English control. A film, *Breaker Morant* (1975), creates its whole theme
around the sacrifice of "Breaker"—a nickname born of his prowess at breaking
horses—and his mates for an alleged atrocity against the Boers. Two of the
three involved, one being the Breaker, were shot, so the film argues, to protect
the diplomatic interests of England in its relations with Germany, which was
making much of the brutalities of the conflict.

8. One chaplain's diary, written in Egypt, has the following note, entered on
Sunday 7 February: "We have no bands so only sang 2 hymns of 'Onward
Christian Soldiers.' . . . I preached to the men from Exodus, the passage of the
children of Israel over the Red Sea, on the words 'Go forward' for we are on
historical ground" (cited in McKernan 1986, 28). General Chauvel, the commander of the celebrated Light Horse in Palestine, made the following comments
concerning the Rev. W. Maitland Woods, the discoverer of the famed Shellal
mosaic now on display in the Australian War Memorial: [Woods] had lectured
throughout the two Mounted divisions and the Imperial Camel Corps on the
Holy Land and had proceeded in creating an interest therein which was not only
of great value to the commanders, as it helped to counteract the boredom of
campaigning in desert or semi-desert country" (Trendall 1973, foreword).

9. An excellent contemporary description of two-up appears in Kenneth
Cook's stark account of life in the mining town of Broken Hill (Cook 1967, 23–
40). The game is extraordinarily simple. It is in fact a game of pure chance.
This is important for understanding its centrality in Australian egalitarian culture. I shall develop the idea, through this and later chapters, that in egalitarianism in its Australian form inequality is valued only insofar as it can be reduced
to a quality in nature. Money—money in gambling specifically—is the morality
of nature. Freed from its fixity in imposed social and political orders—understood as inegalitarian—in gambling, money becomes purely natural, attaching to

human beings through the magical property of luck, which in itself is nature in pure process.

10. On some occasions, however, "Anzac and Turk arranged shooting matches, each contestant firing at a target waved above enemy trenches." Gammage makes the general assessment of the historian, "In short, the Turk was a brave and resourceful but gentlemanly opponent who followed the rules. 'They are the whitest fighters that ever fought,' a 10th Battalion officer decided" (Gammage 1975, 93–94).

11. Immigrants from Turkey to Australia protested at the memorial garden at the time of its inauguration. They protested against current oppressive inequities in Turkey.

12. The mosaic was discovered on April 17, 1917, during the second battle of Gaza. It had been partly uncovered when the Turks dug their trenches.

13. There are, of course, numerous examples of the religious form of modern nationalism. Recent studies concerning Russia are those of Binns (1979), and Lane (1981). Perhaps the holiday most readily comparable to Australian Anzac Day is the American Memorial Day. Warner's study (1961) is still excellent. The kind of analysis he adopts also prefigures later developments in "symbolic anthropology." Of importance is Warner's attention to the Christian symbolic framework of the day. Such ideological embeddedness of Western ritual and ceremonial forms is too often treated by anthropologists in an unproblematic fashion.

14. Australia was urban in its very beginnings, growing out from small coastal centers that became the capital cities. Many of these later settlements were not the places of convict imprisonment—as were Brisbane, Sydney, and Hobart—but they developed under the conditions of powerful state control, planning, and surveillance nonetheless. Adelaide and South Australia are excellent examples. South Australia was, and still is, a highly planned state.

15. Australian prehistorians are concerned about the dating of the arrival of the Aboriginal population in Australia. Estimates waver between 80,000 and 40,000 years. This is undoubtedly important for a wider understanding of human history, but I note its nationalist significance in the popular, white imagination in Australia.

16. Australian Aboriginals are used by white Australians to argue their own ideological positions and descriptions of their society. In this, Aboriginal society becomes little more than their own ideological projection as in an otherwise interesting work on Australian history by Stuart Macintyre (1985, 3–10). He is concerned with drawing attention to the dreadful plight of Aboriginals caused by the European colonization of Australia. He then proceeds to contrast Aboriginal society with English colonial institutions and in effect constitutes Aboriginal society in the contrast. Thus Aboriginal society becomes the negation of English society, or everything English society is not. The procedure of comparison is a false one, common among anthropologists as it is among historians. It is the type of comparison to which this volume is opposed. Leach (1961) has attacked Macintyre's kind of comparison, as has Gluckman (1948).

17. It is frequently commented upon by Australian scholars that the development of an Australian identity in the idea of the bush was usually the act of

urban intellectuals. The bush, then, is a romantic conceptualization adhered to amid the disorder and disruption of city life. This is true, but I stress the congruency of the idea within egalitarian, largely Christian, thought. The bush is the ideal egalitarian world—like the frontier in American egalitarianism— perhaps synonymous with the idea of community in much Western sociological thought. Hughes (1970) discusses the romantic conception of the bush and notes its production in nationalist processes. The argument, however, develops in the course of demonstrating it as myth—that is, false in the sense I have discussed for similar positions taken in relation to the Sinhalese material. My point, of course, is that such ideas as that of the bush have a constitutive function in the structuring of reality and their force is more fully comprehended by placing them in a more encompassing context of egalitarian ideology. A more thorough investigation of the idea of the bush is that presented by White (1981). He demonstrates its intellectualist production and links its formation to the growth of capitalist interest in Australia. White's general argument is a pragmatic, instrumentalist one in which the idea is located in ideological processes of domination in Australia.

18. There was significant opposition to the Australian war effort, especially when the huge loss of life became apparent. The International Workers of the World (IWW), established in America, was later to gain some importance in Australia. It was instituted in Australia in 1907 and had only a few members at first. With the waning of popular enthusiasm for the war a powerful issue developed concerning the possibility of introducing conscription. This seriously divided the nation, and Prime Minister Billy Hughes, who gave his support to conscription—which was not introduced—lost considerable popular support over it. With the conscription issue the IWW in Australia, the "Australian Wobblies," grew in popular following. The following was pasted to walls as early as July 1915:

"TO ARMS!!

Capitalists, Parsons, Politicians,
Landlords, Newspaper Editors, and
Other Stay-at-home Patriots.

YOUR COUNTRY NEEDS YOU IN THE TRENCHES!

WORKERS

FOLLOW YOUR MASTERS!!

(Builders' Labourers'
Song Book 1975, 88)

Some of the resistance to the war effort, which had strong connotations of class distinctions, was also interpreted as an opposition between Protestant and Irish Catholic. This opposition, incidentally, which is still present in Australian political culture, refracts the dualism of Australian egalitarianism, which I shall

examine more closely in the next chapter.   This dualism opposes the structures
of inegalitarianism to those of equality and Protestantism which symbolized—
especially Anglicanism—the powers of ideologically inadmissible political domination and imposition.   The development of the Anzac tradition did not overcome division but intensified it.   Protestants accused Catholics of being traito-
rous.   Anzac came into being at the time of the Sinn Fein uprising in Ireland,
and feelings were high in Australia.   The Irish Catholic population, however, did
go to some lengths to demonstrate their loyalty to Australia and to ward off the
anti-Irish prejudice that is still in evidence in Australia today (McKernan 1980).

Chapter 6

1. Generally, the relation of the service of women to that of men is stressed
in the Anzac traditions.   I note that at the Australian War Memorial the voluntary guides, an important pressure group in Memorial politics, are women.   They
are unpaid and take great pride in their intimate knowledge of the details of the
"relics" and the events surrounding them.

2. The events at the Dawn Service at Canberra also appear to assume a
more religious tone.   It is held within the War Memorial and the people who
gather carry candles.   So far as I know this does not occur elsewhere in Australia
on Anzac Day.

3. In 1922 he sent this telegram to those concerned with planning the
Memorial.   The text is on file in the Memorial archives.

> Concerning telegram being despatched today care needed in fixing
> relation of memorial building to capital which is planned on American
> model to stand on hill behind Parliament with somewhat vague
> function of containing archives of Commonwealth.   Memorial might
> replace it as commemorating starting point of Australian national
> history and far more sacred to Australians than this importation from
> America but do not know if Memorial commemorating war sacrifice
> would be approved for the purpose.   On whole would suggest that
> small separate memorial park better interprets Australian feelings.

4. I draw attention to the epithet "Little Digger" used in reference to
Hughes.   He was a small man, but the diminutive, common in Australian talk
among friends, is also symbolically indicative of his reduction into the body of
the people, a point upon which I shall enlarge subsequently.   The frequent use of
the diminutive in Australia is consistent with its egalitarian ideology.

5. Hughes became extremely unpopular over the issue of conscription and
other aspects of his political opportunism.   I do think, however, that he did,
despite his unpopularity in many circles, achieve a symbolic import in the
traditions of Anzac, which transcended what he represented during his active
political career.

6. Mateship is the aspect of Australian culture that has received the most
discussion and around which an intense folklore exists.   It has been explicitly
linked with egalitarianism.   Ward (1966), a historian, virtually repeats the folklore but attempts little analysis.   Encel (1970) seems to be confused on egalitarianism as a whole, more or less assuming that inegalitarianism refutes the

universality of it as an ideological form. To my mind the best discussion of mateship in Australia and one that sets it firmly within world egalitarian ideological forms is that by Oxley (1978).

7. The Australian emphasis on autonomy is not merely an instance of marked individualism. It is, as I will show, central to an understanding of Australian insubordination, but it contributes as well to a marked authoritarianism which some may observe among Australians. This authoritarianism appears also in the officiousness of those in bureaucratic positions. I suggest that much of the authoritarianism and officiousness of Australians flows, not from a commitment to authority or the ideals of bureaucratic systems per se, but from the stress on autonomy. In this sense individualistic autonomy, when located in certain kinds of structure such as the military, can become accentuated, even given an opportunity for "perfect" realization. I am implying that the military can be a symbol of autonomy gained as well as autonomy lost.

8. The internal order of many hotels in Australia could be interpreted as modeling aspects of the social order. The front bar, or public bar or saloon bar, is workers' space. The lounge bar is regarded as superior and is likely to be where the "suited" members of Australia's male population may gather—bureaucrats, professionals, business people, and so on. The development of the pubs as discos attractive to Australia's youth is beginning to alter this arrangement drastically. Such aspects of the internal ordering of hotels as may be apparent dissolve on Anzac Day.

9. The exhibits tend to stress the heroism of the Vietnam veterans. They share an identity with the exhibits of the Second World War in the Memorial. There have been changes in the internal organization of the memorial generally so that even the First World War exhibits are, in their display, beginning to conform to the ideas stressed in the exhibits for the later wars. The place, in my view, is being radically "cleaned up," and the First World War exhibits are beginning to lose their marked symbolic ambiguity, an ambiguity that pointed to the futility of war and its great suffering and also pointed to the transcendence of ordinary Australians out of all that suffering. The Memorial is beginning to glorify war in a manner ultimately refused by many of the Anzacs.

10. Australians exercised perhaps worse and murderous mayhem at the end of the war in Palestine, in response to the killing of a New Zealander by an Arab. The official historian, Gullett, recognized the difficulty of the event for his legend-making exercise. The mayhem occurred at Surafend, and Gullett, while condemning it, nonetheless finds the opportunity even here to valorize Australian nationalist ideals of autonomy and mateship. He describes the revenge of the New Zealanders and their support by Australians thus:

> The war task was now completed and they, a band of sworn
> brothers tested in a hundred fights, were going home. To them the
> loss of a veteran comrade by foul murder, at the hands of a race they
> despised, was a crime which called for instant justice. They were in
> no mood for delay. In their movement against Surafend, therefore,
> they felt that while wreaking vengeance on the Arabs, they would at
> the same time work off their old feeling against the bias of the
> disciplinary branch of General Headquarters, and its studied omission
> to punish Arabs for crime. They were angry and bitter beyond sound

reasoning. All day the New Zealanders quietly organized for the work in Surafend, and early in the night . . . surrounded the village. In close support and full sympathy were large bodies of Australians. . . . Many Arabs were killed, few escaped without injury; the village was demolished.

The Anzacs, having finished with Surafend, raided and burned the nearby nomad camp. . . . General Headquarters demanded the men who had led the attack and had been guilty of the killing. The Anzacs stood firm; not a single individual could definitely be charged (Gullett 1938, 789).

11. To be precise, Birdwood was born in India.

12. Prominent persons in the business elite of Australia are active in sporting activities. This is not advertising alone but, I suggest, an attempt to assert their dominance as a fact of nature. Alan Bond, a well-known property developer, is at present a hero in Australia, valorized as the person who won the America's Cup, a yachting trophy. The cup was displayed in museums and art galleries throughout Australia. Bond, of course, did not sail in the yacht; he provided the money.

13. Warner (1961, 247–51) discusses the symbolic significance of Lincoln in Memorial Day in the United States. It is apparent from this account that Lincoln symbolizes both state and people and conjoins them. Australia has no such comparable figure. The Anzacs as collective symbolic heroes, as I have stressed repeatedly, stand outside the state, independent as the nation. Other points of contrast between Memorial Day and Anzac Day can be noted on the basis of Warner's description. Most significant in my view is the important part taken by the various church denominations and ethnic associations. Memorial Day seems to be a celebration of the powerful pluralist feature of American egalitarian democracy. Such pluralist aspects are not nearly so apparent on Anzac Day, at least at present.

14. There is at present a growing struggle in Australia between unions and managements over the demarcation of work, whereby an individual's job is rigidly defined. The practice, supported by the unions, protects jobs and secures their incumbents against the threat of unemployment. The ontology of Australian egalitarian individualism is rising to ideological consciousness in the present situation—in T-shirts, for example, emblazoned with the slogan "Resist to Exist."

15. At the 1986 Anzac Day ceremonies in Maroubra, a suburb of Sydney, a deputy prime minister and various other senior politicians were to be seen in the body of the "worshipers" facing the Wall of Remembrance. The service was led by a major in the Salvation Army (personal communication).

16. The preparations for the Bicentennial indicate an attempt by the representatives of the state to overcome the people-state opposition I have described. This is most evident in the symbolism inscribed into the new Parliament House, which will be opened in 1988. The building has been designed by an American firm of architects, with some local Australian assistance. It has been built into Capitol Hill and therefore merges with the earth and rises from it. The building symbolizes the naturalization of the state, an aspect of the state resisted in

Anzac nationalism. In the process of this naturalization I note that the building will have inscribed on its walls the names of 400 ordinary Australian citizens chosen from those sent in by the public. The idea is an appropriation of the egalitarian enshrinement of Australian war dead at the Australian War Memorial. I have my doubts as to whether the symbolism of the new Parliament House will in effect represent a final resolution of the kind of people-state opposition I have been essaying. Some Australians refer to the building as the "big bunker"—the last line of defense of the state.

17. Jeans (1981, 56) describes the outcry during the stone-laying ceremony at the Sydney memorial on 19 July 1932, "The Catholic coadjutor Archbishop of Sydney, Dr. Michael Sheehan, not only denounced the proposed religious ceremony as predominantly Protestant, but also the 'Crucifixion of Civilization, which was 'offensive to ordinary Christian decency. What we object to particularly is the figure of a nude woman on the Cross, a perfectly nude woman, which is revolting and immoral in a memorial like that.' "

18. The full title of the book by Anne Summers is *Damned Whores and God's Police*. The outline of her critique fits with my interpretation of the dominance of Australian men through a particular egalitarian ideological form.

Chapter 7

1. During the seven months following Blainey's initial statement at the town of Warnambool in the state of Victoria, approximately 368 newspaper articles, reports, and editorials appeared on the subject of Asian immigration that were directly connected to Blainey's statements. Some 222 letters to the editor in response from the public were published during the same period. (Markus and Ricklefs 1985, 119–42).

2. The White Australia policy was probably not finally relinquished until the Vietnamese boat people cracked the wall of Australia's defenses during the 1970s. Important surveys of the White Australia policy are those of Palfreeman (1967) and London (1970). Wilton and Bosworth (1984) give an excellent critical account of developments during recent years and the emergence of multiculturalism. They argue that the old values of mateship and meat pies have declined. This may be so, but as I shall indicate in this chapter, egalitarian logic is very much in full swing.

3. In certain quarters there was strong opposition of a staunchly English liberal kind to these acts. Thus the lead article in the Sydney *Morning Herald* of 24 April 1861 stated, "The Chinese Bill, of course, could never be accepted by any score of educated Englishmen—barbarian, unchristian, unconstitutional— opposed to the law of nations—disgraceful to the colony among colonies— contemptible for the violence of its spirit and its impracticability in application. As a measure, it cannot be mended, and, were we inclined to submit to its adoption as a matter of discretion, we should convert it from a permanent into a temporary law, leaving it, with all its imperfections, to go down in due time to the limbo of all villainy."

4. Blainey has published a number of histories of Australia. These include *A Land Half Won* (1980); a book on the Australian Aboriginals, *The Triumph of*

the *Nomads* (1975); and two books based on a television series, *The Blainey View* (1982). A significant aspect of these books is Blainey's fascination with technology and with the pragmatics of living. He displays his own intense rationalism, which is very much a part of Australian nationalism, to which of course he is an important contributor. Blainey is now professor of history at the University of Melbourne.

5. I use the word *folk* in the context of the development of analytical histories of folk or popular cultural and social forms that represent an attempt to strike through the nature of realities and modes of thought very different from those of the present day. I refer of course to the kinds of work exemplified by such French historians as Marc Bloch and, most recently, Le Roy-Ladurie. Blainey and the Melbourne school generally have been responsible for strongly nationalistic writing that is aimed at the production of an understanding of the past to construct an identity in the present. Ian Turner defends the Melbourne "radical nationalist" tradition against its various critics from the New Left in Australia, arguing that it fits the interests of the Australian working class. He rejects the significance of the charge that Australian nationalism in its populist style is an example of "bourgeois-liberal hegemony" (Turner 1979, 10). I am in some agreement with the Australian New Left except that I consider many of them to be open to their own charge (see Kapferer and Kapferer, 1986). Australian nationalist ideas, in their egalitarianism, define Australia's political culture as a whole. It should be confronted as such, not dismissed through a kind of sloganeering to which some in the New Left are prone (McQueen 1970; Connell 1977).

6. Dumont (1980, 42, 399) makes use of Evans-Pritchard's work among the Nuer in his study of caste, specifically the notions of "situational selection" and "segmentation." In his use of "segmentation" he concentrates on its idea of divisibility rather than the corporateness or solidary character of the groups thus formed. Dumont argues that the latter emphasis is that of English anthropology. My view is that notions of segmentation and corporateness of groups are produced within an English egalitarian ideology and that even ideas such as segmentation are not reducible to the empirical situation of the Nuer, as Dumont claims.

7. There are a number of excellent critiques of multiculturalism in Australia and their relation to forms of ideological political domination. Some of the best are those of Rizvi (1986), Bullivant (1981), Lepervanche and Bottomley (1985).

References

Original Sources

The Dipavamsa, translated by Hermann Oldenberg. New Delhi: Asian Educational Services, 1982.

The Mahavamsa, translated by Wilhelm Geiger. London: Pali Text Society, 1980.

The Rajavaliya, edited by B. Gunasekera. Colombo: Government Printer, 1900; reprinted 1954.

The Thupavamsa, translated by N.A. Jayawickrama. London: Luzac and Co., 1971.

Newspapers and Weekly Journals

Australia Today: From the Heart of the Nation (Sydney)
Canberra Times
Frontline (Madras)
Hansard (Australia): (Canberra: Government Printer)
Lanka Guardian (Colombo)
Divaina (Colombo)
Private Eye (London)
Sydney Morning Herald
The Daily News (Colombo)
The Hindu Organ (Jaffna)
The Island (Colombo)
The National Times (Sydney)
The Sun (Colombo)

Books and Articles

Adam-Smith, Patsy
  1978   *The Anzacs*. Melbourne: Thomas Nelson.

Ames, Michael
  1963   "Ideological and Social Change in Ceylon." *Human Organisation* 22(1):45–53.

Anderson, Benedict
  1983   *Imagined Communities: Reflections on the Origin and Spread of Nationalism*. London: Verso.

Ardener, E. W.
    1973   "Some Outstanding Problems in the Analysis of Events." A.S.A. Conference Paper. Mimeographed.

Bailey, F. G.
    1960   *Tribe, Caste and Nation: A Study of Political Activity and Political Change in Highland Orissa.* Manchester: Manchester University Press.
    1969   "Parapolitical Systems." In *Local-level Politics: Social and Cultural Perspectives*, edited by Marc J. Swartz. London: University of London Press.

Barnett, Steve
    1975   "Approaches to Change in Caste Ideology in South India." In *Essays on South India*, edited by Burton Stein. Honolulu: University Press of Hawaii.

Barnett, Steve, and Martin G. Silverman
    1979   *Ideology and Everyday Life.* Ann Arbor: University of Michigan Press.

Barth, Fredrik
    1969   Introduction and "Pathan Identity and Its Maintenance." In *Ethnic Groups and Boundaries*, edited by Fredrik Barth. London: Allen & Unwin.

Bean, C. E. W.
    1981   *The Official History of Australia in the War of 1914–1918*, vols. 1–6. St. Lucia, Brisbane: University of Queensland Press.

Bechert, Heinz
    1977   *William Geiger: His life and Works.* Colombo: M. D. Gunasena.

Beck, B.
    1972   *Peasant Society in Konku: A Study of Right and Left Subcastes in South India.* Vancouver: University of British Columbia Press.

Berreman, G. D.
    1963   *Hindus of the Himalayas: Ethnography and Change.* Berkeley: University of California Press.

Berreman, G. D., and Louis Dumont
    1962   [Discussion of] "Caste Racism and Stratification." *Contributions to Indian Sociology* 6:122–24.

Béteille, A.
    1986   "Individualism and Equality." *Current Anthropology* 27(2):121–34.

Binns, C. A. P.
    1979   "The Changing face of Power: Revolution and Accommodation in the Development of the Soviet Ceremonial System," pt. 1. *Man*(n.s.) 14:585–606.

Blainey, Geoffrey
    1966   *The Tyranny of Distance.* Melbourne: Sun Books.
    1975   *The Triumph of the Nomads.* Melbourne: Macmillan.
    1980   *A Land Half Won.* Melbourne: Macmillan.
    1982   *The Blainey View.* Melbourne: Macmillan.
    1984   *All for Australia.* North Ryde, Sydney: Methuen Haynes.

Bloch, Marc
    1973 *The Royal Touch: Sacred Monarchy and Scrofula in England and in France.* London: Routledge & Kegan Paul.

Bourdieu, Pierre
    1977 *Outline of a Theory of Practice.* Cambridge: Cambridge University Press.

Brown, Kevin
    1984 "A Bad Year for Avocados: Blainey and Immigration." *Arena* 67:78–92.

Bryson, John
    1985 *Evil Angels.* Melbourne: Penguin Books.

Builders' Labourers' Song Book.
    1975 Camberwell, Victoria: Widescope.

Bullivant, B. M.
    1981 *Race, Ethnicity, and Curriculum.* Melbourne: Macmillan.

Burgmann, Verity
    1984 "Writing Racism Out of History." *Arena* 67:78–92.

Butler, A. G.
    1945 *The Digger: A Study in Democracy.* Sydney: Angus & Robertson.

Carrithers, Michael
    1983 *The Forest Monks of Sri Lanka: An Anthropological and Historical Study.* Delhi: Oxford University Press.

Cassirer, Ernst
    1979 *Symbol, Myth, and Culture: Essays and Lectures, 1935–1945,* edited by D. P. Verne. New Haven: Yale University Press.

Chamberlain, Chris
    1983 *Class Consciousness in Australia.* Sydney: Allen & Unwin.

Clark, C. M. H.
    1968 *A History of Australia,* vols. 1–3 Melbourne: Melbourne University Press.

Clifford, James, and George E. Marcus, eds.
    1986 *Writing Culture: The Poetics and Politics of Ethnography.* Berkeley: University of California Press.

Cohen, Abner
    1974 *Urban Ethnicity.* London: Tavistock Publications.

Cohen, B. S.
    1983 "Representing Authority in Victorian India." In *The Invention of Tradition,* edited by Eric Hobsbawn and Terence Ranger. Cambridge: Cambridge University Press.

Collins, H.
    1985 "Political Ideology in Australia: The Distinctiveness of a Benthamite Society." In *Australia: The Daedalus Symposium,* edited by Stephen R. Graubard. North Ryde, Sydney: Angus & Robertson.

Collman, J.
    1979   "Fringe Camps and the Development of Aboriginal Administration in Central Australia." *Social Analysis* 2:38–57

Committee for Rational Development
    1984   *Sri Lanka: The Ethnic Conflict.* New Delhi: Navrang.

Connell, R. W.
    1977   *Ruling Class, Ruling Culture.* Cambridge: Cambridge University Press.

Connell, R. W., and T. H. Irving, eds.
    1980   *Class Structure in Australian History.* Melbourne: Longman Cheshire.

Connell, R. W., and others
    1982   *Making the Difference.* Sydney: Allen & Unwin.

Conway, R.
    1985   *Great Australian Stupour.* Melbourne: MacMillan.

Cook, Kenneth
    1967   *Wake in Fright.* Ringwood, Australia: Penguin Books.

D'Alpuget, Blanche
    1982   *Bob Hawke: A Biography.* Sydney, Penguin Books.

Das, Veena
    1982   *Structure and Cognition: Aspects of Hindu Caste and Ritual.* Delhi: Oxford University Press

Dhammaruchi, Sedawatte
    1979   Foreword to *Eelam—The Truth*, by Madihe Pannaseeha Maha Nayaka Thero. Colombo: Swastika Press.

Dirks, N.
    1987   *The Hollow Crown.* Cambridge: Cambridge University Press.

Dissanayaka, T. D. S. A.
    1983   *The Agony of Sri Lanka.* Colombo; Swastika Press.

Douglas, Mary
    1966   *Purity and Danger.* London: Routledge & Kegan Paul.

Dumont, Louis
    1977   *From Mandeville to Marx.* Chicago: University of Chicago Press.
    1980   *Homo Hierarchicus.* Chicago: University of Chicago Press.
    1986   *Essays on Individualism.* Chicago: University of Chicago Press.

Durkheim, Emile
    1965   *The Elementary Forms of the Religious Life.* Translated by Joseph W. Swain. New York: Free Press.

Encel, Sol
    1970   *Equality and Authority: A Study of Class, Status, and Power in Australia.* Melbourne: Longman Cheshire.

Encel, Sol, and Lois Bryson
    1984   *Australian Society.* Melbourne: Longman Cheshire.

Epstein, A. L.
    1958   *Politics in an Urban African Community.* Manchester: Manchester University Press.

Evans-Pritchard, E. E.
    1937 *Witchcraft, Oracles, and Magic among the Azande.* Oxford: Oxford University Press.
    1956 *The Nuer.* Oxford: Oxford University Press.

Fabian, Johannes
    1983 *Time and the Other.* New York: Columbia University Press.

Farmer, B. F.
    1963 *Ceylon: A Divided Nation.* London: Oxford University Press.

Feyerabend, Paul
    1978 *Against Method.* London: Verso.

Foigny, Gabriel de
    1676 "A New Discovery of Terra Incognita Australis." In *Journey Through Utopia;* by Marie Louise Berneri. London: Freedom Press, 1982.

Foucault, Michel
    1979 *Discipline and Punish: The Birth of the Prison.* Harmondsworth: Penguin Books

Gammage, Bill
    1975 *The Broken Years.* Ringwood, Australia: Penguin Books.

Geertz, Clifford
    1973 *The Interpretation of Cultures: Selected Essays.* New York: Basic Books.
    1979 " 'Internal Conversion' in Contemporary Bali." In *A Reader in Comparative Religion*, 4th ed., edited by William A. Lessa and Evon Z. Vogt. New York: Harper & Row.

Geiger, Wilhelm
    1984 *The Dipavamsa and Mahavamsa and Their Historical Development in Ceylon.* Colombo: Trumpet Publishers.

Gellner, Ernest
    1983 *Nations and Nationalism.* Oxford: Basil Blackwell.

Girard, René
    1977 *Violence and the Sacred.* Translated by P. Gregory. Baltimore: Johns Hopkins University Press.

Gluckman, Max
    1948 *The Sociological Theories of Bronislaw Malinowski.* Rhodes Livingstone Paper 16. Manchester: Manchester University Press.
    1954 "Rituals of Rebellion in South-East Africa." Frazer Lecture. Manchester: Manchester University Press.
    1958 *Analysis of a Social Situation In Modern Zululand.* Rhodes Livingstone Paper 28. Manchester: Manchester University Press.
    1961 "Anthropological Problems Arising from the African Industrial Revolution." In *Social Change in Africa*, edited by Aidan Southall. London: Oxford University Press and International African Institute.

Gombrich, Richard
    1971 *Precept and Practice: Traditional Buddhism in the Rural Highlands of Ceylon.* Oxford: Clarendon Press.

Gramsci, Antonio
   1971   *Selections from the Prison Notebooks.* Translated by Quintin Hoare
          Geoffrey and N. Smith. London: Lawrence & Wishart.

Greenwald, Alice
   1978   "The Relic of the Spear: Historiography and the Saga of Dutthagamani."
          In *Religion and Legitimation of Power in Sri Lanka*, edited by Bardwell
          L. Smith. Chambersburg, Pennsylvania: Anima Books.

Gullett, H. S.
   1938   *The Australian Imperial Force in Sinai and Palestine 1914—1918.*
          4th Edition, Sydney: Angus & Robertson.

Gunasekera, B.
   1900   Preface to *The Rajavaliya*, edited by B. Gunasekera. Colombo: Gov-
          ernment Printer (reprinted 1954).

Gunasinghe, Newton
   1984   "Open Economy and Its Impact on Ethnic Relations in Sri Lanka." In
          Sri Lanka: The Ethnic Conflict, by the Committee for Rational Devel-
          opment. New Delhi: Navrang.
   1985   "Perceptions and Solutions." *Lanka Guardian* (Colombo) 8:1.

Gunawardana, R. A. L. H.
   1978   "The Kinsmen of the Buddha: Myth as Political Charter in the Ancient
          and Medieval Kingdoms of Sri Lanka." In *Religion and Legitimation
          of Power in Sri Lanka*, edited by Bardwell L. Smith. Chambersburg,
          Pennsylvania: Anima Books.
   1982   "Total Power or Shared Power." Paper presented at the Seminar for
          Asian Studies, Peradeniya University.
   1984   "People of the Lion: Sinhala Consciousness in History and Historiog-
          raphy." In *Ethnicity and Social Change in Sri Lanka*, a Publication
          of the Social Scientists' Assocation. Colombo: Karunaratne.

Hacking, Ian
   1982   "Language, Truth, and Reason." In *Rationality and Relativism*, edited
          by Martin Hollis and Steve Lukes. Oxford: Basil Blackwell.

Handelman, Don and Lea Shamgar-Handelman
   1986   "Shapes of Time: The Choice of a National Symbol." Conference Paper:
          "Symbolism through Time." Wenner-Gren Foundation International
          Symposium no. 100, Fez, Morocco, January 12–21.

Handelman, Don and Bruce Kapferer
   1980   "Symbolic Types, Mediation, and the Transformation of Ritual Con-
          text." *Semiotica* 30.

Hassan, R., and G. Tan, eds.
   1986   *Asian Migrants in Australia: A Socioeconomic Study.* Discussion
          Paper 12. Adelaide: Centre for Development Studies, Flinders Uni-
          versity of South Australia.

Heesterman, J. C.
   1985   *The Inner Conflict of Tradition: Essays In Indian Ritual, Kingship,
          and Society.* Chicago and London: University of Chicago Press.

Hegel, Georg Wilhelm Friedrich
   1952   *Hegel's Philosophy of Right.*   Translated and annotated by T. M. Knox.
          Oxford: Clarendon Press.

Hiller, Peter
   1981   *Class and Inequality in Australia.*   Melbourne: Harcourt Brace.

Hirst, John B.
   1983   *Convict Society and Its Enemies.*   Sydney: Allen & Unwin.

Hobsbawm, Eric
   1983   Introduction to *The Invention of Tradition*, edited by Eric Hobsbawm
          and Terence Ranger.   Cambridge: Cambridge University Press.

Hobsbawm, Eric, and Terence Ranger, eds.
   1983   *The Invention of Tradition.*   Cambridge: Cambridge University Press.

Hughes, Robert
   1970   *The Art of Australia* Ringwood, Australia: Penguin Books.
   1987   *The Fatal Shore.*   London: Collins Harvill; New York: Alfred A. Knopf.

Inglis, K. S.
   1965   "The Anzac Tradition."   *Meanjin* 1 (March):25–44.
   1967   "Australia Day."   *Historical Studies* 13(49):20–41.
   1985   "A Sacred Place: The Making of the Australian War Memorial."   *War
          and Society* 3(2):99–106.

Jayarajan, Paul
   n.d.   "Historical Truths of the Legend Relating to Prince Vijaya."   Colombo:
          The Colombo Apothecaries.

Jayawardena, V. Kumari
   1972   *The Rise of the Labor Movement in Ceylon.*   Durham, N.C.: Duke
          University Press.
   1984a "Ethnic Consciousness in Sri Lanka: Continuity and Change." In *Sri
          Lanka: The Ethnic Conflict*, by the Committee for Rational Develop-
          ment.   Delhi: Navrang.
   1984b "Some Aspects of Class and Ethnic Consciousness in Sri Lanka in the
          Late Nineteenth and Early Twentieth Centuries."   In *Ethnicity and
          Social Change in Sri Lanka*, a publication of the Social Scientists'
          Association.   Colombo: Karunaratne.
   1985   *Ethnic and Class Conflicts in Sri Lanka.*   Colombo: Centre for Social
          Analysis.

Jeans, D. N.
   1981   "The Making of the Anzac Memorial, Sydney: Towards a Secular
          Culture."   In *Australia 1988: A Bicentennial Bulletin* 4 (November)

Kapferer, Bruce
   1969   "Norms and the Manipulation of Relationships in a Work Context."
          In *Social Networks in Urban Situations*, edited by J. Clyde Mitchell.
          Manchester: Manchester University Press.
   1983   *A Celebration of Demons.*   Bloomington: Indiana University Press.
   1986a Foreword to *Creating Culture*, edited by Diana Austin.   Sydney: Allen
          & Unwin.

1986b "Pragmatic Power and the Transcendent Ideal: Sorcery and State Buddhism in Sri Lanka." Paper Presented at the Chandra Jayawardena Memorial Conference, Macquarie University, Australia, 25 April.

1987 "Nationalism and Transcendence." Address to the Israeli Anthropological Association, February.

Kapferer, Judith, and Bruce Kapferer
1986 "The Making of the Organic School: A Critique." *Curriculum Perspectives* 2:20–22.

Kedourie, Elie
1985 *Nationalism.* London: Hutchinson.

Kemper, S.
1980 "Time, Person, and Gender in Sinhalese Astrology." *American Ethnologist* 7:744–58.

Kitley, P.
1979 "Anzac Day Ritual." *Journal of Australian Studies* 4 (June):58–69.

Lane, Christel
1981 *The Rites of Rulers: Ritual in Industrial Society.* London: Cambridge University Press.

Leach, Edmund
1961 *Rethinking Anthropology.* London: Athlone Press.

Lepervanche, Marie M. de
1984 "Immigrants and Ethnic Groups." In *Australian Society,* edited by Sol Encel and Louis Bryson. Melbourne: Longman Cheshire.

Lepervanche, Marie M. de and Gill Bottomley
1985 *Ethnicity, Class, and Gender in Australia.* Sydney: Allen & Unwin.

Le Roy-Ladurie, Emmanuel
1978 *Montaillou: Cathars and Catholics in a French Village 1294–1324.* Translated by B. Bray. London: Scholar Press.

Levi-Strauss, Claude
1966 *The Savage Mind.* London: Weidenfeld & Nicolson.
1969 *The Elementary Structures of Kinship.* Boston: Beacon Press.

Liyanagamage, A.
1978 "A Forgotten Aspect of the Relations Between the Sinhalese and Tamils." *Ceylon Historical Journal* 25:95–142.

London, H. I.
1970 *Non-White Immigration and the "White Australia Policy."* Sydney: Sydney University Press.

McCarthy, Dudley
1983 *Gallipoli to the Somme: The Story of C. E. W. Bean.* Sydney: John Ferguson.

Macintyre, Stuart
1978-79 "The Making of the Australian Working Class." *Historical Studies* 18:233–52.
1985 *Winners and Losers.* Sydney: Allen & Unwin.

McKernan, Michael
   1980   *The Australian People and the Great War.* Melbourne: Thomas Nelson.
   1986   *Padre: Australian Chaplains in Gallipoli and France.* Sydney: Allen &
   Unwin.

McQueen, Humphrey
   1970   *A New Brittania.* Ringwood, Australia: Penguin Books.

Malinowski, Bronislav
   1926   *Myth in Primitive Psychology.* London: Psyche Miniatures General
   Series, no. 6.
   1945   *The Dynamics of Culture Change,* edited by Phyllis Kaberry. London:
   Oxford University Press.

Manor, James, ed.
   1984   *Sri Lanka in Change and Crisis.* London: Croom Helm.

Marcus, Andrew, and M. C. Ricklefs, eds.
   1985   *Surrender Australia.* Sydney: Allen & Unwin.

Marriott, McKim
   1976   "Hindu Transactions: Diversity Without Dualism." in *Transaction and
   Meaning,* edited by Bruce Kapferer. Philadelphia: ASA Essays in Social
   Anthropology, vol. 1.

Mayer, A. C.
   1966   "The Significance of Quasi-Groups in the Study of Complex Societies."
   In *The Social Anthropology of Complex Societies,* edited by Michael
   Banton. A.S.A. Monographs no. 4. London: Tavistock.

Mendis, G. C.
   1946   *The Early History of Ceylon.* Calcutta: YMCA Publishing House.

Mitchell, J. C.
   1956   *The Kalela Dance.* Rhodes-Livingstone Paper 26. Manchester: Manchester University Press.
   1987   *Cities, Society, and Social Perception: A Central African Perspective.*
   Oxford: Clarendon Press.

Mosse, G. L.
   1970   *The Crisis of German Ideology: Intellectual Origins of the Third Reich.*
   London: Weidenfeld & Nicolson.

Munn, N.
   1970   "The Transformation of Subjects into Objects in Walbiri and Pitjantjatjara
   Myth." In *Australian Aboriginal Anthropology,* edited by Ronald M.
   Berndt. Nedlands, Perth: Australian Institute of Aboriginal Studies,
   University of Western Australia.

Nairn, T.
   1977   *The Break-up of Britain: Crisis and Neo-Nationalism.* London: Verso.

Obeyesekere, Gananath
   1975   "Sorcery, Premeditated Murder, and the Canalization of Aggression in
   Sri Lanka." *Ethnology* 14(1):1–23.
   1979   "The Vicissitudes of the Sinhala and Buddhist Identity through Time
   and Change." In *Collective Identities, Nationalisms, and Protest in*

Modern Sri Lanka, edited by Michael Roberts. Colombo: Marga
Institute.

1981 *Medusa's Hair*. Chicago: University of Chicago Press.

1984a *The Cult of the Goddess Pattini*. Chicago: University of Chicago
Press.

1984b "Political Violence and the Future of Democracy in Sri Lanka." In *Sri
Lanka: The Ethnic Conflict*, by the Committee for Rational Development. Delhi: Navrang.

O'Flaherty, W. D.

1973 *Asceticism and Eroticism in the Mythology of Siva*. Oxford: Oxford
University Press.

1976 *The Origins of Evil In Hindu Mythology*. Berkeley and Los Angeles:
University of California Press.

Oxley, H.

1978 *Mateship in Local Organisation*. St. Lucia, Brisbane: University of
Queensland Press.

Paine, Robert, ed.

1981 *Politically Speaking*. Philadelphia: Institute for the Study of Human
Issues.

Palfreeman, A. C.

1967 *The Administration of The White Australia Policy*. Melbourne: Melbourne University Press.

Pannaseeha, M.

1979 *Eelam—The Truth*. Colombo: Swastika Press.

Parkin, David, ed.

1985 *The Anthropology of Evil*. London: Tavistock Publications.

Parkin, F.

1982 *Governing the Cities: Australian Experience in Perspective*. Melbourne: Macmillan.

Peiris, Ralph

1956 *Sinhalese Social Organisation*. Colombo: Ceylon University Press
Board.

Ponnambalam, Satchi

1983 *Sri Lanka: The National Question and the Tamil Liberation Struggle*.
London: Zed Books.

Premadasa, R.

1986 *The Silent Sea*. Translated by N. Sri Wijesinghe. Colombo: Dayawansa
Jayakody.

Rabinow, P.

1986 "Representations are Social Facts: Modernity and Post-Modernity in
Anthropology." In *Writing Culture: The Poetics and Politics of
Ethnography*, edited by James Clifford and George E. Marcus, Berkeley:
University of California Press.

Ricklefs, M. C.
   1985   "Why Asians?" In *Surrender Australia*, edited by Andrew Marcus and
          M. C. Ricklefs. Sydney: Allen & Unwin.

Ricoeur, Paul
   1963   "Symbole et temporalité." *Archivio di Filosofia*, nos. 1 and 2.
   1967   *The Symbolism of Evil*. Boston: Beacon Press.
   1978   "Can There Be a Scientific Concept of Ideology?" In *Phenomenology
          and the Social Sciences: A Dialogue* edited by Joseph Bien. London:
          Martinus Nijhoff.

Rizvi, F.
   1986   *Ethnicity, Class, and Multicultural Education*. Geelong, Victoria:
          Deakin University Press.

Roberts, M.
   1980   "The Past in the Present: The Asokan Persona as a Persisting Paradigm
          of Authority in Sinhalese Political Culture." M.S.
   1982   *Caste Conflict and Elite Formation*. Cambridge: Cambridge University
          Press.

Roberts, Michael, ed.
   1979   *Collective Identities, Nationalisms and Protest in Modern Sri Lanka*.
          Colombo: Marga Institute.

Robertson, J.
   1938   *With the Cameliers in Palestine*. Sydney: Angus & Robertson.

Robinson, Marguerite
   1968   "The House of the Mighty Hero; or, The House of Enough Paddy?
          Some Implications of a Sinhalese Myth." In *Dialectic in Practical
          Religion*, edited by Edmund Leach. Cambridge: Cambridge University
          Press.

Ross, Jane
   1985   *The Myth of the Digger*. Sydney: Hale & Iremonger.

Russell, Bertrand
   1959   *My Philosophical Development*. London: Allen & Unwin.

Russell, Jane
   1982   *Communal Politics under the Donoughmore Constitution, 1931–1947*.
          Dehiwala, Sri Lanka: Tisara Prakasakayo.

Sackett, Lee
   1985   "Marching into the Past: Anzac Day Celebrations in Adelaide." *Journal
          of Australian Studies* 17:18–30.

Sahlins, Marshall
   1981   *Historical Metaphors and Mythical Realities*. Ann Arbor: University
          of Michigan Press.
   1985   *Islands of History*. Chicago and London: University of Chicago Press.

Schneider, D. M.
   1968   *American Kinship: A Cultural Account*. New York: Prentice-Hall.

Seneviratne, H. L.
   1978   *Rituals of the Kandyan State*. Cambridge: Cambridge University Press.

Seymour, A.
    1962   *The One Day of the Year*. Melbourne: Currency Press.

Silva, K. M. de
    1977   *Sri Lanka: A Survey*. Honolulu: University of Hawaii Press.
    1980   *History of Ceylon*. Colombo: University of Colombo Press.

Siriwardena, R.
    1984   "National Identity in Sri Lanka: Problems in Communication and
            Education." In *Sri Lanka: The Ethnic Conflict*, by the Committee for
            Rational Development. Delhi: Navrang.

Siriweera, W. I.
    1984   "The Dutthagamani—Elara Episode: A Reassessment." In *Ethnicity
            and Social Change in Sri Lanka* Social Scientists' Association. Co-
            lombo: Karunaratne.

Smith, A. D.
    1981   *The Ethnic Revival*. Cambridge: Cambridge University Press.
    1986   *The Ethnic Origins of Nations*. Oxford: Basil Blackwell.

Smith, Bardwell L.
    1979   "The Ideal Social Order as Portrayed in the Chronicles of Ceylon." In
            Religion and Legitimation of Power in Sri Lanka, edited by Bardwell
            L. Smith. Chambersburg, Pennsylvania: Anima Books.

Social Scientists' Association (Sri Lanka)
    1984   *Ethnicity and Social Change in Sri Lanka*. Colombo: Karunaratne.

Southwold, Martin
    1985   "Buddhism and Evil." In *The Anthropology of Evil*, edited by David
            Parkin. London: Tavistock Publications.

Stanner, W. E. H.
    1956   "The Dreaming." In *Australian Signpost*, edited by T. A. G. Hunger-
            ford. Melbourne: R. W. Cheshire.

Stirrat, R. L.
    1984   "The Riots and the Roman Catholic Church in Historical Perspective."
            In *Sri Lanka in Change and Crisis*, edited by James Manor. London:
            Croom Helm.

Summers, Anne
    1985   *Damned Whores and God's Police: The Colonisation of Women in
            Australia*. Ringwood, Melbourne: Penguin Books.

Suriyakumaran, Professor
    1984   "The Anatomy of National Identity." *The Island* (Colombo), 21 July.

Tambiah, S. J.
    1976   *World Conqueror, World Renouncer: A Study of Buddhism and Polity
            in Thailand against a Historical Background*. Cambridge: Cambridge
            University Press.
    1986   *Sri Lanka: Ethnic Fratricide and the Dismantling of Democracy*.
            London: I. B. Tauris.

Taussig, Michael
   1980 *The Devil and Commodity Fetishism in South America.* Chapel Hill:
          University of North Carolina Press.

Thompson, E. P.
   1978 *The Poverty Of Theory and Other Essays.* London: Merlin Press

Thornton, E. M., and R. Niththyananthan
   1985 *Sri Lanka, Island of Terror: An Indictment.* Middlesex, U.K.: Eelam
          Research Organisation.

Tocqueville, Alexis de
   1968 *Democracy in America.* Translated by George Lawrence; edited by J.
          P. Mayer and Max Lerner. London: Collins.

Tönnies, Ferdinand
   1955 *Community and Association.* Translated and supplemented by C. P.
          Loomis. London: Routledge and Kegan Paul.

Trendall, A. D.
   1973 *The Shellal Mosaic in the Australian War Memorial.* Canberra:
          Australian War Memorial.

Trevor-Roper, H. R.
   1983 "The Invention of Tradition: The Highland Tradition of Scotland." In
          The Invention of Tradition, edited by Eric Hobsbawm and Terence
          Ranger. Cambridge: Cambridge University Press.

Turner, I. A. H.
   1979 "Australian Nationalism and Australian History." *Journal of Austra-
          lian Studies* 4(June):1–11.

Turner, V. W.
   1957 *Schism and Continuity in an African Society.* Manchester: Manchester
          University Press.
   1967 *The Forest of Symbols.* Ithaca, N.Y.: Cornell University Press.
   1969 *The Ritual Process.* London: Routledge & Kegan Paul.
   1974 *Dramas, Fields, and Metaphors.* Ithaca, N.Y.: Cornell University
          Press.

Valeri, V. O.
   1985 *Kingship and Sacrifice: Ritual and Society in Ancient Hawaii,* translated
          by P. Wissing. Chicago and London: University of Chicago Press.

Wallman, Sandra
   1981 "Refractions of Rhetoric: Evidence for the Meaning of 'Race' in Eng-
          land." In *Politically Speaking,* edited by Robert Paine. Philadelphia:
          Institute for the Study of Human Issues.

Wallman, Sandra, ed.
   1979 *Ethnicity at Work.* London: Macmillan.

Ward, Russel
   1966 *The Australian Legend.* Melbourne: Melbourne University Press.

Warner, W. Lloyd
   1961 *The Family of God: A Symbolic Study of Christian Life in America.*
          New Haven: Yale University Press.

Weber, Max
　　1978　*Economy and Society: An Outline of Interpretive Sociology.* Berkeley: University of California Press.

White, Richard
　　1981　*Inventing Australia: Images and Identity, 1688–1980.* Sydney: Allen & Unwin.

Wilton, Janis, and Richard Bosworth
　　1984　*Old Worlds and New Australia: The Post-War Migration Experience.* North Ryde, Sydney: Penguin Books.

Wirz, Paul
　　1954　*Exorcism and the Art of Healing in Ceylon.* Leyden: E. J. Brill.

Wright, P.
　　1985　*On Living in an Old Country: The National Past in Contemporary Britain.* London: Verso.

Yalman, N.
　　1967　*Under the Bo Tree.* Berkeley: University of California Press.

Index

Aborigines: 3; false comparison of, 238n16; as nationalist metaphor, 142–143, 214

Adam-Smith, Patsy, 127, 173

Ames, M., 108

Anderson, Benedict: 2, 4–5, 95, 140–141, 232n4; and print capitalism, 94

Anthropological comparison, 23–26

Anzac (Australian and New Zealand Army Corps): 29, 235n2; Christian symbolism in, 126–136; and indiscipline, 170, 171, 173; legend of, 121, 125–126; symbolic female and male symbolism of, 180–181; significance of Turks in, 129–131, 188

Anzac Day: 129; and American Memorial Day, 238n13, 242n13; feminism and, 150, 181; legend of, 121, 122; as day of nation, 121, 151–153; as instrument of political control, 145–147; male symbolism in, 180; military symbolism of, 160, 168–169; rite, 137, 149–150, 151–153

Australia Bicentennial, 242n16

Australia Day, as day of state, 121, 169

Australian War Memorial: 122; and new Parliament building, 242n16; "relics" in, 132–133; secular religious form of, 138–139

Autonomy: Australian ideas of, 124, 143, 154–155, 170–173, 178, 241n7; drink and, 157–161; state denial of, 186; national difference and loss of, 190–191

Bailey, F. G., 219

Barnett, S., 220n3

Barth, F., 98

Bean, C. E. W.: 126, 146, 236n3; ritualist empiricism of, 122, 236n4; and individualist ontology, 122–125; secular attitude of, 136; and White Australia, 184–185

Bechert, H., 81

Beck, Brenda, 220n3

Berreman, G., 219

Bhalluka: relation to Dutugemunu, 63; killed by Phussadeva, 64, 116–117

Binns, C. A. P., 209, 238n13

Blainey, Geoffrey, 133, chapter 7

Bloch, Marc, 13

Bosworth, Richard, 206, 243n2

Bottomley, Gillian, 244n7

Bourdieu, Pierre, 47

Bryson, John, 143

Buddhism: in nationalist religion, 5–6, 98–99; as modern ideology of class power, 108–111

Buddhist revival, fundamentalism, 5, 38, 97

Bullivant, B. M., 244n7

Burgmann, Verity, 207

Bush: romance of, 238n17; as symbolic of egalitarian natural unity, 141, 143